THE POLITICS OF POLICE DETENTION IN JAPAN

CLARENDON STUDIES IN CRIMINOLOGY

Published under the auspices of the Institute of Criminology, University of Cambridge; the Mannheim Centre, London School of Economics; and the Centre for Criminology, University of Oxford.

Recent titles in this series:

Dangerous Politics: Risk, Political Vulnerability, and Penal Policy

Annison

Urban Legends: Gang Identity in the Post-Industrial City

Fraser

Punish and Expel: Border Control, Nationalism, and the New Purpose of the Prison

Kaufman

Speaking Truths to Power: Policy Ethnography and Police Reform in Bosnia and Herzegovina

Blaustein

Prisoners, Solitude, and Time

O'Donnell

The Politics of Police Detention in Japan

Consensus of Convenience

SILVIA CROYDON

OXFORD
UNIVERSITY PRESS

OXFORD
UNIVERSITY PRESS

Great Clarendon Street, Oxford, OX2 6DP,
United Kingdom

Oxford University Press is a department of the University of Oxford. It furthers the University's objective of excellence in research, scholarship, and education by publishing worldwide. Oxford is a registered trade mark of Oxford University Press in the UK and in certain other countries

Impression: 1

Published in the United States of America by Oxford University Press
198 Madison Avenue, New York, NY 10016, United States of America

British Library Cataloguing in Publication Data
Data available

Library of Congress Control Number: 2015960857

ISBN 978–0–19–875834–1

Printed and bound by
CPI Group (UK) Ltd, Croydon, CR0 4YY

For my parents,
who can now hold something
of my labours in their hands,

And my husband,
who never gave up on me.

General Editors' Introduction

Clarendon Studies in Criminology aims to provide a forum for outstanding empirical and theoretical work in all aspects of criminology and criminal justice, broadly understood. The Editors welcome submissions from established scholars, as well as excellent PhD work. The *Series* was inaugurated in 1994, with Roger Hood as its first General Editor, following discussions between Oxford University Press and three criminology centres. It is edited under the auspices of these three centres: the Cambridge Institute of Criminology, the Mannheim Centre for Criminology at the London School of Economics, and the Centre for Criminology at the University of Oxford. Each supplies members of the Editorial Board and, in turn, the Series Editor or Editors.

Sylvia Croydon's book, *The Politics of Police Detention in Japan: Consensus of Convenience,* contributes much to what has been a dearth of informed knowledge about the Japanese approach to criminal justice. This lack of understanding applies specifically to pre-charge police detention—or more precisely the practice that is commonly referred to there as 'substitute prison'. Japan is to many eyes a foreign country, both literally and metaphorically. But there is also much about it which is culturally familiar and from which all scholars of criminology can learn.

Pre-charge detention stands in Japan at twenty-three days, interrupted only briefly in the first three days with an appearance before a judge. A period of twenty-three days would be regarded as being at the outer limits of acceptable practice by other developed nations, albeit other countries, our own not excepted, have pursued much longer periods in terrorism-related cases. Indeed, one of the most egregious examples of this was in the UK with the former Labour government's 2006 and 2009 Counter-Terrorism Bills. Both of those Bills failed to be enacted but they included periods of ninety and forty-two days detention respectively. Even now a copy of the *Counter Terrorism (Temporary Provisions) Bill*, with its provision for forty-two days detention, lies ready to be enacted if needed in the Library of the House of Commons. The tensions between community and individual interests, and between human rights and political expediency, both so beautifully detailed in Dr Croydon's book, have widely applicable lessons.

The Politics of Police Detention in Japan: Consensus of Convenience places under a microscopic lens the birth, evolution, and transformation of police pre-charge detention. Substitute prison, as it first emerged in the 1908 Prison Law, was to be a stop-gap measure (a warning perhaps for all about the seductive nature of 'temporary provisions'). Dr Croydon's book spans a 150-year period from the Meiji Restoration in the late nineteenth century to a focus on the modern debates in the latter part of the twentieth century. In so doing it avoids the trap of explaining the lengthy pre-charge detention periods merely as reflecting Asian values, but rather traces the key historical decision points which help us to understand why the Japanese situation is as it is today. The complex and contingent social and political landscape is charted in a compelling manner. But the book is also based for the main part on extensive interviews with forty-eight individuals drawn from across the criminal justice spectrum, participant observations, and interviews at sixteen assorted group meetings of relevant parties, and visits to detention centres and court hearings. The interviews include those from international organizations, as well the relevant Japanese executive, legislative, judicial, and special interest groups. These complement the study of documentary sources including Japanese Diet records, government data, discussion papers, and pamphlets, most of which would otherwise be inaccessible to the non-Japanese reader. Apart from the historical chapter, each of the chapters is infused with the observations, clarifications, and colour which her interviewees provided on these secondary sources.

Her extensive study enables a rich picture to emerge of the realities of pre-charge detention in Japan. Since 2009, state-appointed defence attorneys have been available to suspects in serious cases after seventy-two hours of detention, but interrogation can still take place in the absence of these attorneys. The twenty-three-day period is extendable through re-arrest on other charges. Perhaps most striking, there is no legal requirement to make a full electronic recording of interrogations and no pre-indictment police bail. It is also commonplace for voluntary investigation to take place. This is a pre-arrest arrangement where the individual responds to a police request to co-operate with investigators but is subject to no oversight. There is, of course, no right answer to just how long it is reasonable to hold someone pre-charge, albeit holding suspects pre-charge is widespread if not universal. The reasons for such detention are well recognized across jurisdictions, relating to evidential matters, to interrogations, and to crime prevention. Indicting the right person is critical. But equally detention is self-evidently potentially coercive, and extended detention risks other miscarriages of justice occurring. The human rights issues are writ large. Yet Dr Croydon deliberately expresses no subjective or judgmental view as to the reasonableness of twenty-three days, but rather invites the reader to explore and understand how the political establishment and wider Japanese society have come to see such lengthy periods of detention as legitimate. Thus, whilst Japan is rightly the focus of this study, it is not a book solely for the Japanese market; rather it is one for all of us.

Ultimately, the convenience of the lengthy detention periods, with their resultant high confession rate and emergent, often sincere, remorse on the part of offenders, contributes to both a high clear-up rate and can facilitate the processes of rehabilitation and reintegration of offenders. Three matters, as Dr Croydon points out, should not be forgotten. Firstly, that some 40 percent of those subject to police detention are not prosecuted. Secondly, that Japanese police benefit from what David Bayley has described as the authority of unspoken moral consensus; the interaction of expectation this sets up can assist the confession process, whilst establishing a baseline of high moral standards and helping to secure such standards from the police. And thirdly, as Setsuo Miyazawa has documented, Japan enjoys much higher police to crime ratios than other countries. So the situation is both complex and mundane: direct comparisons risk being invidious. But equally, understanding foreign practices can bring invaluable insights into one's own ingrained beliefs about how the world should work. The book manages both to capture the strangeness of Japanese practices, with their *jujutsu* tactics, and the everyday monetary barriers to change which plague all governments. Moreover, as Dr Croydon tellingly concludes, if the Japanese police had access to many of the investigative techniques available to other police forces, some of a contested nature, their reliance on pre-charge detention may not be so profound.

As Editors we commend Sylvia Croydon's book as making significant contributions to the fields of criminology and penology. It is a book to be most warmly welcomed to the *Clarendon Studies in Criminology Series.*

Jill Peay and Tim Newburn
London School of Economics
January 2016

Acknowledgements

There is no end to a study when the subject matter is ongoing; it is just a matter of when you decide the time has come to place the final full stop. For me, it is now, eight years on since my commencement of this research project, that this time has come. Hopefully the finished product will meet at least some of the expectations of the many people to whom I owe a debt of gratitude for helping me along the way.

To begin with, I would like to extend thanks to my doctoral supervisor, Ian Neary, for opening the academic door to me when he took me as a student, for leading me to choose this topic, and for his guidance. During my years as his student I was crazy enough to imagine that he had already written this book and had a 'master copy' lying buried under one of the piles of paper in his office, with the point of our term-time weekly sessions being to enable me to independently reproduce it, matching as many of the words in his copy as possible. I have since seen sense and grown out of this idea, but hopefully my efforts have nonetheless met my former supervisor's expectations to the point that he would not be ashamed to have a copy of this work sit on his shelves. Regardless, I credit a large part of my development as a researcher to all the clues he has given me along my way.

My various examiners at the University of Oxford also deserve thanks. Benjamin Goold and Liora Lazarus for my transfer of status to a DPhil candidate, and then Roger Goodman and Sho Konishi for my confirmation of status, read the material I submitted, and gave me confidence that I am heading in the right direction. At my DPhil viva, I was most privileged to be examined by Arthur Stockwin and John Swenson-Wright. As 'the first sensei of Japanese politics' to my own first sensei of Japanese politics (Kōichi Nakano), the former has always had for me (and no doubt many others too!) the aura of the ultimate intellectual authority in my field. John Swenson-Wright, another of Arthur Stockwin's former students, was also someone I highly regarded as having achieved so much so early in his career (and most kindly hosted me during a spell at Cambridge). Both scrutinized my dissertation in its entirety and provided me with what I saw as some more valuable hints as to how I could improve the word matching of my draft with that imaginary master copy of my book, which, at that point, still very much eluded me.

While my teachers at Oxford shaped my academic journey, it was the benevolence of a number of institutions that made it a reality. The studentships of the Sasakawa and the John Crump Foundations enabled me to focus on my research in the UK, and generous grants from the Japan Foundation, the Japan Foundation Endowment Committee, the Tōshiba International Foundation, and the European Association for Japanese Studies provided me with opportunities to undertake much needed fieldwork visits to Japan, the United Nations Office in Geneva, and the Council of Europe in Strasbourg, as well as to attend two PhD workshops.

My scholarly career took me next to the University of Tōkyō, where I was fortunate enough to have a two-year stint as Japan Society for Promotion of Science Postdoctoral Research Fellow. During this time I had everything I needed to work on this and other research projects, as well as a most inspiring role model in my host professor Junko Katō.

Currently, at Kyōto University, I am blessed to have what is undoubtedly every academic's 'dream job'. Under the wing of the Hakubi Centre for Advanced Research, I have enjoyed unlimited freedom and plenty of resources for research. Director Kōji Tanaka and Program Manager Toshitaka Hori have done everything in their power to support me, even beyond the call of duty, and Hisayo Mizuno and Yujin Asao have kindly attended to my needs on a daily basis. At the Graduate School of Law, my most hospitable host, Shōtarō Hamamoto, has, in addition to undertaking all manner of tedious administrative duties on my behalf, given me invaluable comments on my project which have helped me crystallize its essence. I could also not omit expressing gratitude to all the other professors who let me undertake numerous travel trips and visiting research positions, or to the administrative team—especially Hisano Nakao, Shiori Maeyama, Michiko Shibata, Yui Nagaoka, and Naomi Sawada—who never failed to process my documentation, with a speed that has often left me stunned!

My embarking on the academic path, and this project in particular, owes a great deal to those who inspired me as an undergraduate with their intellect. At a small, but special, campus at Ichigaya in Tōkyō, I enjoyed three years of liberal arts education, of which

I have the fondest of memories. It was there that Kōichi Nakano, whom I have already mentioned, drew me into the world of Japanese politics with his insightful lectures. Apart from him, there were several others who could be singled out as my intellectual parents and whom I would like to mention: Tadashi Anno, whose brilliant mind and unique ways of seeing the world made him truly shine in my eyes; Mari Miura, who instilled in me academic rigour and provided me with an early example of what I could aspire to be; Antoni Üçerler, whose classes gave me a sense of what it must have felt like to attend the Lyceum (only they were better because, unlike Aristotle, he did not deny access to women!), and who also pushed me to dare to believe that becoming a student at Oxford was not beyond my reach; and all the other staff who provided me with such excellent lessons academically and in life, including Christopher Barnett, James Farrer, Thierry Robouam, James Shields, and Richard Werner. Now that I look back, I can see I was extremely lucky to have had so many great teachers.

At the institutions where I have spent time, I have befriended and benefited intellectually from many others—both more senior academics, who gave me guidance and support, and also my peers, with whom I shared experiences (i.e. mistakes!) while commencing the ongoing process of becoming a full-fledged academic. Amongst these are Ken Amor, Nathan Badenoch, John Campbell, Simon Creak, Pierre Donze, Colin Jones, Sookyeon Huh, Shigeru Kōzai, Aaron Miller, Tatsuya Nakanishi, Andrea Ortolani, Paul Scalise, Taisei Shida, Shiho Sugiki, Tomoko Tateya, Ann Waswo, and David Wessels, and all my other Hakubi brothers and sisters who are too many to name here. I hope there are not too many others whom I have forgotten, but should not have done!

I have also incurred a huge debt to my interviewees, without whose remarks the book would have been most uninformed. I was surprised that these busy people even found the time to meet and talk to me, let alone make extra efforts to help me access printed materials and explain their detailed thoughts in writing, which a number did. It goes without saying that any mistakes in interpreting their viewpoints are purely mine. Thank you also to the Japan Federation of Bar Associations and the National Police Agency for allowing me to reproduce material from their pamphlets, to 'ThisParticularGreg' and Mina Bruchon for granting me permission to reproduce their images on the cover and the dedication, respectively, and to Shihei Umehara for consenting to me including a translation of his song.

For helping turn all my work into an actual book, thanks are due to editor Lucy Alexander at OUP, and project manager Gayathri Viswanathan. Both kept me well informed about progress at all times. Moreover, being my first book, the first email from Lucy with positive feedback from reviewers, and the email from Gayathri providing a completion date when I might actually see the finished work, were two of the most exciting emails I will receive professionally! The copy-editor, Kristy Barker, too deserves much credit—without her careful eye passing over it, the writing would be in a much worse shape than it appears before you now.

On the more personal side, I cannot possibly omit from the list of thanks Jun-sensei and Yukiko-okāsan, to whom I remain eternally grateful. I can never repay them for their part in the initiative that brought me from Bulgaria to Gotemba's Fuji Phoenix College, or the kindness that they showed to me during my six years as an undergraduate and beyond. The Fukukawa, Inoue, Matsunaga, Mizuno, and Takahashi families too opened their homes to me time and time again, treating me like a family member. Without them my days in Japan would have been lonely and drab. Undoubtedly, my conversations over the dinner table during the times I spent in their homes played a most valuable role in my learning how to communicate in the Japanese language. But they gave me so much more than this, shaping my whole view of the world.

Finally, I would like to thank my parents, Vanya and Atanas, who gave their all to ensure I had the opportunities that I did when I was growing up in Sofia. As the Bulgarian saying holds, 'the bird lands on your shoulder only once in your life', and they taught me that I should grab chances as they come along. So it was that I ended in Japan. My 'little' brother Alex, too, has always been there for me in difficult times. Most of all, though, I want to thank David—he is a hero for standing next to me after eight years of my manically indulging in the compulsion of putting words in the 'right' order. If it was not for the support I received from him, this book would never have happened.

11 September 2014,
Cambridge, M.A

Contents

List of Figures

List of Abbreviations and Glossary

1908 Prison Law	*Kangoku hō*
2005 amendment	Act on Penal Institutions and the Treatment of Sentenced Inmates, *Keiji shisetsu oyobi jukeisha no shogū nado ni kan suru hōritsu*
2006 amendment	Act on Penal Detention Facilities and Treatment of Inmates and Detainees, *Keiji shūyō shisetsu oyobi hi-shūyōsha nado no shogū ni kan suru hōritsu*
arrestees	suspects held in police custody, prior to having seen a judge
attrition clause	*zengenka jōkō,* clause that provides for the reduction of the use of the substitute prison system
CAT	United Nations Convention against Torture and Other Cruel, Inhuman or Degrading Treatment or Punishment
Civil Centre	Civil Centre Demanding the Abolition of the Substitute Prison and Opposing the Two Detention Bills, *Shimin sentā*
Correction Bureau	*Kyōsei kyoku*, MOJ bureau responsible for directing and supervising correctional facilities
Correctional Association	*Kyōsei kyōkai*, formerly *Keimu kyōkai*, organization devoted to research and public education on penal practices
Council	Correctional Administration Reform Council, *Gyōkei kaikaku kaigi*
Countermeasure to the Two Detention Bills Headquarters	*Kōkin ni hōan taisaku honbu*, JFBA campaign office
CPR	Centre for Prisoners' Rights, *Kangoku jinken sentā*

detention house	*kōchisho*, MOJ remand prisoner facilities
DPJ	Democratic Party of Japan, *Minshutō*
GHQ	General Headquarters, USA civil service and military personnel involved in governing Japan during Occupation
Home Ministry	*Naimushō*
HRW	Human Rights Watch
IBA	International Bar Association
ICCPR	UN International Covenant on Civil and Political Rights
JCLU	Japan Civil Liberties Union, *Jiyū jinken kyōkai*
JCP	Japanese Communist Party, *Nihon kyōsantō*
JFBA	Japan Federation of Bar Associations, *Nihon bengoshi rengō kai*
JRC	Judicial Reform Council, *Shihō seido kaikaku shingikai*
JSP	Japanese Socialist Party, renamed SDP in 1996, *Nihon shakaitō*
Judicial Council	*Hōsei shingikai*
large central prisons	*shūjikan*
lay judge system	*saiban'in seido*
LDP	Liberal Democratic Party, *Jiyū mishutō*
MOJ	Ministry of Justice, currently *Hōmushō*
Nagoya Prosecution	Nagoya District Public Prosecutors Office, *Nagoya chihō kensatsu-chō*
New Council	Council Concerning the Treatment of Remand Prisoners, *Miketsu kōkinsha no shogū nado ni kan suru yūshikisha kaigi*
NPA	National Police Agency, *Keisatsu-chō*
Penal Institutions Bill	*Keiji shisetsu hōan*, bill submitted in the 1980s–90s by MOJ as part of the Two Detention Bills

Police Boards	Boards of Visitors for Inspection of Police Custody, *Keisatsu ryūchi shisetsu shisatsu iinkai*
Police Detention Institutions Bill	*Ryūchi shisetsu hōan*, bill submitted in the 1980s–90s by NPA as part of the Two Detention Bills
police houses of custody/police cells	*keisatsu no ryūchijō*
Prison Boards	Boards of Visitors for Inspection of Penal Institutions, *Keiji shisetsu shisatsu iinkai*
Proposal	Proposal to Serve as a Framework for Amending the Prison Law, *Kangoku hō kaisei no kosshi to naru yōkō*
RCC	Relief Contact Centre, *Kyūen renraku sentā*
remand prisoners	suspects held in detention by order of a judge
Research Group, cited as KRKK	Correctional Legislative Research Group, *Keiji rippō kenkyū kai*
SDP	Social Democratic Party, formerly the JSP, *Shakai Minshutō*
Special Higher Police	*Tokubetsu kōtō keisatsu*, known shortly as *Tokkō*
substitute prison	*daiyō kangoku*, currently appears in law as substitute detention (*daiyō shūyō*)
suspects	includes arrestees and remand prisoners, and could refer to either or both; where it is not clear from the context, the more precise terms 'arrestee' or 'remand prisoner' are used
Two Detention Bills	*Kōkin ni hōan*
UNHRC	United Nations Human Rights Committee

Note on Conventions

All Japanese technical words are translated into English in the text, with the original Japanese being noted at the first usage and those terms that recur frequently appearing in the Abbreviations and Glossary section. Where possible, the translation of Japanese legislation is the MOJ's own, as appearing at <www.japaneselawtranslation.go.jp>. Unless otherwise noted, all other translations are the author's.

All names appear in the text as first name and then family name, or simply family name, as per the usual Western convention. Unlike some publications regarding Japan, note that here this convention is extended to include Japanese names.

Macrons have been used to mark Japanese long vowels.

1
Introduction

> The purpose of government is to enable the people of a nation to live in safety and happiness.
>
> Thomas Jefferson

> It behooves every man who values liberty of conscience for himself, to resist invasions of it in the case of others: or their case may, by change of circumstances, become his own.
>
> Thomas Jefferson (again)

'You're nicked!'—In every country in the world, there is a period of time during which it is recognized as justifiable for the police to detain and question suspects. That they are permitted to do this for a time sufficient to conduct their investigation is seen as indispensable to the end of finding the truth of the case and delivering justice, both in the name of the directly affected victims and in that of society more broadly. At the same time, the detained party, having not been charged, let alone had their guilt established in court, is still technically innocent, which commands that their liberty is not curtailed unduly. It is also generally seen in a civilized society as desirable that suspects not be put under unnecessary pressure, nor be subjected to torture or cruel or inhumane treatment, which is an ever-present danger of police detention. Indeed, even well-meaning investigators could, in their passion for a result and possibly even subconsciously, cross the fine line between robust questioning and coercive interrogation.

Determining the duration for which it is fair to detain an individual in police custody before either bringing a charge against them or releasing them thus entails a delicate balance of competing considerations. On this matter, it is clearly the case that different people will adopt different perspectives. Ultimately, though, each state is forced to specify what it deems to be an appropriate compromise between the rights of the detained individual and the concerns of the wider community. Regardless of where the line is drawn—and it is perhaps unsurprising that states around the world have not settled on a unified position on the matter—the way in which a state incorporates the various societal views on police detention into its criminal justice legislation in making this choice promises to be most illuminative about the role human rights play in policy-making.

This book examines the processes through which such police detention policy decisions are made in Japan. The duration for which criminal suspects can be held in police custody prior to being indicted there is the longest amongst developed nations—as much as eight times more than is typical. Exploring what lies behind this markedly divergent choice promises to shed important light on how a state sets the boundary between encroaching on the liberty of individuals and the security of the community—a dichotomy that clearly arises much more widely than in the case of police detention. With this being the case, the present study will also contribute broader theoretical lessons regarding the implementation of rights more generally. Indeed, whether Japan's police custody arrangements are found to be due to the structure of the decision-making process, or to some deeper underlying cultural reason, or to a combination of both (or possibly something else entirely), insight will be gained into how such factors are likely to affect other cases of human rights protection and promotion.

Part of the grander motivation for this work is to offer something of a response to a rallying cry made by political philosopher Michael Freeman that the social science of human rights wakes up. The call in question, made first in a 2002 publication *Human Rights* and then again in a chapter appearing in a 2005 edited volume entitled *The Legalization of Human Rights*, is based on an observation that the study of human rights is currently too legalistic, with social scientists, under the influence of scientific positivism, having shunned the concept for far too long. There is too little, Freeman laments, in the way of explaining variations in respect for human rights across different times and places, or the gap between human rights ideals and the realities of human rights violations. Maintaining that only social science is equipped to provide systematic evidence on which to base our assumptions about how human rights can best be protected, he urges political scientists, anthropologists, and sociologists to employ their skills and knowledge to the end of informing this important area. Given that there is a long-standing stalemate in the legalistic debates surrounding what is an especially distinctive system of police custody in Japan, it seems that this is precisely the kind of subject matter Freeman would envisage as more productively being addressed through a political science approach.

Japan's Police Detention System in Perspective

To put Japan's police custody arrangements into an international context, Figure 1.1 presents a comparison of the legally sanctioned periods amongst developed nations for detention of criminal suspects by the police before either a charge must be brought against them or they are released. In particular, this displays the maximum number of days of police detention permitted under the relevant domestic laws for each of the thirty-four members of the Organization for Economic Co-operation and Development (OECD).[1] As shown, the majority of the OECD members permit a period of pre-indictment police detention of less than eight days—within Europe and North America in particular, most countries permit no more than four days. (In fact, the European Union recommends only two days.) Only three OECD member states permit longer detention periods: Australia at twelve days,[2] South Korea at twenty days, and finally, at the top of the list at twenty-three days, Japan.

This lengthy period of permissible police detention is not just a legal quirk; suspects are typically not charged or released quickly in practice either. Official figures show that in 2010 the average period of detention for each arrestee in police cells was as great as 26.3 days (and has been higher over the previous decade).[3] It has even been reported that in certain cases, suspects have been detained for months before being charged. That such eventualities

[1] Note that these figures exclude exceptional terrorism measures, which often allow much longer detention, but which are rarely used.

[2] While the law in Australia only permits twenty-four hours of questioning, suspects can be held for longer than this in practice due to the latter period of time not having to be measured continuously; the law also permits periods of 'dead time' where a suspect is held between bouts of interrogation. Thus, although something of an anomaly, in a 2007 precedent, as a result of the law allowing such flexibility, a suspect was held for as long as twelve days.

[3] In particular, over the years 2006–9, the average number of days was 28.0, 27.4, 27.3, and 26.9, respectively. Source: *Keiji shūyō shisetsu hō no jisshi jōkyō ni tsuite* (On the Implementation of the Act on Penal Detention Facilities and Treatment of Inmates and Detainees), NPA, May 2011.

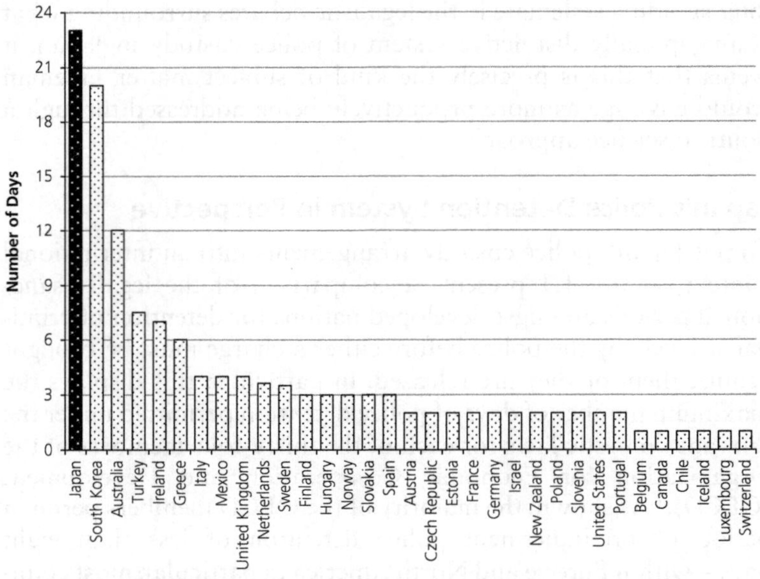

Figure 1.1. Legally sanctioned period of pre-indictment police custody

Sources: Reports produced by USA Department of State, Bureau of Democracy, Human Rights and Labor; Liberty; European Criminal Bar Association; and Foreign and Commonwealth Office (various years).

can occur is because twenty-three days is the maximum period of pre-indictment detention under only a single charge—arrestees can be detained even longer than this. Specifically, if an incident under investigation involves multiple crimes (such as an illegal break-in, a rape, a murder, a robbery, and arson), then the authorities may arrest a suspect repeatedly without releasing them, meaning that the period of detention in police custody is potentially indefinite.

Of course, being able to detain suspects for an adequate duration before charge is widely seen as crucial to the effective operation of the police in carrying out their duties to investigate crimes and protect the public. Indeed, there are a number of clear advantages to taking the perpetrator of a crime quickly off the streets and into custody, such as preventing the destruction of evidence, reducing flight risk, and stopping further crimes being committed. Moreover, in order to have a better chance of bringing those who have committed crimes to justice, it is essential for police to have enough time to gather evidence and interrogate the suspect to the point that they can be confident that they indict the right person. Nonetheless, none of these arguments are unique to Japan, and so do not explain why it has elected for such a lengthy duration of police detention as compared to other developed countries.

From the point of view of human rights protection, prolonged police detention of suspects is problematic because the ills it can bring go well beyond the unavoidable restriction of liberty. To begin with, as is the case with detention of any kind, there is a possibility that the detainer abuses the detainee, either physically or psychologically, torturing, threatening, humiliating, or intimidating them. Moreover, since suspects are completely under the control of the detaining authority, the latter dictates whether or not procedural requirements are met with regards to lawyer consultation and medical care, for example. Finally, it might also transpire that the inmate does not know what rights they are entitled to (or they might not understand these because of a language or another barrier), and the police officer can consequently abuse the suspect by using their ignorance against them.

Importantly, in the case of police detention, as highlighted at the outset, in addition to the means being in place for such abuse to happen, there can be a strong incentive for the investigative authorities to resort to it. Particularly in cases where there is little hard evidence to support their case, an investigator has the obvious motivation of extracting a self-incriminating confession from the suspect, so as to increase the likelihood of a conviction in court, ultimately helping to raise the crime clearance rate. The desire to obtain such a confession could clearly lead to an investigator treating a suspect unfairly, including in non-direct ways, such as only accepting those of their statements that fit a picture developed about the case beforehand. Finally, there is very little comeback for the detainee, as the police officer is in charge of what evidence leaves the detention cell, so even when an abuse happens, it will be hard for the victim to prove it.

Whilst it might seem prejudicial towards Japan to next introduce arbitrarily some further aspects of its criminal justice process, when discussing the prospect for suspect mistreatment in prolonged police detention there, it would equally be an omission to not even mention that the Japanese procedure lacks several of the safeguards against abuse with which many other countries are equipped:

- Firstly, suspects in Japan, even if they are exercising their right to silence, have a duty to sit and listen to the questions and comments of the investigator; they cannot leave the questioning room or stop the interview. This is set out in the Code of Criminal Procedure, Article 198, Paragraph 1, which stipulates that '... the suspect may, *except in cases where he/she is under arrest or under detention* [emphasis added], refuse to appear or after he/she has appeared, may withdraw at any time'.
- Secondly, in the case of those in Japan who do not have the means to hire a defence counsel, the right to a state-appointed one is only available to those in crimes carrying the death penalty or imprisonment for a maximum of three or more years, whose trials would require one. Moreover, this right does not accrue until after an initial arrest period of seventy-two hours, during which time questioning is still permitted. In cases where the maximum penalty is less than three years' imprisonment, a state-appointed lawyer is not made available until after indictment.
- Thirdly, even if the suspect has a lawyer, the investigation can make it difficult for the suspect to have access to them during questioning through their control of when and where interviews take place. There is nothing in the law that requires the investigators to only conduct their questioning when the suspect's lawyer, if he has one, is present.
- Fourthly, there is a lack of transparency about what happens in the Japanese questioning room, as there is no legal requirement for the investigation—as there has famously been in Britain since the introduction of the Police and Criminal Evidence Act in 1984, for example—to make a full electronic recording of the interrogation.
- Fifthly, there exists no option for police bail, so the suspect cannot avoid detention before the investigators come to a decision about whether to proceed with the case or not. Bail is available as a matter of right only upon indictment.

Clearly, all these factors compound the potential for suspect abuse stemming from the length of the detention. Additionally, whilst not strictly part of the police detention period, it is pertinent to note that, prior to arresting a suspect, the Japanese police and prosecution commonly make use of a spell of 'voluntary investigation'. More specifically, unaware that only an official warrant for apprehension obliges them to co-operate with investigators, many suspects succumb to what constitute in law mere *requests* to do so. In practice, this means that, even before they are arrested, suspects can face hours of interrogation in a police cell, possibly across several days. During this time, investigators are not under the judicial oversight that would follow arrest, and many of the risks for abuse associated with interrogation in police detention are present.

To bring the focus back to the matter at hand, let us conclude by making the evident observation that the longer the period of police detention, the greater the risk that police officers and prosecutors unfairly take advantage of detention for the sake of investigation. In the case of Japan concretely, regardless of whether the additional procedural issues raised above are taken into consideration or not, the chance of investigator-led abuse taking place over twenty-three (or more) days is higher than it would be if the period of police detention was shorter, as it is in most other developed countries. Indeed, it is precisely because of the inherent risks of police detention that it has become a widely accepted procedural principle internationally that during the early stages of detention suspects are transferred to facilities independent of the investigation—investigators who need to continue questioning a suspect are required to do so in these other facilities, following the rules for visitations there.

The question thus arises as to why it is that Japan diverges with regards to suspects' rights protection, and how its choice of prolonged police detention is legitimized.

Additional Motivation for Studying Police Detention in Japan

Beyond the principal aim of providing theoretical lessons on human rights implementation, there are several further benefits to the present study of police custody in Japan.

Firstly, by examining in depth how the police detention policies in Japan have been forged, this work will enrich the understanding of a criminal justice system whose efficiency, as measured according to almost any criterion, is remarkable. For a start, within the member states of the OECD, Japan is known to have amongst the lowest rates of all manner of crimes.[4] Even taking into account the extent to which crime might be under-reported there, it is generally acknowledged that these figures are reflective of the true rate of crimes in Japan being below that of most other developed nations. Of course, crime rates are determined by more complex societal issues than simply what form a criminal justice system takes, and so it would be too much of a leap to posit a direct link between Japan's low crime rate and its police detention duration. It is possible, however, to put forward arguments that relate crime clearance rates to the way in which crime is tackled. And on this front, too, Japan's criminal justice system consistently returns higher figures than seen in other developed countries.[5] Moreover, Japan has managed to maintain these figures in the face of trends which might have been expected to take it in the opposite direction over its recent history: urbanization in the post-war period, and then economic contraction and rising unemployment through its Lost Two Decades of the 1990s and 2000s. At the same time, and

[4] To give one important example first, Japan's homicide rate of 0.4 per 100,000 people annually is the second lowest in the OECD (with only Iceland having a lower rate), and is significantly below the OECD average of 2.2. Source: *OECD Better Life Index*, which recorded data from 2011 or the latest available year, and included Brazil and Russia in addition to the thirty-four OECD members. Available at <www.oecdbetterlifeindex.org>. Similar figures are seen for other crimes. For instance, for the years 2003/4, Japan's victimization rate for ten conventional crimes (burglary; attempted burglary; theft of personal property; robbery; sexual offences; assault and threat; theft of a car; theft from a car; theft of a motorcycle or moped; theft of a bicycle) of 9.9 per cent was also the second lowest amongst OECD members, with the average being significantly greater at 15.7 per cent (Van Dijk, Van Kesteren, and Smit 2008).

[5] For example, in 2009 the clearance rate in Japan for homicide was 98 per cent, and for robbery 65 per cent. In the same year in the USA, the corresponding statistics were 67 per cent and 28 per cent respectively. For the year 2009/10 in the UK, the figures were 86 per cent and 21 per cent. Similar statistics for these three countries are also seen in previous years. With a homicide clearance rate consistently over 95 per cent, only Germany comes close in this measure of crime control. Sources: MOJ White Paper on Crime 2010, Tables 1-1-1-2 and 1-4-2-1, available at <hakusyo1.moj.go.jp/en/59/nfm/mokuji.html>; FBI Uniform Crime Report, Crime in the United States, 2009, Offenses Cleared, available at <www2.fbi.gov/ucr/cius2009/offenses/clearances/index.html>; Crimes detected in England and Wales 2010/11, available at <www.gov.uk/government/uploads/system/uploads/attachment_data/file/116404/hosb1111.pdf>.

most strikingly, Japan has continued to spend significantly less on criminal justice than is typical for a country of its GDP.[6]

In light of these facts, it is hardly surprising that foreign policy-makers have increasingly looked to Japan for inspiration on how to reform their own criminal justice systems. What exactly is the secret behind the efficiency and value-for-money of the Japanese one? The complexity of criminal justice issues in general, and the outlying nature of Japan in particular, means such a question is difficult to answer. As a result, Japanese criminal justice has remained something of an enigma, with many foreign commentators resorting to overly simplistic, idealistic explanations for the exceptional statistics it produces, and others seemingly giving up altogether on connecting what is happening in Japan with the situation in other countries, instead resignedly accepting that it is something from another world. Clearly there are lessons to be drawn from the Japanese approach to criminal justice, though, if one is prepared to probe in detail how things work there. Given that police custody is such an integral part of any criminal justice system, any investigation of the latter would be incomplete without a proper consideration of the role of the former. It is thus hoped that, by explaining how the prolonged period of police detention was established in law and is sustained, this study will contribute to the wider debates on Japan's criminal justice system, and help legislators and legal practitioners outside of Japan more constructively compare their own practices with another, very different, system. Indeed, much of the material from which this study is drawn is not easily available to a non-Japanese-speaking audience.

This investigation also has something to offer the debate on police custody between Japan and the international community, as it is defined by the interactions of the Japanese government with the United Nations (UN) human rights bodies, which have reached something of a stalemate. Evidence of frustration on the part of the UN is easy to find. In a recent UN Human Rights Committee (UNHRC) meeting, for example, Sir Nigel Rodley could not help

[6] See for example the statistical analysis of 'What Does the World Spend on Criminal Justice?', where the correlations between expenditure on policing, prosecution, and court expenditure and GDP for seventy countries are investigated (Farrell and Clark 2004).

but exclaim that trying to talk with Japan on the matter is like trying to hold a 'dialogue with the deaf'.[7] On Japan's part too, the constant criticism of this aspect of their criminal justice system is also starting to grate, as exemplified by the outburst of the Ambassador in charge of Human Rights and Humanitarian Affairs, Hideaki Ueda, who shouted to his audience to 'shut up' at another meeting in Geneva, indignant as he was at the laughter rendered to his defence of Japan's police practices as ones of a proudly modern country.[8] Although quotes of this type are atypical, and certainly stronger than the usual formulaic diplomatic language exchanged in such forums, the relationship is clearly not as healthy as it could be. One cannot help but think that, in order to progress from this point, the time has come to go beyond simple finger-pointing and do, as this book will, a little more digging to gain a richer understanding of why Japan retains its present system. A further advantage of doing this is that it will link these human rights debates with the criminal justice policy ones discussed earlier. With the obvious disconnection between these two discourses, it is something of an omission that they have not been more closely linked before.

Some Important Caveats

To avoid misunderstandings, especially by Japanese officials who might feel that the police detention system of their country is being unfairly singled out, I would like to explicitly spell out from the outset three important caveats.

Firstly, whilst in the discussion above I attempted to explain the pros and cons of holding suspects in police detention, the omission to answer such explicit questions as 'How long is it reasonable to detain a suspect prior to charging them?' and 'In what circumstances would this be appropriate?' is deliberate. Indeed, it has been my goal when writing about this sensitive topic, where there are naturally conflicting concerns and where there has been long-standing domestic and international friction in the Japanese case in particular, to avoid statements or phrases that could be considered subjective or judgmental. This is why, in the section

[7] Author's observation of the UNHRC's 94th Session, during which the fifth periodic report of the Japanese government on the implementation of ICCPR was examined, 13–31 October 2008.

[8] UN Committee against Torture, Consideration of the second periodic report of Japan, 22 May 2013.

'Japan's Police Detention System in Perspective', I took as the starting point the objective observation that Japan's twenty-three-day detention period stands at the extreme of the practices of other developed nations. I do not myself want to posit the rights or wrongs of this, or to present justification for any specific policy, knowing that to do so would inevitably alienate some of the practitioners who form an important part of the intended audience. After all, it is exactly the point of the work to understand how the divergent policy of Japan is legitimized by politicians and society more generally there, and therefore it is more appropriate to leave such discussion to the actors themselves.

Secondly, this book is not starting from the assertion that there is an increased number of human rights violations taking place in Japanese police cells as a result of the prolonged detention period. Rather, it restricts itself to the claim that there is an increased *potential* for abuse resulting from this feature of the Japanese criminal justice system, as well as the various exacerbating factors described in the previous section. To begin with, making a priori claims about actual abuses taking place simply on the basis of the law admitting greater potential for such could not be reasonably justified. After all, there is no rationale for governments—the democratic ones, at least—to commit abuse or to establish or condone a system that systematically abuses people. It must have been precisely the disbelief that the world could doubt the Japanese government's commitment to serving their countrymen that prompted Ambassador Ueda's aforementioned UN eruption—why would anyone think that the government of an advanced, modern democracy, such as Japan, wants to torture its citizens? And, anyway, conducting the substantial amount of research required to measure abuse goes beyond what is necessary to give legitimacy to pinpointing Japan's prolonged police detention as an important case study for drawing lessons about human rights implementation. The fact is that Japan's system, by allowing a prolonged police detention, creates an additional risk of abuse, which could affect anyone in society—even a former UN Ambassador—should they fall suspect to a crime in Japan. This is in and of itself significant enough a reason to render the study worthwhile.

Furthermore, it would be a fair point that other factors may be more crucial in heightening the risk for suspect abuse than prolonged police detention. My third caveat is consequently an acknowledgement that Japan is certainly not unique in that an aspect of its legal framework has an intrinsic potential to generate human rights infringements. As would be attested by a quick glance at the UN human rights bodies' recommendations with regards to their implementation of the International Convention on Civil and Political Rights (ICCPR) or the Convention against Torture and Other Cruel, Inhuman or Degrading Treatment or Punishment (CAT), dangers for human rights abuse lurk in almost every country's criminal justice system. To give just two examples with regard to the detention of suspects in particular, Britain and the USA are certainly far from having completely watertight mechanisms for human rights protection in this area—as extreme cases, think Camp Bastion and Guantanamo. Nonetheless, how other states are performing in this respect is not, and can never be, a reason why abuse risks inherent in a particular system should not be scrutinized. Thus the incentive for placing the Japanese police custody system under the microscope remains.

What Produces Policy Divergences?

Policy divergence, particularly in human rights-related areas, has been studied from a number of perspectives. This section considers what explanations this existing literature has to offer for Japan's police detention practices.

Asian culture

Firstly, the predominant cultural arguments predicting Japan would make legislative choices divergent from other developed countries stem from the so-called 'Asian values' discourse. Loosely put, this strand of theory asserts that East Asian people, because of their culture (which might arise from a Confucian tradition), naturally put a preference on community rights, as opposed to individual ones. Although the heavily politicized version of the Asian values argument put forward by several East Asian leaders in the early 1990s was widely discredited following the Asian financial crisis, and the heterogeneity of the region meant that the broad-brush picture first presented was never taken seriously (Japan distanced itself from the 1993 Bangkok declaration, which was the major enunciation of the Asian values argument, signed by representatives of thirty Asian states), academics remained interested in the possibility of there being multiple legitimate ways of human rights implementation, which might depend on some ingrained value system. In recent years, this area of study has been reinvigorated, with several more refined arguments connecting cultural values and human rights being proposed (Peerenboom 2003: 605, Bell 2006, Avonius and Kingsbury 2008, Tan 2011), suggesting that such theories are still viewed as having explanatory value.

It is not difficult to see how police custody in Japan, and a system of prolonged police detention in particular, fits comfortably into these cultural predictions. To spell this out explicitly, Japan's lengthy detention of suspects in police facilities could be argued to be a by-product of a higher prioritization in Japanese society, or any other East Asian society as a matter of fact, of the right of the community at large to live in and enjoy a safe environment over the right of individual suspects to not be deprived of their freedom for more than the absolute minimum amount of time. The evidence presented in Figure 1.1 does nothing to contradict this claim. In fact, that South Korea, which is the only other OECD member from East Asia, is the only one permitting police detention for a similar length of time to Japan appears to lend substance to the cultural theory.

The problem with such approaches is that they do not set out the specific mechanics through which this distinctive Asian culture manifests itself into actual policies. Even if the police custody policy of Japan does somehow result from a certain Asian tradition, it is still an important exercise to go beyond abstract theorizing to determine how it arises in practice, which the existing body of work does not do. How is it that a certain societal preference leads to a particular choice of legislation? On the other hand, if one were seeking to avoid making generalizations about the motivations of individuals within a particular part of the world, a less prejudicial starting point might be to ask whether there actually is any evidence of the Japanese doing things 'differently' to how those in the West would have done. Could it not simply be the case that the 'Asian choice' made on police custody in Japan was nothing more than the natural conclusion to some decision-making process with given constraints and interests?

Uniqueness of Japanese criminal justice

A second branch of literature relevant to police detention in Japan, if not to South Korea and other East Asian countries, relates the distinctive features of the Japanese criminal justice system to equally distinctive features of Japanese society and national character. As with 'Asian values', such arguments have appeared in various forms over many years, but to summarize, using the words of Cavadino and Dignan,

> although in many ways [Japan's] criminal justice and penal institutions and processes look extremely familiar to Western eyes, the way they operate can often seem surprising since they are still strongly imbued by traditional Japanese attitudes and values. (Cavadino and Dignan 2006: 171)

Whilst the research on Japan's police detention system specifically has to date been somewhat limited, there have been a number of studies on policing more generally which potentially offer insights into it.

One could do worse than to start with the classic work of David Bayley, which has provided to Westerners an influential viewpoint on policing in Japan since first being published in 1976. This work clearly gives the impression that to understand the current system of police custody in Japan, one should recognize the authority of the police there. In particular, Bayley writes that:

> Japanese police officers are not viewed by the community simply as agents of law. They possess enormous moral authority. Their role transcends, though it must not contradict, legal prescriptions. A Japanese police officer is more than a specialist in catching criminals and advising about crime prevention. He acts with the aura of a teacher shaping conduct to conform to community standards . . . (Bayley 1976: 142)

Where this authority comes from, Bayley argues, is a strong communitarian spirit, which elevates to a position of high prestige all government servants, including the police force. In comparing the situation of officers in the USA and Japan, for instance, he asserts that 'American police officers have the authority of man-made law; Japanese police have the authority of unspoken moral consensus' (Bayley 1976: 143). According to Bayley's argument, this recognition of the police's authority goes both ways:

> Awareness that they are a moral rather than just a legal force makes Japanese police officers sensitive to the intangible effects of what they do . . . They recognize that how they do something is as important as what they do. Knowing they are more than legal instruments, they accept the obligation of moral tutors to be upright in word and deed. (Bayley 1976: 144)

It is from such 'deep-seated attitudes towards [the] authority [of the police]', held by both the public and the officers themselves, that '[t]he lack of enthusiasm for abolishing the pre-charge detention system' stems (Bayley 1976: 149). Moreover, for Bayley, the trust in the police is so high that '[a]rrest is tantamount to conviction' (Bayley 1976: 149)—the layman would not envisage that a police officer would arrest an innocent man. In a more recent work, David T Johnson supports this claim, linking the 'stigma of arrest' to the comparatively low arrest rate of Japan (Johnson 2002: 14), which currently stands at less than 20 per cent.[9] Whilst equating arrest and conviction does not actually fit with the reality that approximately 40 per cent of arrests do not result in indictment,[10] when one considers that nearly all trials in Japan end with a guilty verdict,[11] it is unarguable that the police are in a position of great trust when it comes to determining criminal justice outcomes there.

Why is it, though, that the Japanese police might require in particular a system of prolonged detention? Here, it seems that there is a relevance to the cultural importance of confession within Japan. To quote from Bayley again:

> All observers, including police and prosecutors, agree that the primary purpose of detention is to obtain a confession. 'Confession is king,' as a police training manual puts it, because it fits moral imperatives of Japanese society. (Bayley 1976: 146)

Similarly, although Chalmers Johnson attributes the consequently unsurprisingly high confession rate in Japan[12] in part to a coercive

[9] In Japan in 2013, there were 1,314,140 Penal Code offences, but only 262,486 people were arrested. Note that the total number of cases cleared was 394,121, meaning that about a third of cleared cases did not involve an arrest at all. (Source: *Police of Japan 2015*, available at <www.npa.go.jp/english/kokusai/%28full_text%29POJ2015_web_.pdf>.) According to Johnson, this is a stark contrast to the USA, where 'arrest initiates most criminal cases' (Johnson 2002: 13).

[10] Police Detention Administration in Japan, NPA pamphlet, 29 October 2008.

[11] In 2010, for example, the overall conviction rate in both district and summary courts was 99.9 per cent. Even when only taking into account cases in which the accused pleaded not guilty, the conviction rate was still high, being 97.3 per cent in district courts and 96.7 per cent in summary courts. By comparison, in the USA in 2012 the conviction rate was 93 per cent, and in the UK in the year ending March 2014 it was 83 per cent. Sources: Supreme Court of Japan, Outline of Criminal Justice in Japan, available at <www.courts.go.jp/english/judicial_sys/criminal_justice_index/criminal_justice/index.html>, United States Attorneys' Annual Statistical Report for the Fiscal Year 2012, and the Criminal Justice Statistics Quarterly Update to March 2014 issued by the UK Ministry of Justice.

[12] Again in 2010, the confession rate in Japan for ordinary cases appearing for the first time in a district court was 91.2 per cent, and in a summary court was 92.8

police force, he also recognizes Japanese culture as a contributing factor (Johnson 1972). To expand on this, confession is perceived as being part of a culture of apology in which acknowledging one's crime is the first step towards rehabilitation, or, to put it another way, a promise not to offend again (see, for example, Braithwaite 1989). That this is important in Japan, it is argued, is demonstrated by the leniency shown to suspects who confess and show remorse:

> Leniency is considered an appropriate response if the correctional process has begun. The sincerity of confession and remorse therefore becomes a significant factor in deciding whether correction is likely. (Haley 1991: 133)

It is supposedly for this reason that confessions carry such weight in the Japanese criminal justice system, and also that the police are so keen to obtain them.

Such observations encapsulate what Daniel Foote, in another influential work by a Western scholar on criminal justice in Japan, has characterized as 'benevolent paternalism'. The 'benevolent' part of this description refers to the perceived goal of the system being the 'achiev[ement of] reformation and reintegration into society through lenient sanctions tailored to the offender's particular circumstances',[13] and the 'paternalistic' part to the 'substantial [degree of] discretion [granted] to the authorities in both gathering and using information about the offender and the offense' (Foote 1992: 317). In Foote's view, the 'intrusions on personal autonomy' which the Japanese criminal justice system countenances, including the suspect investigation period allowance of up to twenty-three days, are the price Japan pays for succeeding in the

per cent. (Source: Supreme Court of Japan, Outline of Criminal Justice in Japan, available at <www.courts.go.jp/english/judicial_sys/criminal_justice_index/criminal_justice/index.html>.) To put this into context, studies have placed the confession rate in the USA in the range 42–64 per cent, the confession rate in the UK in the range 55–62 per cent, and the confession rate in Australia to be in the range 46–76 per cent: see the discussion in Moston and Engelberg (2011).

[13] Although since Foote's work it has been observed that the benevolent aspect of Japanese justice is decreasing, with the sentences being issued by courts there becoming increasingly punitive, it is generally accepted that sentencing in Japan remains on the more lenient side by international comparison (Garland 2001, Johnson 2007).

attainment of its goal of reintegrating offenders into society. Moreover, relating the premium on confession in Japan to the police custody practices there and the authority of the police, as already highlighted previously, Daniel Foote writes:

> Given the Japanese public's apparent willingness to accept intensive questioning of suspects, at least so long as the investigators maintain a high degree of accuracy in identifying the suspects subjected to arrest and questioning (which the public also appears to trust to be the case), the fundamental approach [towards confession] in Japan is unlikely to change. (Foote 1991: 486)

So it is that one can understand why 'the centrepiece of the investigation is ordinarily the interrogation of the suspect' (Foote 1992: 317), and consequently how the balance of individual rights versus the demands of the community has been settled in the case of police detention in Japan.

Certain aspects of the above schools of thought have received criticism for 'idealization of the other' (by, for example, Murayama 1990, Miyazawa 1992, Johnson 2002, Goold 2004)—either by oversimplifying the approaches of criminal justice officials and their relationship with the wider Japanese community, or by uncritically linking these to outcomes such as the low crime rate. As Goold writes, 'Japan has come to be regarded by [some] scholars as something of a criminal justice utopia, a country in which police officers are treated as beloved members of the community, and prosecutors and judges are loyal servants dedicated solely to the rehabilitation of offenders' (Goold 2004: 14). Such a picture is, for Goold, marred by Orientalism. On a similar theme, the Japanese scholar Kōichi Hamai offers a speculation to contrast with those Western researchers who have asserted that Japan's low crime is a by-product of the high consciousness of social order of its citizens, suggesting that it is perhaps due instead to a mentality based on the concept of *murahachibu*, a practice from Edo Japan whereby the whole village punished those who did not obey the rules and behaved badly by ostracizing them.[14] Perhaps even more strikingly, some scholars question whether the outcomes themselves might on closer inspection not be quite as remarkable as they first appear. For instance, Setsuo Miyazawa comments that in discussing Japan's high crime clearance rate, one should take into

[14] *Asahi Shimbun* interview with Hamai. '*Keimusho kara mieru mono*' (What Could Be Seen from the Prison), 22 January 2013.

account that Japan has many more police officers per crime than other countries do (Miyazawa 2012: 165). Such an observation clearly hints at a more mundane explanation for the success of the Japanese police than some great efficiency on the part of individual officers stemming from intangible cultural factors.

On the other hand, it has also been pointed out that there is something of a circularity to those arguments which place Japan on a pedestal that has kept them relevant. Indeed, so it is said, Japanese police officials themselves are very keen to soak up outsiders' views that present their approach to combating crime and dealing with criminals as unique, and readily attempt to preserve this image through their words and actions. As Aldous and Leishman describe in the case of the police boxes in Japan in particular, 'Western admiration ... often ahistorical, uncritical and counter-intuitive as it is, may to a significant extent have convinced Japanese police officials of the uniqueness and merits of their own system' (Aldous and Leishman 2000: 11). These attempts of the police to live up to the legend have apparently propagated the view of Japan's policing and attitude to crime as *sui generis* to such an extent that the Japanese media—even the more liberal part of it—is, as Ellis et al. observe, 'still saturated with *nihonjinron* [unique to the Japanese people] ideas' (Ellis et al. 2008: 186).

It would be foolhardy to deign that, just because some of the literature focusing on the uniqueness of Japan's criminal justice practices has perhaps been overgenerous in its praise, this area of scholarship has nothing to offer in the way of explaining police detention practices in Japan. However, as with the 'Asian values' strand of arguments, one must be cautious in trying to apply the existing characterizations too hastily, as doing so runs the risk of identifying the outcome with the assumption—'ah, the Japanese must have this unique policy because of the way they do things differently!'.

State resistance to international norms

Moving towards a more mechanical explanation, another branch of literature that is potentially relevant to explaining the divergence of Japan's police custody arrangements from other states comes from the field of international relations, and in particular certain ideas arising from the theory of human rights norm diffusion developed by Keck, Sikkink, Risse-Kappen, and Ropp, amongst others (Keck and Sikkink 1998, Risse-Kappen, Ropp, and Sikkink 1999). This body of work would suggest that the apparent compromising of the rights of suspects in Japan, relative to other developed countries, is simply the result of the Japanese state's self-interest being, if not in direct conflict with the protection of these rights, then at least such that they are sidelined.

To give some more detail, the proponents of this norm-diffusion theory see states' elites as seeking to maintain their sovereignty and local culture, and only responding to pressures to conform with international legal human rights norms in order to gain material or political advantages. In what Risse-Kappen, Ropp, and Sikkink describe as the 'spiral model', resistant states, in their bid to enhance their position, enter into what they consider are only symbolic gestures with regard to international human rights norms, only to find later that it has become impossible for them, with domestic and transnational NGOs constantly exposing the discrepancy between their official commitments and actual practices, to not continue on a path of ever more significant concessions (Risse-Kappen, Ropp, and Sikkink 1999). Ultimately, the model predicts, these initially resistant states come to full compliance with the international human rights standards. It should be noted, however, that the authors leave open room for 'blocking factors' that inhibit progression into the later stages of the spiral model. These might include 'forces threatening the territorial integrity or internal cohesion of the state' and '[lack of] societal "openness" to external processes of argumentation and persuasion' (Risse-Kappen, Ropp, and Sikkink 1999: 258–67).

If the above theory is applied to the case of Japanese police custody, the natural conclusion would be that Japan is a laggard in the area of protecting suspects' rights, still being on one of the earlier stages of the spiral model, and that it is simply a matter of time until its practices converge with those of other developed nations. Given that Japan ratified a number of international human rights treaties in the 1990s, including the UN CAT that explicitly relates to custody arrangements,[15] one would expect that it would eventually align its police detention practices with other states that

[15] See, in particular, Article 11, which states: '[e]ach State Party shall keep under systematic review interrogation rules, instructions, methods and practices as well as arrangements for the custody and treatment of persons subjected to any form of arrest, detention or imprisonment in any territory under its jurisdiction, with a view to preventing any cases of torture.'

have ratified these treaties, such as the majority of the OECD members, reducing the duration of legally permissible police detention in particular—that is, unless one of the so-called blocking factors hinted at by the norm-diffusionists leaves Japan at a final plateau from which change is unlikely.

Thus it is that one can draw inferences about Japan's police custody practices, and what might be expected to unfold in the future. However, there is an obvious gap in the argument, in that it neither provides insight into where to look for blocking factors in specific cases, nor gives clues as to whether and how they would disappear over time. This being the case, it seems that the theory is not on a fine enough scale to interpret the root cause of the divergence in the case under study here. Indeed, the fact that, having ratified most of the key international instruments on human rights, Japan is at a later stage of the spiral model means that it falls precisely into the gap where the norm-diffusionists assert a 'blocking factor' could be relevant. Whatever its analytical convenience, the portrayal of the state as a monolithic blob trying to defend itself against change does not seem adequate. Why, for instance, does Japan not reduce the length of legally permitted police custody in order to harmonize its police detention practices more closely with those of other developed nations, given that in other cases, such as children's rights (Goodman 2000), patients' rights (Neary 2002), and women's rights (Chan-Tiberghien 2004), it has made significant changes in such a direction? Clearly, if one is to answer such questions as 'Is Japan ever going to converge on international norms regarding police detention?' and 'Even if it is going to do so in the future, why is this not happening now?', work remains to be done.

To summarize, each of the three branches of literature discussed in this section leaves a fog surrounding the mechanism leading to the emergence of prolonged police detention in Japan. In the case of culture, whilst this should not be discarded as being unimportant in conditioning the approaches of individuals involved in a decision-making process, it is simply not the case that there is a black box into which one places 'culture' and then turns the handle to discover what statute emerges. A similar point also applies when trying to extrapolate from a characterization of some aspect of Japanese society, however incisive this might be. Moreover, although transnational network theories do not avoid the question of what leads a state to adopt a particular human rights-related policy, the present versions of such rather neglect the possible internal causes for its divergence from those of other developed countries.

An Institutional Approach

Based on the above critique, I contend that in trying to understand Japan's police custody regime, it is important to zoom in, recognizing that the relevant legislation emerged not in isolation, but within a potentially complex social and political landscape that might have evolved over time.

Adopting a social scientific approach to such ends has been strongly advocated in recent years. Specifically, as mentioned at the outset, the political philosopher Michael Freeman has argued that, notwithstanding work such as that of Keck, Sikkink, Risse-Kappen, and Ropp, there is still an appalling general dearth of research on human rights by social scientists (Freeman 2002, 2006). The bulk of today's human rights literature, as Freeman seeks to highlight, consists primarily of descriptions or technical formal analyses of legal instruments, rules, and procedure. That the study of human rights is in such a state is, he argues, the sad result of the social scientists being under the erroneous assumption that objectivity requires them to ignore a concept with normative connotations such as human rights altogether—a consequence of this group of researchers having remained under the spell of the mid-twentieth century's dominant teaching that ethical judgments ought to be removed from their work for being 'unscientific' and 'subjective' (Freeman 2002: 78). Not only did the social sciences neglect human rights, thereby leaving the human rights discourse to the law, but this legalistic tendency itself served to reinforce the estrangement. In Freeman's own words,

> [t]he cost of [the] attempt to universalize the concept of human rights [through the Universal Declaration of Human Rights (UDHR)] was to alienate it from Western philosophy and social science. Natural law was generally in decline [in the post-war period]. The concept of human rights was consequently controversial in philosophy and was largely ignored by the social sciences under the influence of scientific positivism. This left the

discourse of human rights mainly to lawyers. International law is not generally familiar, however, with those disciplines of theory, method and epistemology that are foundational for social science. As a result, the study of human rights was vulnerable to a combination of natural-law idealism and text-based legalism. Human rights became 'legalized', therefore, not only by being written into laws, but also by becoming the near-monopoly of legal science. (Freeman 2006: 49–50)

For him, it is high time that social scientists, and political scientists in particular, step in and restore the balance, by using their familiarity with such concepts as 'development, stability, participation, bureaucracy, interest groups, power relationships, judicial behaviour, popular movements, militarism, public opinion and ideology' for the goal of uncovering factors that either hamper or facilitate human rights implementation so that policies can be devised accordingly (Freeman 2006: 52). By seeking to explain a case of human rights variation through the lens of political science, it is hoped that the present study will offer something to this grand programme.

So, then, let us start to think about how decisions relating to Japan's police detention policy are made. Being of a political nature, many factors other than rights-conflict resolution can also impinge upon the process in question, and so it is important to take a broad view of the issue. Politicians, for example, might want to be seen to be tough on crime, and by reducing lengths of police custody might worry that they would lose votes by appearing to be on the side of the criminals. This is not to say that the political elite have no incentive for introducing international norms that take the side of the suspects domestically. Ratifying related international treaties can bring prestige, and, on a more pragmatic level, can be an important bargaining tool for politicians. Moreover, failure to ensure that their criminal justice system, including the treatment of suspects, meets modern international standards can be acutely embarrassing. Bureaucrats, too, in defending their turf, might be reluctant to yield authority to other organizations. Even campaign groups giving no consideration to logistical or political constraints might scupper their chances of influencing powerful figures through such trivialities as poor organization. Taking this bigger picture into account will enable identification of the processes through which choices relating to prisoners are made and legitimized, together with the constraints upon them. Only by doing this will it be possible to determine the origins of the present police detention practice, and to understand whether and how suspects' rights have been incorporated into the decision-making process.

To go from the concrete to the abstract, what the above tells us is that, in order to elucidate how decisions relating to Japan's police custody practices are made, it is essential to understand the institutional landscape, and how this shapes actors' actions. This being the case, it makes sense to turn to institutionalism. As Putnam notes in his seminal work *Making Democracy Work*, although (new) institutionalism is a diverse church, the majority of its proponents agree on two key points: '[i]nstitutions shape politics' and '[i]nstitutions are shaped by history' (Putnam 1992: 7–8). To expand first on the former, once institutions are in place, key actors will act in such a way as to maximize their utility (that is, behave rationally in line with the incentives the institution prescribes), and outcomes can only be understood by taking this into account. Putnam himself explains, '[o]utcomes are not simply reducible to the billiard-ball interactions of individuals nor to the intersection of broad social forces. Institutions influence outcomes because they shape actors' identities, power and strategies' (Putnam 1992: 8). Regarding the second point, this is based on the acknowledgement that the original institutional landscape did not appear from nowhere, but was left to the current actors by their predecessors. Consequently, in trying to understand the present, it is also important to recognize historical legacies—to say it more plainly, the effects of the past last.

This way of thinking suggests that we would fail to achieve our goal of fully understanding the choices made in Japan today on police custody if we do not acknowledge that these are conditioned by history. Such a perspective has previously proved to be applicable in a range of areas. Indeed, some of the staple works of a Japanese politics student's diet have sought to demonstrate that contemporary Japanese policies can be explained in terms of the Occupation period reforms, or lack thereof. Johnson, for example, famously argues that it is because the Americans left the Ministry of International Trade and Industry with overwhelming powers, thereby allowing it to reinvigorate the policies and institutions that had evolved in the Meiji and Taishō periods, that the Japanese economic miracle happened (Johnson 1982). Furthermore, although Samuels' study differs from Johnson's in that he depicts the same Ministry as actually having its hands tied in terms of being able to intervene into the energy market from the measures left in place by the Occupation, it is precisely these measures to which he attributes the persistence of an energy policy that the government might have benefited from changing in the second half of the twentieth century (Samuels 1987). In recent years, these two studies have been criticized for overplaying historical factors, but with respect to such a transformative period of Japanese history as the Occupation, few would deny that the upheaval that it brought had a profound effect on Japan, or that its impact on Japan's institutional framework has been long-lasting. (This is not to imply that the Occupation was the only pivotal point of Japan's history.)

Although not strictly pinpointing historical resonance as the determining factor in legislative outcomes, another area of theory relevant to this point is that of institutional inertia in Japan. As Amyx has described in the case of the Japanese financial sector, due to the informal networks developed between bureaucrats and practitioners, the institutions of Japan show a high degree of 'stickiness' (Amyx 2004). That is, despite sometimes overwhelming pressure to change a policy, this might be a long time coming, and insubstantial when it actually occurs. Similarly, Krauss and Pekkanen identify a number of features of the Japanese political landscape that remained unchanged following the major electoral reform of 1994 (Krauss and Pekkanen 2011). One can extrapolate from such work that, once an institutional arrangement is established in Japan, it is likely to be durable. So, again, this leads us to the conclusion that to understand how a particular part of the legal framework arose, one will have to look a long way back to find its origins. In particular, it would be negligent to ignore the possibility that there have been points in history which, if not predetermined Japan's future, then at least set it on a course from which deviation is unlikely to occur.

Accordingly, this book seeks to characterize the institutional context of Japan's police detention system, and describe how this has been shaped by and evolved through history. The promise of adopting this institutional approach is that it will yield great understanding of the mechanisms through which the prolonged police detention policy came about. With the striking conflicts between the individual rights of suspects and the good of the wider society already described, it is inevitable that different groups participating in the decision-making process will take positions that are diametrically opposed. This will make it easy to determine whose views the police detention policy represents, and where the balance of power in suspects–community rights decision-making in Japan lies. Let it be noted that the interactions that will be examined—between, inter alia, the bureaucracy, the legislature, and the bar—are features common to many political systems. It is thus not unreasonable to expect that the study will achieve the aforementioned goal of illuminating some general factors relevant to human rights implementation, making it more widely beneficial than simply explaining the particular case.

Finally, and stating that the following is only possible with the benefit of hindsight, in the process of clarifying what is at the root of Japan's policy of prolonged police detention, this book will also explain why, despite there having been a broad-based consensus there since the 1970s on the need to update the regulatory framework for prisons, such reform was not forthcoming for three long decades. To the extent that many of the eventual changes in this framework were generally seen as 'improvements' in the treatment of prisoners by domestic and international rights advocates, accounting for this delay promises to yield a supplementary lesson on the factors likely to hamper human rights implementation. By formulating such a conclusion, this book will provide a further service with regard to Freeman's exhortation that social science is brought to bear in this area.

Methodology

Towards the goal of explaining Japan's police custody divergence, this book undertakes two lines of enquiry. Firstly, it traces the historical process through which the present-day system of prolonged police detention emerged, identifying the critical junctures in this policy's evolution. It then examines relevant recent legislative reform attempts, so as to determine what it is about the current institutional landscape that explains its persistence.

The historical component focuses on the questions of why the choices leading to Japan's present lengthy police custody were made and what constraints these left to future generations. It begins with the period just after the Meiji Restoration, when the foundation of Japan's modern-day institutions was laid. Specifically, it seeks to identify what basis there might be for prolonged police detention in the newly created laws of this period. Of course, assuming a priori that there was nothing before the Meiji period that might have played a role in shaping today's police detention practices might seem deterministic. However, in the sense that the Meiji period is when Japan moved from being an isolated feudal state to one more akin to its present-day incarnation, with fundamental changes impacting social structure, the legal and judicial system, politics, the economy, the military, and foreign relations, it seems a natural starting point for the present investigation.

This investigation continues up to the Allied Occupation Forces reforms. In particular, it investigates how, in the first half of the twentieth century, police detention was applied in practice, as well as how it was debated in parliament and more generally, and then determines the impact on the policy of the multitude of changes that took place during the Occupation. The primary purpose of this is to describe the playing field at the start of the post-war period, though it should be noted that building up the historical account of police detention in this way is of value in itself, since very little has appeared on this part of the story outside of the Japanese literature. All that being said, with the ultimate goal being to characterize the modern debates surrounding police custody in Japan, it is not the intention to overly dwell on the early developments. Rather, once I have identified the key historical aspects of the criminal justice context, I will move on to exploring the more recent situation in depth.

For the second aspect of the study, which concerns the modern reform attempts, it is essential to determine the positions of the key institutional actors and their relative power in the decision-making process. As the central tool in this direction, an in-depth analysis is conducted of the various episodes over the past thirty years when reform of the police detention policy was on the table as part of a broader legislative review—firstly across the 1980s and 1990s, and then again in 2005–6. Although it is not strictly necessary to focus on these periods in order to understand the relevant actors' positions on the issue of police custody, there is no question that great insights can be drawn from them. This is because it is at points of legislative reform that actors are forced to distil and prioritize their demands, and so display their true colours. It is not only the standpoints of actors that are revealing, though; the bargaining strategies adopted can also tell a story—who is prepared to give what away, and who is prepared to get into bed with whom.

An important step in proceeding with the above programme is choosing the actors on which to focus attention. Since it is impossible to consider everybody who could possibly have played a role in shaping the police detention system, it is necessary to be somewhat selective. Here, I choose to place the spotlight on players with a particular stake in police custody from each of the following categories:

1. *Bureaucracy.* I scrutinize the ideology and follow the actions of the National Police Agency (NPA) and the Ministry of Justice (MOJ), the former of which holds jurisdiction over the investigation of suspects and the latter of which is responsible for general criminal justice affairs. Note in particular that this choice of actors includes the Public Prosecutor's Office, which is administratively part of the MOJ (though is independent of the authority of the Justice Minister).
2. *Judiciary.* Examining the attitudes within the judiciary is appropriate as well, insofar as it has a mandate not only to later conduct the trials of those suspects who become indicted, but also to decide at an early stage upon arrest whether, where, and for how long suspects are to be detained.
3. *Legislature.* No study of policy-making can legitimately omit paying attention to the dynamics within the legislature, which in the Japanese case were largely determined for almost fifty years until 2009 by the leading Liberal Democratic Party (LDP), with the Democratic Party of Japan (DPJ), amongst other parties, more recently starting to play a role of increased prominence.
4. *Interest groups.* Such actors are also relevant to consider, with the Japan Federation of Bar Associations (JFBA), which has an interest in the protection of the rights of its clients, being the first most obvious of these, with a particular concern in suspect detention decision-making.
5. *International organizations.* In today's age of globalization, it is also essential to consider the impact on domestic policies of international organizations—in this case, those concerned with human rights, such as the intergovernmental UN and the NGOs, Amnesty International and Human Rights Watch (HRW).

Actors of each of these types have been seen to be relevant to decision-making in Japan in general, and so, potentially, they could play a role in the present case as well. Of course, similarly to the issue of choosing a starting point discussed previously, there is a danger that actors not appearing on the above list have also influenced the process of formation of the current police detention arrangement, particularly during the earlier period when the policy-making landscape was different. This being the case, when empirical findings suggest it is important to consider the role of actors not hitherto named, I do not shy away from doing so.

Since, as stated in the previous section, the explanation of the emergence and establishment of Japan's modern police detention system presented in this book automatically serves to reveal the cause of a delay in the implementation of prisoners' rights, a few words are in order on this connection. To wit, the study of police detention conducted here incorporates the documentation of three failed Prison Law (*Kangoku hō*) revision attempts in the 1980s and 1990s, on the one hand, and the corresponding success in the mid-2000s. This being the case, it immediately offers the chance to conduct a within-case comparison that will shed light on the prison issue. Why exactly was it that reform took so long to achieve? Comparing and contrasting the two sets of reforms with differing outcomes allows the crucial factor to be isolated.

The findings of my investigation are based on a range of primary and secondary sources. For my narrative on police custody during the period between the Meiji Restoration and the end of the Allied Occupation, I rely primarily on existing Japanese-language scholarship on this subject. In particular, I summarize the research of Japanese social and legal historians. The availability of such work for me to draw on in my construction of the complete story of the emergence of Japan's current police custody policies is extremely useful, since the period under my investigation spans nearly 150 years, with official materials for the earlier stages of this history being difficult to access and direct fieldwork being literally impossible to conduct. As for my analysis of the developments in the post-Occupation era, although there I still refer to Japanese-language academic literature from time to time, I depend chiefly on primary sources, collected mainly during one seven-month and one three-month-long field trip to Japan—from early July 2007 until the end of January 2008 and from the beginning of January until the end of March 2009, respectively—but also intermittently during my stay in Japan since November 2009. These sources include:

- Numerous semi-structured in-depth interviews, each lasting between one and three hours, with: MOJ, NPA, and Tōkyō Metropolitan Police officials; serving prosecutors and prosecutors from within the administration of the Tōkyō High Public Prosecutors Office; ex-judges and senior judges in active duty; former justice ministers, a shadow justice minister, and other legislators from the LDP, DPJ, and Social Democratic Party (SDP); a political secretary; lawyers and JFBA spokesmen; convicted inmates, including a death-row inmate with a record of a later contested police detention confession; rehabilitated convicts; a prison warden, a prison guard, and a prison nurse; academics; a media member; and representatives of professional and non-professional non-governmental organizations (NGOs). These NGOs include not only the Relief Contact Centre (*Kyūen renraku sentā*, RCC), which is specifically designed to help suspects and to campaign for their rights, but also those advocating prisoners' and other undermined groups' rights, such as the Centre for Prisoners' Rights (*Kangoku jinken sentā*, CPR), United Prisoners, the Anti-Death Penalty Forum 90, the Japan Civil Liberties Union (*Jiyū jinken kyōkai*, JCLU), and Amnesty International Japan. (Further details appear in the Interviews section at the end of the book.)
- Participant observation in domestic and international gatherings on this and relevant topics, including most notably a series of JFBA meetings on the Realization of Reform of the Criminal Detention System and the UNHRC's October 2008 examination of the Japanese government's fifth periodic report on the progress towards the implementation of the ICCPR, whereby the issue of Japan's prolonged detention was discussed.
- Visits to the Tōkyō Detention Centre, Tōkyō Metropolitan Police, and Fuchū Prison, and attendance at various court hearings involving confessions obtained in police custody.
- Printed material, including official government data, National Diet minutes, White Papers, pamphlets, and newspaper articles.

Gathering information from a diverse pool of informants, experiences, and written material allowed me to become familiar with the issues involved and to formulate as balanced a view as possible of the factors that produced Japan's policy of prolonged police detention.

What Lies Ahead

To preview the argument developed in the ensuing pages: Japan's policy of prolonged police detention is a by-product of a path dependency process, and more specifically the positive feedback mechanism triggered by the combined legacies of two critical junctures in the evolution of Japan's suspect detention policies.

The first defining event in Japan's historical progression to the establishment of its modern-day police detention arrangements was the instituting into law of the so-called 'substitute prison' (*daiyō kangoku*) article. This statute, which was adopted as part of the 1908 Prison Law, stated that 'police cells (*ryūchijo*) could be used in lieu of prisons [that is, MOJ detention facilities, today known as *kōchisho*]'. As is set out in Chapter 2, however, this step did not in itself yield the system of prolonged police detention as we see it today. Indeed, at the time, the principle of an un-convicted person's rights was still not very well embedded into the Japanese criminal justice procedure, and, with no measures such as *habeas corpus*, there were few restrictions on the authority of the police. Consequently, although lengthy police detention was common from Meiji up until the arrival of the Allied Forces, it was not the substitute prison article that was seen as being at its root. Rather, using their quasi-judicial powers in conjunction with the infamous Peace Preservation Law (*Chian iji hō*), which the pre-war militarist authorities had promulgated as a tool in their bid to suppress popular dissent, the police had great leeway to arrest, try, and imprison individuals outside of the court system, and they would do so extensively. As to why the substitute prison article was adopted, this followed from an incongruity between the MOJ's criminal procedural requirements and the earlier detention strategy of the Home Ministry (*Naimushō*). Concretely, with the introduction of preliminary examination during the transitional Meiji period, a demand that necessitated suspects be detained nearby courts was created. In the absence of a sufficiently dispersed network to meet this need, due to the Home Ministry's concentration on the development of large central prisons (*shūjikan*), from a practical point of view it was necessary that police cells were allowed to be used temporarily instead in some cases. Thus it was that the substitute prison article was placed into legislation, albeit supposedly only as a stop-gap measure.

This modest origin notwithstanding, the substitute prison article would come to occupy a much more prominent role in the Japanese criminal justice process following the post-war Occupation reforms. Indeed, the Americans tried to prevent the arbitrary and prolonged police arrest and abusive interrogation that was rampant in pre-war Japan by stripping the police of its Peace Preservation Law and enacting a new Constitution and Code of Criminal Procedure. These two statutes were much more suspect rights-conscious than those they replaced, with the revised Code of Criminal Procedure in particular dictating that, similarly to the USA, suspects should be held for no longer than seventy-two hours in police custody prior to being brought before a judge. Although not written explicitly in law, the documentary evidence that exists clearly suggests the Americans would have expected that, if further detention was deemed necessary by the judge, the suspect would be transferred to facilities independent of the investigative authorities. However, by neglecting to reform the Prison Law and, in particular, its substitute prison article, they left a legal loophole permitting the return of suspects to police custody after having seen a judge for up to a further twenty days. This oversight, which gave a continued legal basis for the practice of using police cells rather than MOJ facilities for detaining suspects, could thus be seen as the second pivotal point in the emergence of Japan's present system of prolonged police detention.

Over the decades following the changes of the Occupation, a self-reinforcing expansion mechanism for substitute prison would kick in, firmly establishing this measure within the Japanese criminal justice process. On the one hand, the NPA were quick to take advantage of the gap the occupiers left with the substitute prison article, and would increasingly turn to it as a means of retaining control over suspects during investigations. Being the guardian of social safety and order, it was relatively easy for the Agency to attract significant sums from the national budget for constructing new facilities that enabled this practice to be increased. The MOJ, on the other hand—more focused on managing the growing problems arising in its overcrowded prisons—found it helpful and convenient for the NPA to take on some of the burden of suspect detention. Indeed, not only did this reduce the pressure on the MOJ to supply the quantity of detention centres adequate for the demand that the criminal justice process produced, but it also meant the Ministry could convert some existing detention facilities into prisons, so as to alleviate the creaking prison system. The initial evidence regarding these positions is presented in Chapters 3 and 4, which explore the actions of the two government departments during the Prison Law reform process. This is then distilled in Chapter 5, which goes on to explain how the mutually symbiotic relationship that developed between the NPA and MOJ was key to the embedding of the substitute prison system—with these two actors content for almost every new demand for a suspect detention facility to be met by the NPA, it would become increasingly difficult and costly for a change to take place.

Once started, this process of self-reinforcement found little resistance, not least because even the main opponent to substitute prison—the JFBA—found the support for abolition amongst its members dwindle over time. The bar's campaign for the use of substitute prison to be reduced, and eventually ceased, had been ongoing throughout the decades following the Association's inception in 1949. As discussed in Chapter 3, this stand against the system would culminate in the Prison Law reform process of the 1980s and 1990s when, through the political opposition, the lawyers' organization put an ultimatum to the government that this piece of legislation could not be amended without a substitute prison attrition clause being included. In the more recent reform process in the mid-2000s, covered in Chapter 4, though, they did not adopt such a stance, and consequently allowed the MOJ and NPA to pass legislation that meant the status quo would be maintained. Although the political position of the JFBA was arguably weaker and so taking such a hard line was not seen by all its members as a viable option in the latter period, the change in strategy also reflects an evolution in how the typical lawyer saw police custody. As a young, liberal organization in the 1970s, most of the JFBA's members were idealistic and stood passionately against substitute prison as a matter of principle—this remains the Association's official public line even today. However, as is expanded upon in Chapter 5, many of the newer members of the profession who have seen this system as the norm throughout their careers hold a more pragmatic attitude towards it. With the enormous expansion of the network of police cells and interview rooms across the country, they (and indeed their clients) describe how it is actually preferable on the grounds of convenience, especially visitation proximity, for suspects to be held in NPA facilities, rather than in MOJ ones. So it is that the growth of substitute prison in itself has served to reduce one of the potential obstacles, that is, a united opposition of the bar, to the continuation of this trend.

There are several additional, background factors that facilitated the entrenchment of substitute prison that arise in the historical accounts of Chapters 3 and 4, and which are detailed in Chapter 5. The first two of these relate to the MOJ and NPA's popular images as institutions: the former being seen, at least with regard to its responsibility for prison management, as the agency that brings to localities dangerous criminals; the latter as the citizens' guardian. This difference in image meant that there was a significant electoral disincentive for politicians to divert resources in the direction of the MOJ for building facilities incorporating detention centres, whereas it was much easier for it to gain approval by boosting the budget of the NPA. Furthermore, the difference in image impacted on the relative ability of each department to maintain detention capacity. In the case of the MOJ, it often faced local 'not in my backyard' resistance when attempting to build new facilities, meaning it had to overcome an even greater hurdle than simply finding the wherewithal for construction. By contrast, the NPA's new facilities often saw a 'definitely in my backyard' welcome. The next factor was that, not viewing substitute prison as fundamentally problematic, judges routinely granted approval to the prosecution's requests, being made on the grounds of investigative efficiency, for suspects' continual detention in police custody. Finally, the lack of public interest in the substitute prison issue could also be seen as one of the reasons for the limited impact of international and domestic advocacy groups. Unable to garner widespread popular support, these organizations failed to gain leverage in the Diet.

The story of substitute prison would not be complete, however, without a consideration of the potential impact upon it of the latest criminal justice change in Japan—namely, the introduction of the so-called lay judge system (*saiban'in seido*). This programme is undertaken in Chapter 6, which explores how both criminal justice debates and practices are changing as a result of this new development. It concludes that substitute prison is fated for change, as the transparency of interrogations becomes increasingly important and investigators turn away from the pursuit of confessions to other methods of collecting evidence.

Beyond the impact on the rights of suspects, that the substitute prison article appeared in the Prison Law and was so tied to the management of prisons meant that the developments previously described also had a significant impact on the implementation of convicted prisoners' rights. Indeed, as will be detailed in Chapter 3, since it was impossible for the authorities and the JFBA, represented in the Diet by the LDP and the DPJ respectively, to reach an agreement on whether to retain or abolish the substitute prison article, the whole project of updating the Prison Law came to a standstill for nearly thirty years. This deadlock was, as elucidated in Chapter 4, only resolved following a major scandal at Nagoya Prison involving inmate fatalities, when the pressure on the MOJ to finally make a change to the near-hundred-year-old Prison Law increased dramatically. To achieve this, the MOJ, together with the NPA and the ruling LDP, were compelled to adopt a new strategy of splitting the Prison Law revision process into two stages—first dealing with the less problematic part of the legislation for convicted inmates in a constructive manner, and then, after only a very limited consultation incorporating its possible opponents, pushing the remainder on police custody through the Diet. The broad positive response concerning the advancements in prisoners' rights protection of the first part of this change, which had an easy passage through the Diet, was in stark contrast to the continued objections of substitute prison abolitionists to the second. This provides conclusive proof that it was indeed substitute prison that had been the spanner in the works of the Prison Law reform.

Following the presentation of the evidence that supports the above picture, space is devoted, in Chapter 6, to a consideration of the future prospects for the substitute prison system, and in particular what impact might the recent introduction of lay judges have upon it. Finally, in the conclusion of Chapter 7, a return is made to the grander questions raised above regarding the significance of Japan's divergence on the issue of police detention to criminal justice issues and human rights implementation more generally.

2

Origin of the Modern System of Police Custody

> If you can look into the seeds of time, and say which grain will grow and which will not, speak then to me.
>
> William Shakespeare, Macbeth

> Mez quant ja est la chose fecte, ne peut pas bien estre desfecte. ['But when a thing is already done, it cannot be undone'.]
>
> Fourteenth-century French proverb

Towards comprehending how the prolonged police detention of suspects in modern-day Japan arose, this chapter traces back its origin in history. Without wanting to suggest that seeds could not be found by studying the criminal justice practices that existed in the days of the secluded Tokugawa regime and even earlier, the starting point here is the Meiji Restoration—for the Meiji oligarchy's attempts to mould a new state brought changes to all aspects of Japanese society, many of which are seen as having played a crucial role in shaping today's policies. From here, this historical part of the study of police custody in Japan continues up to the end, and the immediate aftermath, of the American Occupation. With this part of the story having been told, all will be in place for the exploration of the more recent police detention debates that will follow in subsequent chapters.

Administrative Musical Chairs and the Birth of Substitute Prison

Whilst seeking to retain order in a tumultuous environment, the Meiji authorities oversaw a radical transformation in the administration of criminal justice, whereby a feudalistic system was replaced by a codified one modelled on those of the leading Western powers. During this period, jurisdiction for prisons would pass from the Ministry of Justice (MOJ) to the Home Ministry and back again—a reshuffling of duties that had the residual effect of police cells being permitted to be used as a substitute for prisons. Although objections that criminal suspects could be abused if detained by the police during the pre-trial phase were raised prior to the promulgation of Japan's first Prison Law in 1908, the so-called 'substitute prison article' would nonetheless be included in this legislation to make up for the shortage of cells suitable for suspect detention in the prison network that had been developed hitherto.

After a brief false start at the beginning of the Meiji period, the management of prisons would be entrusted to the newly formed MOJ, which oversaw the preparation of aspirationally modern regulations for governing detainees that gave a special place to unsentenced inmates. Initially, in 1869, jurisdiction over prisons had been assigned to the Ministry of Criminal Affairs (*Gyōbushō*), which was one of the bureaucratic agencies that the ruling elite had tried to resurrect from the ancient Great Council of State (*Dajōkan*) during its short-lived attempt at revival-style modernization. With the momentum to reform along more Western lines growing, in only two years the Ministry of Criminal Affairs underwent a metamorphosis to become, together with the Bureau of Censorship (*Danjōdai*), the MOJ.[1] Leading the development of the penal system within this government department was Shigechika Ōhara. Attempting to bring about a more humane prison regime than that in place under the Tokugawa Shogunate (1603–1868), in creating his 1872 Illustrated Prison Rules (*Kangoku soku narabi ni zushiki*), Ōhara combined ideas from the ancient, Confucian-based system of benevolent treatment of subjects (*ritsuryō*)[2] with some of the prison administration practices that he had witnessed in the British colonies of Singapore and Hong Kong (Maeda 2004: 31–2, Botsman 2005: 146–54). These

[1] At the time of its formation, the MOJ was known in Japanese as *Shihōshō*. After the Second World War it would go through several incarnations, being labelled *Hōmuchō* in 1948 and *Hōmufu* in 1949, before arriving at its modern title of *Hōmushō* in 1952 (Stockwin 2003).

[2] This code contained both penal (*ritsu*) and administrative (*ryō*) law, and was intended to nurture morality within the populace, thereby creating citizens living virtuous lives according to Confucian values, with *ritsu* relating to the chastisement of evil and *ryō* relating to the promotion of righteousness (Ishii 1980: 22).

instituted a distinction in treatment, which had not existed prior to the Restoration, between unsentenced and sentenced inmates, and to house the former group in particular, Ōhara's rules proposed a special type of prison—the detention centre (*kansō*). The latter measure was intended to alleviate the extreme overcrowding that had arisen in the temporary premises for holding unsentenced inmates that had been created from rundown estates in the immediate aftermath of the Meiji restoration—indeed, within these improvised facilities, as many as fourteen or fifteen people were being held on a single Japanese *tatami* mat (Niwayama 1981: 112–13).

Prisons, however, did not remain under the MOJ's control as, soon after the establishment of the Home Ministry in 1873, the office of their administration was transferred there.[3] This shift was not an outcome that was idly arrived at, but one that had been actively sought by the Home Ministry, and also facilitated by the political climate of the time. Indeed, Toshiyoshi Kawaji, who was a key figure in the establishment of the Japanese police force, had actively petitioned for such a change. Kawaji's justification for this was that, since the MOJ had been granted jurisdiction over courts, there was a need to compensate the Home Ministry so as to ensure that criminal justice duties were balanced between the two government departments (*Daikasumi kai* 1971: 605). Moreover, Home Ministry officials saw taking responsibility for prisons as part of the Ministry's duty to maintain 'public safety and order' (*chian*). In particular, with many of the functions that had previously been performed by the feudal lords now being its concern, the Home Ministry was charged with keeping a handle on the widespread social unrest occurring in the confused and turbulent transitional time of the start of the Meiji era (Jansen and Hall 1989). With increasing crime and jail-breaks being a common threat, the Home Ministry contended that it would be in a better position than the MOJ to maintain control over the prison system (*Daikasumi kai*

[3] This would take place in several steps. First, by the end of November 1874, the jurisdiction of all prisons for both sentenced and unsentenced inmates was moved to the Home Ministry, with the exception of the detention centres for unsentenced inmates that were physically attached to the MOJ and the courts. Then the control of these detention centres was also brought under the remit of the Home Ministry, with the last of them—a new facility whose construction on the grounds of the MOJ had been completed in 1975—being transferred in 1876 after a petition to this effect had been filed by the Tōkyō Metropolitan Police.

1971: 605). The decision was argued to make sense from a practical point of view too, as the prefectural authorities, to which the administration of individual prisons was entrusted, were also supervised by the Home Ministry (*Daikasumi kai* 1971: 605). The reason why the Home Ministry's campaign was successful, it has been suggested, was that the wind was blowing in the right direction politically. In particular, following the 1873 resignation of the first Justice Minister Shimpei Etō and other influential figures in the government due to their part in the debate over invading Korea (*Seikanron*), the Home Minister Toshimichi Ōkubo faced little opposition in claiming the office of prisons (Inata 1971: 13).

Under the Home Ministry, the emphasis of Japan's detention strategy changed, ensuring that Ōhara's 1872 Prison Rules would never be fully implemented. Being perhaps too ambitious in their scope, even before the time came for the regulations in question to be put into practice, Treasury budgetary concerns (*Ōkurashō*) had limited the extent of their application (Röhl 2005: 760), meaning that unsentenced inmates did not receive the treatment envisioned by the criminal justice pioneer Ōhara. However, it has also been argued that this position was actually a pretext on the part of the government, which was seeking to move away from the populist British legal model to a more European-style system as part of its ongoing bid to maintain political control, of which the creation of a Home Ministry was a part (Niwayama 1981: 112–13). In particular, various uprisings of disgruntled former *samurai*, culminating in the 1877 Satsuma Rebellion, were generating many political prisoners.[4] To house these, on the encouragement of Motohiro Onoda—a high-ranking police official who had studied the prison systems of Europe—the Home Ministry devoted resources to building large central prisons of the kind found in Belgium and France (Niwayama 1981: 112–13, Röhl 2005: 760). Unlike the other prisons of the time, these also had the distinction of being administered directly by the central government, rather than the prefectures.[5] With large central prisons becoming the focus of the Home Ministry's detention policy, development of the other types

[4] At the end of the Satsuma Rebellion itself, 2,700 were incarcerated (Röhl 2005: 760).

[5] The Home Ministry built such facilities in a number of locations, first in Tōkyō (1879) (this is the forerunner of the Tōkyō Detention Centre) and Miyagi (1879) (the current Miyagi Prison), then in Kabato, Hokkaidō (1881); Sorachi, Hokkaidō (1882); Miike, Fukuoka (1883); Kushiro, Hokkaidō (1885) (today's Kushiro Prison); and another one in Abashiri (1891) (today's Abashiri Prison).

of facility required to fulfil Ōhara's vision—including detention houses for unsentenced inmates—was neglected.

Parallel with these developments, in 1874 the Home Ministry introduced a continental European-style police force, which would be strengthened over the next two decades in order to keep on top of the mounting political turmoil. The establishment of a centralized police along French lines was overseen by the aforementioned Kawaji (who would later become known as the 'father of the Japanese police'). Based on his first-hand observations of what was the oldest force in Europe, and together with his grander vision of the role of the police as a 'nursemaid', his ideas were explained in a 1873 report and book entitled *Hand and Eye of the Police*, whose legacy would be long-lasting (Tipton 1997: 47). Following Kawaji's initial work in setting up the Japanese police force, during the 1880s the latter would see a dramatic expansion, crucial to which was the powerful military leader and Home Minister of the time, Aritomo Yamagata. As was the predominant trend amongst the elite of the day, Yamagata sought a transition for the police from the initial French model of the 1870s to a German one (Jansen and Hall 1989: 646, Tipton 1990: 41), to this end enlisting the assistance of Berlin police captain Wilhelm Höhn (Ishii 1958: 461, Pedlar 1990: 169, Aldous 1997: 24). Höhn's proposal that the police force would function better if it was more widely spread led to 11,047 'residential police boxes' (*chūzaisho*) and 1,255 'police boxes in Tōkyō' (*hashutsujo*) being established over a ten-year period from 1888,[6] and he also instigated rigorous training for the numerous new recruits needed to man them (Jansen and Hall 1989: 646, Jansen 2009: 401).

This increase in police presence was matched by an increase in its authority. An early, and widely applied, instrument of police power was the 1885 Summary Trial Regulations for Police Offences (*Ikeizai sokketsu rei*), which permitted the head of a police station to conduct immediate trials for offences against the police within their jurisdictional district (Ames 1981: 10, Röhl 2005: 144). Since the Penal Code of the time left room for a broad interpretation of what constituted a crime against a public official,

[6] Figures taken from *Japanese Community Police and Police Box System*, NPA. Retrieved on 18 January 2014 from: <www.npa.go.jp/english/seisaku1/Japanese CommunityPolice.pdf>. (See also Smethurst 1974: 9, Aldous 1997: 24, Aldous and Leishman 2000: 3–6.)

these regulations made it particularly easy for the police to arbitrarily impose its power (Aldous 1997: 27). Bolstering the police in such a way allowed the oligarchs to quash the growing opposition to their regime coming from groups such as the Freedom and Popular Rights' Movement.[7] Further measures introduced to the same end included the 1886 enhancement of the political wing of the police's powers[8] and the 1887 Peace Preservation Ordinance (*Hōan jōrei*), which included provisions to prevent uprisings and social order disturbances.[9] Implemented immediately and with vigour, the Peace Preservation Ordinance served as the basis for deporting 570 people from Tōkyō within three days of its issuance (Smethurst 1974: 10, Jansen and Hall 1989: 658).

Meanwhile, the houses of custody attached to the broadening network of police stations were designated as a type of prison that could be used for the temporary detention of those awaiting trial. Concretely, the 1880 Code of Criminal Instruction (*Chizai hō*) prepared by the MOJ imposed new demands on the detention system, with, in particular, a preliminary examination[10] stage necessitating that defendants be held in close proximity to the courts, so as to facilitate the pre-trial investigation of the preliminary judge. It would not, however, be possible to accommodate this need using the existing detention houses, since the Home Ministry had not developed a number sufficient to do so, with its focus continuing to be on large central prisons. To fill this gap, when the Prison Rules were amended in 1881, houses of custody (*ryūchijo*)

[7] This movement spread throughout the 1870s and 1880s, its aim being to loosen the control of the central establishment. Its members advocated a British-style government, that is, one with political parties and a cabinet organized by the majority party, which is answerable to a national assembly.

[8] This was achieved through the Regulations Governing the Organization of Local Government Officials of 1886, under which the Political Police (*Kokuji keisatsu*) was replaced by a Higher Police (*Kōtō keisatsu*) section.

[9] A brief background discussion on this topic can be found in the National Archives of Japan, available at <www.archives.go.jp/ayumi/kobetsu/m20_1887_01.html>.

[10] Preliminary examination is a non-public procedure by a judge undertaken prior to a court trial, in which it is decided whether there is sufficient ground for proceeding to trial, and what items require further examination for the purposes of the trial. Such a process is the hallmark of French criminal justice, and was adopted in Japan not only as part of its ongoing attempt to modernize its laws, but also due to its resonance with traditional practices there. More specifically, the role of the public prosecutor in the French system resembled that of the feudal magistrate, in that they were responsible for both gathering evidence and impeaching suspects.

attached to local courts and police stations (specifically, *keisatsu no ryūchijo*)—the latter of which there were many by this time—were incorporated into the prison system.[11] Given that police facilities were becoming ubiquitous, and the vast majority of these would have had accompanying cells, this was clearly a convenient way for the Home Ministry to respond to the demand created by the MOJ's new Code without its having to embark on a dramatic prison-building spree.

From 1884, the Home Ministry further granted through a unilateral ordinance that, in addition to this role of suspect detention, police cells could be used to incarcerate those serving sentences of less than ten days in lieu of a fine. Since police cells were not considered a type of prison in which sentenced inmates could normally be held, this practice of using them for such was the beginning, literally, of what would become the 'substitute prison' system. As the police force grew, so did the use of its facilities as prisons, for both unsentenced and sentenced detainees, and this multipurpose nature meant that the treatment of the two classes of prisoner was sometimes confused or abused (Satō 2005: 31). The ensuing criticism forced the Home Ministry to issue rules in 1887 to ensure a stricter distinction between how unsentenced individuals, who were simply awaiting the next step in the criminal justice process, and sentenced inmates were held (Satō 2005: 32). Moreover, the second amendment to the Prison Rules, made in 1889, further relaxed the restrictions on unsentenced inmates—allowing them, for example, to buy their own food.[12] Nonetheless, the practice of using police cells for holding both unsentenced and sentenced inmates continued into the next decade.

As the modernization of the criminal process continued, an expansion of the preliminary examination meant that dependence on the use of police cells for suspects increased further still. Specifically, in 1897, the MOJ ordained that the preliminary examination stage of the criminal process was extended beyond the larger cities, to which it had originally been restricted, to courts nationwide (*Shihōshō* 1939: 175). In smaller localities, however, there were no facilities available for defendants to be held after having received a detention order. There were also no prospects for local governments to provide such from their own pockets and no desire

[11] *Kangoku soku*, 1881, Article 1, Clause 1.

[12] Penal Institutions of Japan, Correction Bureau, MOJ pamphlet, p. 37. Retrieved on 15 January 2014 from: <www.moj.go.jp/content/000079580.pdf>.

from the central administration to fill the funding gap or send detention officers to every location where they might potentially be needed, sometimes just for a handful of suspects. Given that, in jurisdictions where there were no detention houses (under the 1889 revision of the Prison Rules, what were formerly *kansō* were now denominated *kōchikan*), there was already the practice of detaining unsentenced individuals in police stations instead, it was agreed by the MOJ and the Home Ministry that it would not be problematic to continue this. As a result, with the preliminary examination sometimes lasting for periods of several months, suspect detention in police cells became even more prevalent than hitherto.

Whilst the use of police cells for defendants had, as noted above, already been permitted since 1881, some observers were concerned that the Prison Rules' specification that this be only for temporary periods was no longer being reflected by current practices, whereby in certain jurisdictions there might be no prospect for suspects to be moved into detention houses independent of the police. For instance, in a leading law journal of the time, it was protested that:

> Criminal defendants detained by a writ should not just be detained in any prison. If a defendant is restrained for convenience in police cells, and if the distinction between the police and the prison organs is not made clear, with the defendant's detention being managed by custodial personnel who are also involved in the investigation of the said crime, then there is a danger of the latter treating the defendant with a feeling of spite and cruelty, and furthermore, the interests of the defendant might be obstructed. (*Kangoku zasshi* 1897: 25–7)

In the same article, it was underlined that the detention house was seen as the proper place of detention, and that the use of police cells for defendants, although not explicit in the Prison Rules, should be understood as something of an exceptional measure:

> Article 1 of the Prison Rules recognizes that the cells within police stations are a type of prison, but it is clear that this needs to be interpreted in a narrow way, and that it is simply the case that the temporary detention of criminal defendants detained by writ in police station cells sometimes cannot be helped. (*Kangoku zasshi* 1897: 25–7)

This was such a hot topic partly because there were at the time an extremely large number of individuals being detained for preliminary examination.[13] Perhaps more significantly, though, the changing nature of police detention—from unavoidable and temporary to sometimes prolonged as a matter of course—was seen as retrogressing to a pre-trial detention arrangement that left suspects more open to coercion by the police. Indeed, the reduction of police abuse of detention had been one of the intentions of introducing a preliminary examination procedure, with which initial fact-finding and remand decision were placed in the hands of the court, in the first place (Matsuo 2004: 50–2).

Jurisdiction over prisons would be passed from the Home Ministry to the MOJ at the turn of the century in April 1900, a move which was justified in several ways. Indeed, as Keigo Kiyoura—the Justice Minister of the time—strategically pointed out, the Home Ministry had become somewhat overburdened with duties, running as many as seven separate departments compared to the MOJ's one—the Civil and Criminal Affairs Bureau (cited in Masajirō 1961: 226). Whilst this was a situation that had even led some to raise the issue of abolishing the MOJ altogether, in fighting his Ministry's corner, Kiyoura contended that placing the administration of prisons within the latter would help to balance the responsibilities of the two Ministries, and was anyway a natural move given the tight link between the preliminary examination that the MOJ already managed and the office of detention (*Keimu kyōkai* 1943: 316). A complementary justification to this was that the transfer of prisons would be advantageous from a diplomatic standpoint. After all, the modernization of Japan's criminal justice procedures had been one of the preconditions of its ending arrangements of extraterritoriality in the mid-1890s.[14] The separation between policing and prison administration, in addition to the promulgation of a Penal Code and a Code of Criminal Procedure, could thus be understood as a natural result of Japan trying to Europeanize its criminal justice system (Tōkyō Sankai 1974: 7). Such could be inferred from the comment of MOJ official of the time Shigeo Wakayama, who cautioned:

[13] A total of 28,879 individuals were held for preliminary examination in 1897 alone (Barrows 1901: 139).

[14] Although the Anglo-Japanese Treaty of Commerce and Navigation which promised the ending of extraterritoriality was signed in 1894, it came with conditions, including one that rendered the first twelve years a probationary period for Japan.

> If the revised treaties are implemented, and foreigners are detained in [the inferior and coarse conditions of] today's police cells, this will become a seed for complaints and grievances that would no doubt create serious problems. (Wakayama 1899: 28)

Notwithstanding the legitimacy of these arguments, given the Home Ministry's overwhelming influence, it is perhaps more important to identify why it was prepared to relinquish its hold on prisons at this point in time, since without its blessing, it is unlikely that such a proposal would ever have transpired. The account of this part of the story later given by a consortium of Home Ministry officials explained that this was a result of the changing societal circumstances:

> Recall that the original rationale for prisons having been placed with the Home Ministry at the beginning of Meiji was because it was the organ most suited to managing the situation during the period of great social confusion and instability, with organized escapes of groups of inmates, and frequent incursions on prisons . . . It was only natural that afterwards, once public safety and order was more stable, the jurisdiction of prisons was moved back to MOJ, as it originally has a strong link with the office of prosecution. (*Daikasumi kai* 1971: 605)

The darker interpretation of the same episode, however, is that even though the regime was facing new challenges from nascent labour and socialist movements, the growing powers at the Home Ministry's disposal meant it no longer needed the prison system as a tool to retain social control (Satō 2005: 32). In particular, two new laws established in 1900—the Administrative Enabling Law (*Gyōsei shikkō hō*) and the Public Order and Police Law (*Chian keisatsu hō*)—gave the police legal grounds for arresting individuals without recourse to the Code of Criminal Procedure, reducing the value of maintaining authority over prisons for the Home Ministry, and so it was satisfied to pass it over. Doing so also freed it from the obligation to create facilities to fulfil the requirements induced by the MOJ's changes to the criminal procedure.

Regardless of the underlying cause for it, this reorganization saw the Bureau of Prisons (*Kangoku kyoku*) being placed under the MOJ, though the detention arrangements for suspects would not change, meaning that the phrase 'substitute prison' could, for the first time, be applied to unsentenced detainees as well. Although there was a clear desire within the MOJ to take on the office of prisons, it did not have the capability to do so in a single step. This was because the prison network that would be bequeathed to it by the Home Ministry did not enable the detention of suspects close to courts, which had become even more essential than before, given the recent expansion of the preliminary examination. Moreover, the option was not available to the MOJ, as it was to the Home Ministry, of using houses of custody instead. Indeed, since police cells were still required for arrestees and were actually attached to police stations, they could not be transferred to the MOJ as other prisons were, and even if the court facilities had remained a type of prison, there were not enough numbers of them at all. As a compromise, although police cells would no longer be classified as a type of prison, it was agreed that prisoners could still be held there when needed—but these facilities would remain under the control of the Home Ministry, with the MOJ playing only a supervisory role. This practice was formalized in 1902 with a law ordaining that local police authorities should be reimbursed by the MOJ for expenses incurred in accommodating detainees (such as for food, clothing, sanitation, and other daily necessities). The new arrangement meant that, substantively, little changed for suspects; only the responsibility for their detention had been passed from the Home Ministry to the MOJ. And, whilst the practice of substituting police cells for other facilities could, as indicated previously, be traced to earlier in the Meiji period, it was now that 'substitute prison' was truly given birth to.

When the MOJ came to propose legislation for prisoners shortly afterwards, the planned continuation of the use of police cells as a substitute for prison proved contentious. Indeed, although the Ministry was keen to push ahead with creating a statute corresponding to its new office, the physical infrastructure of prisons for unsentenced inmates still lagged behind the demands of the criminal procedure. As a result, so that police cells could still be used more widely than for just detaining arrestees, the bill submitted to the Diet by the MOJ to create Japan's earliest prison legislation—the 1908 Prison Law—permitted, through what would henceforth be known as the 'substitute prison article', that:

> The facilities belonging to the police stations can be used to substitute prisons, provided that a convicted person sentenced to penal servitude or imprisonment shall not be detained therein continually for one month or more.[15]

[15] Prison Law, Article 1, Paragraph 3.

As a consequence, concerns about using police cells as a cover for MOJ detention centres, which had been expressed ever since the introduction of the practice, continued to be raised during the subsequent deliberations—for, although the proposed law was widely viewed as the modern legal instrument that those who commissioned it had hoped for (Röhl 2005: 769), critics argued that the substitute prison article meant that suspects would not be adequately protected from such abuses as had occurred under the previous system, when police and prisons were both under the Home Ministry's jurisdiction. Concretely, Takuzō Hanai[16] criticized the substitute prison article as 'the [proposed Prison Law's] greatest shortcoming', and Keizaburō Miyako[17] questioned:

With regards to substitute prison, why is it necessary for it to be applied in the houses of custody attached to police stations? . . . There have hitherto been some gross malpractices taking place there; we have all heard that abuse sometimes occurs. [The proposed provision] states that for up to one month, it is fine to use police cells as a substitute for prisons, but if this happens, there is an extreme danger that further malpractice will occur. Do those concerned [with putting this measure into law] think that there won't be such problems, or do they simply think that it cannot be helped for such to happen?[18]

Despite these objections, the government prevailed, thereby establishing the substitute prison article in law. In justifying the need to incorporate this measure, which he saw as an improvement on what had appeared in earlier regulations, the Prison Law's innovative architect, Shigejirō Ogawa, explained that:

The [government's] intention is to, as far as possible, not continue to use [police cells] as prisons in the future. In reality, though, it is not possible to build a prison at every location where a criminal case might be dealt with in a court, and for this reason it cannot be helped that occasionally the necessity will emerge to use the cells in the police station of that place as a substitute for prison. It is anyway the case that the malpractices that occur in police cells happen on account of the imperfect conditions that exist there. Since we will be using them as a substitute prison, however, we

[16] A high-profile lawyer who became a politician of progressive persuasions, advocating for the realization of universal suffrage, for instance. Later he would serve as President of the Tōkyō Bar Association and would be appointed to various legal research commissions, including the Legislative Council of the MOJ.

[17] Also a lawyer and law academic.

[18] 24th Imperial Diet Session, House of Representatives, Minutes of the deliberation of the Committee on the Prison Law Draft Bill and Four Other Matters, 5 March 1908.

will try as hard as we can to prevent bad practices, and limit the abuses occurring there as much as possible.[19]

Moreover, since detention in police custody of anyone apart from those suspects awaiting trial was meant to be a short-term exception rather than the norm,[20] the practice of the MOJ reimbursing the relevant local police authority for expenses incurred in accommodating detainees under the substitute prison system, which had been legislated for during the earlier reorganization, would continue. So would the practice of the MOJ overseeing the police's detention operation, albeit that this duty was hardly ever undertaken in practice, and a 1913 ordinance would ordain that supervision was only necessary in case of a specific need (Kamoshita 1971: 99). Finally, whilst the MOJ did not present a specific strategy for reducing the application of substitute prison, it has been argued that the Diet discussions indicate the legislators' intent would most likely have been that the detention capabilities of court houses be increased to meet demand (Satō 2005: 48).

Slightly contradicting the impression given by this discussion prior to the promulgation of the Prison Law, that is, that police detention was something that ideally would not have been included in the legislation and should only be applied when absolutely required, however, was the Home Ministry's simultaneous issuance of an instrument that had the opposite character. Indeed, on the very same day in 1908 as the Prison Law passed the Diet, the Police Crimes Punishment Ordinance (*Keisatsu-han shobatsu rei*)—the precursor of today's Minor Offences Act—was enforced by the Home Ministry. In conjunction with the Summary Trial Regulations for Police Offences, this enabled police chiefs to impose on-the-spot penalties of imprisonment for up to thirty days. This imprisonment penalty would be executed in the police's houses of custody, in their capacity as a substitute for prison (Satō 2005: 39).

To summarize, the substitute prison system that resulted from this period of history had its origins in a misalignment in the 1880s and 1890s between the development of Japan's criminal procedure by the MOJ and its detention system by the Home Ministry: the former requiring an extensive network of small facilities be

[19] Ibid.

[20] Note, for example, that Ogawa wrote in 1911 that 'detention in police houses of custody is not to exceed a short few days' (*Keisatsu kangoku gakkai Tōkyō shikai* 1894: 194).

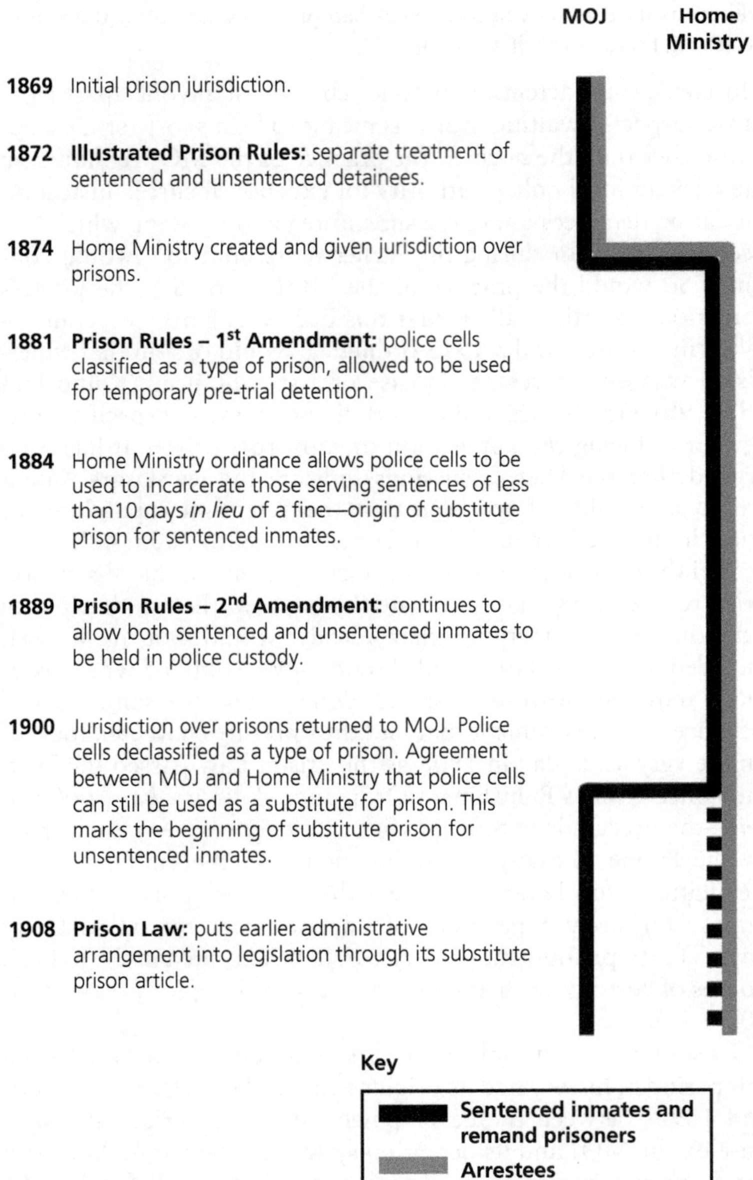

Figure 2.1. Prison jurisdiction through the Meiji period

built close to courts, and the latter concentrating on establishing large central prisons. The system of substitute prison became further established when, at the end of the nineteenth century, the use of police cells in lieu of prisons could not be discarded even after jurisdiction over criminal detention was passed back to the MOJ. (The developments of this period are summarized in Figure 2.1.) As a counterfactual thought, one might imagine that had prison administration remained in the hands of the MOJ throughout the Meiji period, it might well have been the case that this practice, which would later become highly controversial, would never have been introduced.

A Tool for Political Oppression in the Pre-war Period

Over the next few decades, the Home Ministry oversaw a continued increase in the powers of Japan's burgeoning police force. These enabled the detention of individuals for extended spells in police cells, as well as their sentencing, without access to the courts ever being granted. Despite the growing unease within legal circles about these repressive measures, there would be few checks on their application in practice.

Government fears about opposition movements in the first half of the twentieth century saw the political wing of Japan's police force significantly strengthened. Although the actual numbers of police officers per capita were still lower in Japanese urban areas than in major European capitals during this period, since its inception the police had seen extensive growth and succeeded in permeating municipalities. For instance, by 1914 there had been 858 police stations established in Tōkyō alone, which compared with only ninety-one in the more populated Paris (Westney 1982: 333). The motivation for cultivating this extensive police presence was to manage growing unrest and threats to the regime, mainly from socialists and anarchists. Specifically to this end, the so-called 'Higher Police' (*Kōtō keisatsu*), whose original duties had been the monitoring of 'organisations, meetings, newspapers, magazines, documents and other publications concerned with politics' (Tipton 1990: 45), had in 1904 been bolstered by the Home Ministry, and given the broader remit of '[investigating and controlling] social movements and [suppressing] radicals spreading dangerous foreign ideas' (Neary 1989: 42). Moreover, following a number of disturbances instigated by socialist and anarchist activists, including the 1908 Red Flag Incident[21] and the 1910 Kōtoku Incident,[22] a 'Special Higher Police' (*Tokubetsu kōtō keisatsu*, known in short as *Tokkō*)—often referred to by the more sinister designation 'The Thought Police' (*Shisō keisatsu*)[23]—was created, with a reach and powers to take action against citizens that were even more extensive (Tipton 1997).

Together with the physical expansion of the police force, there was an explosion in the amount of police detention being undertaken. To a large degree, this resulted from the Home Ministry's instigation of what is considered 'one of the chief symbols of police suppression' in the pre-war period, also described by the liberal *Asahi* newspaper as 'evil'—the 1925 Peace Preservation Law[24] (Mitchell 1973: 340). Even though the police could already avail itself of various authoritarian measures, the Peace Preservation Law went further, allowing the detention of individuals under such vague terms as their having altered the elusive 'national essence' (*kokutai*).[25] In practice, this meant that socialism, communism, and other ideologies were criminalized, and, as a consequence, the twenty years between 1925 and 1945 saw the use of the substitute prison system—particularly by the Special Higher Police—go through the roof. Indeed, over this period, close to 70,000 suspected ideological offenders were detained in police cells for interrogation, confession, and to serve criminal sentences, including over 1,600 communist election campaigners on a single day in March 1928 (Mitchell 1976, Nishimura 2006). Of these, many were held for minor infractions, for which they could be sentenced by a police chief and held for up to thirty days (as per the 1908 Police Crimes Punishment Ordinance introduced previously), sometimes repeatedly for months on end, whilst the police officers—not unlike the Spanish Inquisition—went about the

[21] A riot in Tōkyō after leaders of a socialist march were arrested, which led to the resignation of the Home Minister.

[22] An assassination attempt on the Emperor by anarchists and socialists.

[23] Officially the Special Higher Police (*Tokubetsu kōtō keisatsu*).

[24] These were subsequently revised to include increasingly draconian provisions in 1928 and 1941.

[25] According to the concept of 'national essence', from the point of Japan's creation a relationship of voluntary affection and trust was established respectively between the emperor, a descendant of the Sun Goddess, and the people, his eternal subjects. Just as the emperor, the patriarch of the whole nation, was bound to be benevolent, the people had the duty to be loyal to him, else Japan would see its demise. This concept was promoted by the Meiji authoritarians as the basis for the emperor's sovereignty, although in reality it was the former who held the substantive power.

business of 'converting' them away from what the authorities saw as their dangerous political convictions.

As a result of these developments, although somewhat wary of expressing their opinions in public, jurists became heavily critical of substitute prison. The most frequently communicated fault of the relevant article of the Prison Law was that it facilitated 'unjust' police detention (Satō 2005: 39). Fearful of personal consequences, however, critics were often reluctant to openly attack police practices. For example, Seiichirō Ōno, a professor of Tōkyō Imperial University renowned for his work on criminal law, felt it necessary to censor some of his more stringent criticisms, which included his allegation of police torture, when publishing an article in 1930 in a special issue on police detention of the prominent legal journal *Hōritsu jihō*. The omitted words of this article have since been uncovered to reveal that Ōno originally wrote:

> The problem of treading on human rights within the criminal justice system did not start today, but recently there have been illegal arrests of labour movement members, anarchists and communists, and we hear that the police's authority is being abused with torture and violence . . . The biggest problem of all with regards to illegal arrests . . . is the current application of police station cells, . . . [and t]he Prison Law needs to be amended in order to abolish the substitution of police cells for prison . . . This would be the best way to prevent illegal arrests taking place . . . [Reforming the current system of police custody] is the most pressing issue of our criminal policy. (Ōno 1930: 3–6)

Other scholars, activists, and politicians produced similar articles for the same issue of this journal. These included Izutarō Suehiro from Tōkyō Imperial University, who, through an open letter to the incumbent Justice Minister entitled 'Do You Not Have Objections Even to This?',[26] requested a government inquiry into the current system of police detention.

It should be highlighted that at this point of history the chief problem being raised with the substitute prison system was not the conflict it induced between the police's investigation and pre-trial detention duties. Rather, the point of contention was that it could be applied in such a way that individuals may be sentenced and imprisoned in police cells without ever being granted the

[26] Full title: '*Kore demo sashitsukae nai no deshō ka? – Keisatsu ryūchijo ni tsuite Watanabe Shihō Daijin he no kōkaijō*' (Do You Not Have Objections Even to This? – An Open Letter to Justice Minister Watanabe regarding the Police's Houses of Custody) (*Suehiro* 1930: 20).

protections of the ordinary criminal procedure. Indeed, the Code of Criminal Procedure, updated in 1922 following a protracted revision process aimed at aligning it more closely with the German-inspired Meiji Constitution, was seen as relatively progressive, 'enhanc[ing] the procedural rights of the accused and role of defense counsel' (Haley 1998: 71). However, in response to investigators' complaints that this Code and its predecessor placed too many restrictions on their activities (Matsuo 2004: 74), the Home Ministry soon afterwards introduced the aforementioned 1925 Peace Preservation Law. This marked a dramatic strengthening of the police's powers to arrest individuals, convict them in summary trials, and then detain them in its own houses of custody by appeal to the substitute prison article. Applying this law and the rest of its arsenal of powers, the police was able to almost completely sidestep judicial proceedings, so much so that 90 per cent of the tens of thousands of individuals detained under the Peace Preservation Law in particular never saw a trial in court.[27] The substitution of police cells in place of prisons, of course, still included their use for unsentenced individuals, as had been the reason for the introduction of the substitute prison article in the Prison Law. However, since the police did not have to rely on the ordinary criminal procedure for its business of maintaining social control, and since with preliminary examination defendants were already anyway placed under the control of an investigator until trial, it was the substitution of police cells for the imprisonment of sentenced inmates—and the complete circumvention of the Code of Criminal Procedure—that attracted the bulk of criticism during this period.

The pre-war Japanese administration of justice has been characterized as 'Janus-faced', with elements of both an authoritarian and a humanitarian nature (Mitchell 1992), though there can be little disagreement about which side of this divide police detention during the period falls into. Indeed, the harsh social control laws enacted in this era contributed to a dramatic increase of abuse of and within police custody. Whilst the detention and coercion of unsentenced individuals in police cells was by no means exceptional,[28] the area highlighted as especially problematic by

[27] For instance, during the period 1928–43, of the 67,156 arrested, only 6,024 were prosecuted (Soeda 2007).

[28] Perhaps the most famous such case was the notorious Yokohama Incident of 1942–5, in which sixty journalists and researchers were arrested and coerced into false confessions by the Special Higher Police. It is recognized even in the decision determining the third reinvestigation upon appeal of the Yokohama Incident that

critics was the widespread use of police facilities for holding, and often abusing, sentenced inmates—the majority of whom had been convicted in quasi-judicial proceedings orchestrated by the police. What voices of opposition there were, however, proved ineffective in halting the rise of such practices.

Occupation Reforms: Job Half Done

During the Occupation of Japan, one of the Allied Forces' first priorities was to seek a reduction in the coercive powers the police had gradually accrued in the pre-war period. Having taken early action on this front, including removing the Peace Preservation Law, the occupiers then proceeded on their mission towards the democratization of Japan through fundamental legislative change. In the area of criminal justice in particular, their efforts would see a reform of the pre-trial process through an amendment of the Code of Criminal Procedure and also a reorganization of the police force. The Prison Law, however, would be left untouched. As a result, the substitute prison system would survive, albeit with its use taking on a new form in the post-war period.

To the end of bringing a radical change to the policing of political activities and police detention practices in Japan, only just over a month after General Douglas MacArthur arrived in the autumn of 1945, the newly instituted General Headquarters (GHQ) sent to the domestic government an instruction relating to the 'Removal of Restrictions on Political, Civil, and Religious Liberties'.[29] In this 'human-rights directive', GHQ demanded immediate repeal of the Peace Preservation Law and Thought Control Law (Ideological Prisoner Custody and Surveillance Law), which it clearly viewed as having been at the root of police malpractice. It also called for instantaneous release of all those currently detained under such measures, abolition of the secret police (and other parts of the Home Ministry concerned with thought crimes), removal of various high-ranking Home Ministry officials, and prohibition of 'the physical punishment and mistreatment of all persons detained, imprisoned, or

upon being taken to the police station's cells and whilst in detention there, those who were arrested on suspicion of infraction of the Summary Trial Regulations for Police Offences were subjected to torture a number of times, and because of this conceded to signing false confessions.

[29] Memorandum for: Imperial Japanese Government. Through: Central Liaison Office, Tōkyō. Office of the Supreme Commander of the Allied Powers (SCAPIN-93), 4 October 1945. Retrieved on 9 February 2014 from: <www.ndl.go.jp/modern/e/cha5/description03.html>.

under protection and surveillance'. The speed with which this edict was released testifies to how pressing this matter was for GHQ.

That installing due process in Japan was a central aim of the occupiers was further highlighted by the centrepiece of the post-war reforms—the 1947 Constitution. This statute included a number of measures designed to safeguard against the abuse of human rights, including as many as ten specific measures concerning Japan's criminal process. Some of the motivation for this came from the occupiers' view that:

> The most serious abuses of individual rights in Japan have been through the uncontrolled actions of the various police agencies, particularly the [Special Higher Police] and the [Military Police (*Kempei-tai*)] and the conduct of the prosecutors. All manner of abuses have been practised by the police and prosecutors in the enforcement of general law, but primarily in the enforcement of the Thought Control Law. It is not unusual for people to be incarcerated for months and years without charges being filed, during all of which time attempts are made to force confessions from the accused.[30]

Consequently, several of their proposed articles were particularly related to police detention procedures, spelling out that arrests could only be made following the issuance of a warrant from a competent judicial officer, that suspects should be informed of charges against them and immediately provided counsel, that the reason for a suspect's detention should immediately be shown in court, that torture and other cruel punishments were 'absolutely forbidden', and that forced confessions could not be admitted as evidence in court. Arguably the specifics of these recommended articles were inspired by recent developments in the USA, notably the 1943 McNabb ruling, which ordained that confessions obtained during a long period of police detention were inadmissible as evidence in court. Moreover, explicit measures such as these represented a marked change for the protection of rights during criminal proceedings, given that the mere two articles pertaining to this area in the Meiji Constitution being replaced were somewhat hollow, relegating all specifics to the more easily

[30] 'Memorandum for Chief of Staff. Subject: Comments on Constitutional Revision Proposed by Private Group' (also known as the Rowell Remarks after its author Lieutenant Colonel Milo Rowell, Director, Department of Legal Affairs, Public Administration Bureau, Government Section, GHQ), Article 5, 11 January 1946. Retrieved on 13 February 2014 from: <www.ndl.go.jp/constitution/e/shiryo/03/060shoshi.html>.

changeable legislation.[31] Nonetheless, when it came to the promulgation of the new Constitution in 1946, the draft prepared by the Americans passed the Diet almost without debate.

By the time the new Constitution was promulgated, work to update other Japanese legislation had already begun. For those charged with the latter task, it was necessary to assess what changes needed to be made to ensure the appropriate protection of the newly guaranteed rights in practice, including of course those for individuals held in police detention. One of the places in which the Occupation forces found serious failures related to this issue in particular was the Code of Criminal Procedure, and they saw the introduction of a new one as crucial in eradicating these shortcomings. To begin with, in order that the determination of guilt happens in a public court, which was a right guaranteed by the new Constitution, the Americans were keen for Japan to move towards a more adversarial style of trial[32] and do away with the pre-war preliminary examination system, which they also determined to be the cause of protracted pre-indictment detention. To safeguard the rights of suspects, the Americans further proposed replicating the New York system in which the investigative authorities were required to bring suspects before a judge without delay (Satō 2005: 43).

Despite a fight from the Japanese side, when the new Code of Criminal Procedure was enacted in 1948, it would indeed contain measures that would entail judicial involvement in detention decisions at a much earlier stage than had been the case hitherto. When making their initial plans with regard to the Code of Criminal Procedure at the end of 1945, the Japanese legal representatives had already shown they were aware of which way the wind was blowing by providing for an abolition of the preliminary examination.[33] At the same time, however, they called for the

[31] For instance, with regard to pre-trial proceedings, the relevant text simply read that '[n]o Japanese subject shall be arrested, detained, tried or punished, unless according to law'.

[32] The adversarial style of trial involves advocates for the disputing parties (usually the state and defendant in criminal trials) representing their interests to an impartial judge or jury who determines the truth about the case. This is in contrast to Japan's hitherto more inquisitorial system, many elements of which would arguably remain despite the Occupation reform, such as the judge himself being actively involved in the examination of evidence.

[33] This was through the '*Hanzai sōsa ni kan suru jinken yōgo no gutaiteki hōsaku*' (Concrete Measures for Human Rights Protection Relating to the Criminal Investigation) prepared by the Small Committee for Second Consultation Relating to Items (*Dai ni shiimon jikō kankei shōiinkai*)—a measure which

investigative organs' increased coercive authority by, for instance, recognizing detention by prosecutors for up to four months, and by police for ten days (Odanaka 1977: 44–5)—such a measure was seen by some as a necessary replacement for enabling the investigation to find the truth through interrogation, without having to resort to means outside of the criminal procedure (Matsuo 2004: 53–4). However, once the Constitution, with its principle of no arrest without a warrant, was promulgated, the Japanese authorities were left with little room for manoeuvre. Indeed, although they initially interpreted the Constitution's 'competent judicial officer' as including high-ranking police officials, a rapid learning process ensued, through which this illusion was replaced with an understanding closer to the Americans' original intent. Consequently, the Japanese eventually, rather reluctantly, accepted the procedural element of *habeas corpus* in the new Code of Criminal Procedure. Specifically, the revised legislation required that a suspect be brought within three days before a judge, who may issue a warrant for him to be detained for a maximum of twenty further days before indictment (precisely, an initial ten-day period, with a possible ten-day extension).[34]

As already indicated in their human rights directive, another place where the Americans saw change as needed was the concentration of power in the Home Ministry, and the Bureau of Police in particular. Indeed, already having had its wings clipped at the start of the Occupation, the Home Ministry was completely dismantled by the end of 1948. In its place, the Occupation authorities installed three new ministries and a politically neutral National Public Safety Commission (*Kokka kōan iinkai*). A key part of this reorganization was the creation of a replacement for the defunct Bureau of Police. Perhaps its most important input to this process was the 'Report of the Metropolitan Police Planning Commission' prepared by former New York Police Commissioner Lewis J Valentine. Valentine was strident in his criticisms of the lack of democracy in Japanese police policies and organization. Apart from being appalled by what he saw as 'barbaric' detention practices, including the holding of sick and juvenile inmates with adult reoffenders, he particularly highlighted the problem of the police holding judicial powers—points that had also been taken forward

also included a proposal to terminate the Administrative Enabling Law and the Summary Trial Regulations for Police Offences.

[34] Articles 75, 207, and 208. Although for cases involving 'Crimes Related to Insurrection, Foreign Relations or Public Disturbance', an additional five days of pre-indictment detention was permitted.

in the Constitution and Code of Criminal Procedure redesign. Following Valentine's report, it was strongly urged by the Public Safety Section of GHQ, which was overseeing the reform of Japan's police force, that this organization see a comprehensive decentralization (Eiji 2002: 297–9). Whilst a tussle between the Government Section and G-2 on this matter, in which MacArthur himself had to step in to arbitrate, meant that this recommendation was not completely followed, the police force was nonetheless broken down into a multilayered structure, with governance on national, regional, and prefectural levels and, at the bottom, 1,400 independent local forces.[35] In addition, a National Rural Police System (*Kokka chihō keisatsu*) was created, and moreover, the police was not placed under a ministry, but rather the newly formed National Public Safety Commission (Leishman 1999: 112). Together with the corresponding restriction of police functions to more basic crime control, this restructuring clearly represented a turning of the page in the history of the Japanese police.

In the same period, preparations had also been taking place with regard to reforming the Prison Law, and to this end an amendment bill was presented to the Justice Minister by a MOJ Prison Law Revision Investigation Committee (*Kangoku hō kaisei chōsa iinkai*) set up for drafting such in 1947. Although on the surface this adopted a radical line on substitute prison, the accompanying caveats meant that it did not represent a real step away from the existing practice. Indeed, preliminary ideas for this new legislation had been formulated by a group of civil experts put together in 1946 by the Correctional Association (*Keimu kyōkai*, currently *Kyōsei kyōkai*),[36] which were reflected in the proposal's clear distinction between those merely suspected of having committed a crime and those convicted. Going much further than the earlier panel's position that 'the content of the substitute prison article should be made more full and improved', though, the MOJ Committee

[35] This reform was encapsulated in the Police Act (*Keisatsu hō*, Act No. 196 of 1947) and the Police Duties Execution Act (*Kesatsu-kan shokumu shikkō hō*, Act No. 136 of 1948).

[36] The Correctional Association had its offices within the MOJ at this time. It was the descendant of an organization that had been formed in 1899 by the merging of the Prison Association of Great Japan (*Dai Nippon kangoku kyōkai*) and the Police Prisons Institute (*Keisatsu kangoku gakkai*), two professional bodies involved in debating penology during the Meiji reforms—*Kangoku kyōkai*. When it accepted its modern-day name of *Kyōsei kyōkai* in 1957, its offices were moved to Nakano, Tōkyō (Correction Library of Japanese Correctional Association pamphlet, October 2004).

somewhat eye-catchingly went on to declare that '[s]ubstitute prison should be abolished'.[37] What took the gloss off this recommendation, however, was the proposal's subsequent concession (in the same article), due to the impossibility of making an immediate change, that 'in the meantime, the continuation of the existing practices should be allowed'. This was extremely frustrating for some, including Committee member Bunsaku Nakao, who commented that:

> The clause about substitute prison abolition is one that grabs your attention. This system is naturally rife with bad practices and has thus come to be regarded as a cancer of penal administration. However, because of the necessity to use it in practice, this reality was ignored [by the Committee]. Nonetheless, because this cancer obstructs the future revision of the penal system, it is all the more important that on a revision occasion such as this things are not left as they are. This is why the outline proposal included a measure towards substitute prison abolition, even though there was recognition that to reach this end an extremely large number of small prisons needs to be built and this cannot happen overnight, meaning that it also had to provisionally allow the continuation of the current system. I cannot stop praying, though, that the day comes when the demands of the proposal, which are indispensable for the true regeneration of the penal system, are realized. (Nakao 1948)

Passion aside, however, this argument distinctly echoed the remarks made by the government on substitute prison at the time of the Prison Law's promulgation four decades earlier, and suggested that consideration of the abolition of substitute prison was once again being put on hold.

Ultimately, the proposed clause regarding the abolition of substitute prison was never realized anyway, since as time passed by, Prison Law revision slipped down, and eventually off, the agenda. Rather than by any objections raised by American or Japanese legal experts with the content of the Prison Law Revision Investigation Committee's work, though, the stalling of the reform process can be explained by the change of American priorities in occupied Japan and the concomitant change in the balance of power between the different GHQ sections (Niwayama 1981: 117–18). Specifically, leadership within GHQ had hitherto rested with the Government Section (*Minsei kyoku*), which had been faithfully trying to promote democratization in all social spheres, and under which the limited action that was taken with regard to revising the Prison Law had happened. However,

[37] *Kangoku hō kaisei yōkō* (Prison Law Amendment Proposal), Article 1, Paragraph 6, 26 August 1947.

with American fears of the communist threat, both inside Japan and across East Asia, growing, the G-2 Section of the General Staff (*Sanbō dai ni bu*) saw an increase in importance, becoming the most prominent section by the end of 1948. As a result of the G-2's emphasis on the maintenance of public order and peace—for which the supposedly already purged Special Higher Police were secretly used! (*Daikasumi kai* 1970: 798)—the scheduled Prison Law revision was placed on the back burner.

This omission to amend the Prison Law demonstrates how it was not, at the time, seen as relevant to police detention by the Americans, who would leave Japan confident that their reforms had put an end to the pre-war abuse of suspects. Indeed, as has already been described, the occupiers were determined to eradicate such problems, and towards this end, as well as removing the repressive legal instruments previously used by the police, they spared no effort in providing constitutional guarantees for the rights of suspects in a newly designed criminal procedure. Given the strength of the resolve to make progress in this area, it is clear that the Americans would not have let the matter rest were they aware of any outstanding changes needed to secure a police detention system in Japan similar to their own. In particular, it is most likely that, having instigated the changes that they did, the Americans would have expected that the maximum length of time that a suspect could be held in police detention would be three days, that is, the length of time they allowed in the Code of Criminal Procedure prior to a suspect's mandatory presentation to a judge. Furthermore, the signs are that they would have further anticipated, as was the case in the American system at the time (and as it remains today), that the suspect would then be transferred to detention facilities independent of the investigation, that is, one of the MOJ's detention centres. And, even though this was not specified in the Code of Criminal Procedure explicitly, there is little doubt that this interpretation was for them a matter of course. Against this background, that there was a lack of prioritization given to the Prison Law reform, to the point where it went unmade, attests to the fact that it was not seen as being linked to the police detention issue.

However, with the 1908 Prison Law still in place at the end of the Occupation, the limitations on police detention left by the Americans were less than they had envisaged. Indeed, with the substitute prison article having escaped the occupiers' attention, a suspect could still legally be detained under a single charge in police cells for up to twenty-three days before indictment—this being the

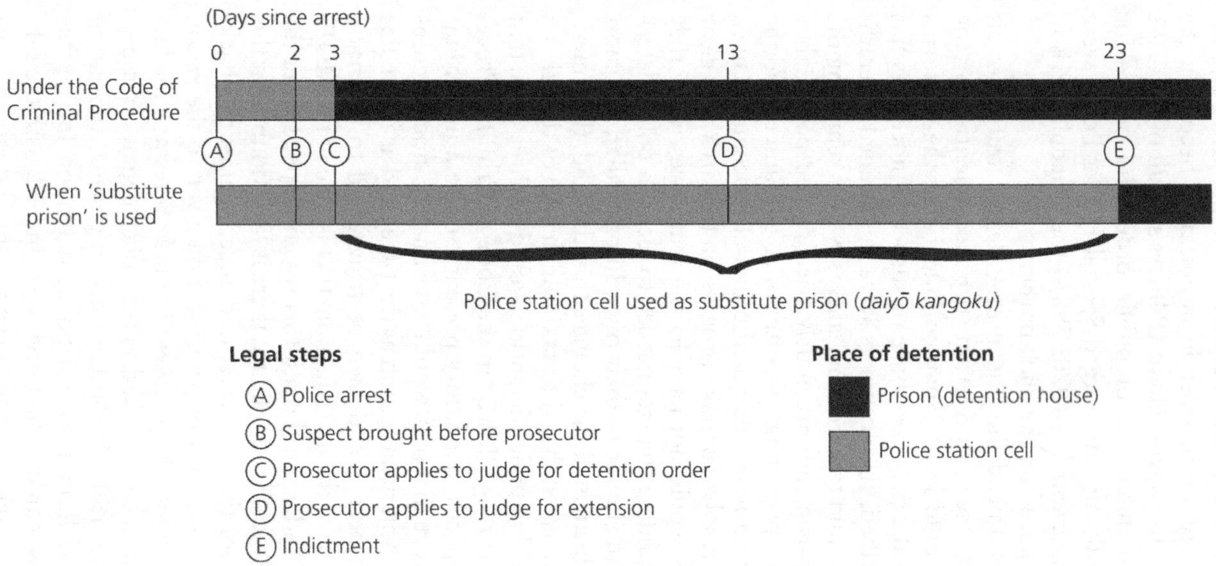

Figure 2.2. Procedure for pre-indictment detention of criminal suspects

case when, after having been presented before a judge at the point of elapse of seventy-two hours since arrest, the suspect is returned straight back to police cells for detention until the prosecutor's time allowance for deciding whether to press charges—of an initial ten days, and another ten days by extension—expires (see Figure 2.2). As will be illuminated subsequently, it is this form of the substitute prison system that has remained until the present day, and that is the origin of Japan's having the longest period of pre-indictment police detention in the developed world.

The Scene Being Set, Enter the Players

Although the fate of Japan's post-war criminal procedure had been determined by 1948, two of the future key combatants with regard to police detention were by this time yet to emerge. It would not be long, however, before they did. On the one hand, there was the creation of a new central police organization—the NPA, a body which represented a partial backtracking from the earlier police reform. And on the other, there was established, as a further consequence of the Constitutional reform, an autonomous national lawyers' association—the JFBA. Once the post-war character of police detention started to reveal itself, this latter organization would soon embark upon a campaign to close the loophole in the system left behind by the Americans.

Soon after the Occupation ended in the early 1950s, in a controversial move to recentralize the force so that it was more manageable and better able to cope with the unsettled social environment of the time, Japan's police experienced a second post-war restructuring. In particular, the 1954 version of the Police Act saw smaller forces being amalgamated into prefectural and major metropolitan-sized units, co-ordinated by a single national organ, the NPA (Nakahara 1956)—a structure which persists to this day.[38] Such a reform was justified on the grounds that the arrangements ordained in the 1948 Police Act resulted in inefficiencies, both financially and in terms of co-ordinating the multitude of local forces (Nakahara 1956: 587, Hunter 1984: 168). According to Shigeru Yoshida, the Prime Minister at the time of the revision, these were not just administrative problems, as the small local forces were sometimes simply not able to maintain control over their jurisdictions, for example by being unable to

[38] For further details, see NPA pamphlet 'Organisation & Resources'. Retrieved on 17 February 2014 from: <www.npa.go.jp/english/kokusai/2013POJ%281-5%29.pdf>.

prevent communist elements taking over their stations (Yoshida 2007: 144–5). For those on the left of the political spectrum, however, when the notion of re-centralizing the police was raised, it was seen as an attempt by the growing conservative movement within the Japanese authorities (which had also seen increased support from the Americans during their later years in Japan) to shift the policing situation away from the democratic ideals of the early Occupation and closer to the pre-war authoritarian one (Ames 1981: 12). Their objections forced Yoshida to extend the Diet session three times in order to conclude the debate of the bill, and would see socialist politicians trying to prevent the speaker from physically entering the house for this to take place (Sasaki-Uemura 2001: 173). Moreover, once pushed through parliament, the new law would even be challenged in court concerning the legitimacy of its promulgation and the unconstitutionality of its content, albeit that this action was unsuccessful (Itoh and Beer 1978: 41).

Despite widespread disapproval, the Japanese government again tried to strengthen the powers of the police at the end of the decade; even though they would not manage to do so, the discussion this action triggered highlighted that, once again, police detention was becoming a matter of contention. Specifically, in 1958, as part of Prime Minister Nobusuke Kishi's preparation to renegotiate the USA–Japan Security Treaty, a new police Duties Execution Act was put on the table (Calder 2008: 137). Similarly to the 1954 Police Act, this was criticized by socialist politicians and media as 're-establishing the police State' (cited in Sissons 1959: 34). However, in contrast to the earlier legislation, this time its opponents did succeed in blocking the bill. The principal concern was that many of the provisions were vague and left room for abuse by the police, which was seen as a risk too far for some. Indeed, despite the various recent reforms, in the post-war period the force continued to hold a reputation for stepping over the line of its more restrictive current legislation—a point which even the government could not deny, with its spokesman declaring in the Diet that 'I propose to get to grips with this problem. It appears to be a question of educating the police. I propose to drive home to every policeman the points brought out in these debates' (cited in Sissons 1959: 43). Moreover, during the debates, attention would be focused on the use of police detention for suspects, with cases highlighted where police officers had been proven in court to have forcefully extracted false confessions, as well as some in which people had been erroneously detained in police cells (Sissons 1959: 43–4).

The policing profession was not the only one to undergo great changes during this era, for, to take a step backwards in time, the Occupation also saw an overhaul for the bar. With the 1947 Constitution declaring that '[n]o person shall be arrested or detained ... without the immediate privilege of counsel',[39] there was an immediate guarantee that the work of lawyers would be increased in the future. It would not be until the passing of the 1949 Practicing Attorney Law, however, that the present role of lawyers in Japanese society would really be established. In particular, this law transferred control over lawyers from the MOJ to local and national bar associations, granting the bar independence from the government for the first time in Japanese history (Hattori 1963: 136–7). Moreover, in contrast to the voluntary national lawyers' organization that had existed since before the war, from 1949 the JFBA was granted the power to recruit new lawyers and impose disciplinary action for professional misconduct (Hattori 1963: 136–7).

In addition to its regulatory duties, the JFBA would also soon establish itself as a defender of human rights within the Japanese criminal justice system. One of the central causes it adopted was the improvement of suspect detention practices, challenging in particular the police's use of substitute prison. The Association's earliest public declaration against the continued use of this system can be traced to 1958—precisely when the hubbub surrounding the revision of the Police Duties Execution Act arose. It would subsequently, in 1964, go on to adopt the first of a series of resolutions for its abolition. The JFBA saw the police's capitalizing on the relevant article in order to hold suspects under its own control for as long as twenty-three days as increasing the risk of forced confessions, and questioned how it could be reconciled with Article 38 of the Constitution, which stated that '[c]onfession made under compulsion, torture or threat, or after prolonged arrest or detention shall not be admitted in evidence'. Although it took nearly a decade for the JFBA to adopt its official position on the substitute prison system and start raising such criticism of it—perhaps for the reason that, as explained by Satō, it took a few years for problems with the substitute prison system in relation to remand prisoners and the revised Code of Criminal Procedure to surface (Satō 2005: 44)—as the organization encountered a growing number of cases in which their clients complained of having been pressured by the

[39] Article 34.

investigation to sign a false confession,[40] its concerns about the substitute prison would only increase. And, as a result, subsequent years would see the JFBA frequently locking horns with the NPA.

Conclusion

The legal basis for the system of police detention that remains in force in Japan today resulted from an omission on the part of the American occupiers to abolish the substitute prison article. This clause had only been included in the 1908 Prison Law so as to enable the continuation of a practical arrangement agreed upon at the time when responsibility over prisons passed from the Home Ministry to the MOJ. However, whilst the application of the substitute prison article was seen as a problem domestically in the pre-war period, it did not catch the eye of the Americans, who saw rather that the solution to the arbitrary and prolonged police detention and abusive interrogation that was rampant before their arrival lay in the restriction of police powers and promulgation of a new Constitution and Code of Criminal Procedure. Although this new legislative framework introduced the notion of *habeas corpus*, requiring that suspects be brought to a judge within three days of their arrest, the Americans' failure to revise the Prison Law meant that the substitute prison article provided a legal loophole permitting the subsequent return of suspects to police custody for up to a further twenty days. It is this oversight that would set Japan on the path towards its current practice of using police cells, rather than MOJ facilities, for detaining suspects as standard. Indeed, having been stripped of the majority of its repressive powers, the police would find that the substitute prison article was something of a hidden gem and would, as will be demonstrated in later chapters, go on to habitually apply it as a most convenient investigative tool. Had the duty of prisons not been passed about during the Meiji period, or the objections to the substitute prison article's inclusion in the Prison Law been heeded at the time of its promulgation, or the post-war revision of the latter statute been completed with an abolition clause, however watered down this might have been, then the police detention picture in Japan might now look quite different.

[40] An early famous example being the Okunishi case of 1961, in which Masaru Okunishi was acquitted after reportedly having provided a confession under coercion. Subsequently, the prosecution would appeal this verdict successfully in 1969, with this decision being upheld by the Supreme Court in 1972 and Okunishi being sentenced to death. Later still, in 2005, after four decades on death row, Okunishi was granted the right to a further retrial.

3

A Tale of Two Detention Bills

A state is better governed which has few laws, and those laws strictly observed.

René Descartes, Discourse on Method

Where there is no law there is no freedom.

John Locke, The Second Treatise of Government

Despite its seemingly exceptional character in law, over the decades following the post-war reforms, the use of substitute prison expanded rapidly to the point that, by 1980, as many as 90 per cent of suspects were detained in this way. The first time that the political spotlight was placed on this phenomenon was when plans for an overhaul of the antiquated Prison Law started to be made in the late 1970s. The key issue throughout the entire duration of subsequent discussions, which ran until the early 1990s, was the legislative regime for criminal suspects, with the Ministry of Justice (MOJ) and National Police Agency (NPA) each drafting a bill for the detainees in their care. That the police saw fit to take such a step for regulating the already controversial substitute prison arrangement was met with outcry from lawyers from the Japan Federation of Bar Associations (JFBA) and opposition politicians. As several high-profile failures of the system were exposed, domestic concerns would snowball, and be echoed throughout the global human rights community.

This epoch thus provides a perfect lens through which to determine where each of the key actors stood on substitute prison, why they did so, and also how they interacted with each other on this issue. As such, it allows conclusions to be drawn about the reasons for the increased use of substitute prison in the post-war period. The present chapter is focused on reaching this end, which will in turn start to explain substitute prison's modern-day entrenchment. The evidence set out here serves the additional purpose of demonstrating the tangible impact of the debates surrounding substitute prison on Japan's system of incarceration more generally.

Two Bills or Not Two Bills

Beyond the contentious issue of whether substitute prison should continue to exist at all, perhaps the most hotly debated question in the police detention debate of the period of interest in this chapter was whether it was the legal status or the place of detention that should be the key determinant of which was the authority with legitimate jurisdiction over suspects detained in police cells.

On the one hand, it was argued that, having seen a judge, the rights and obligations of suspects, whether they were being held in police facilities or MOJ detention centres, should be determined by the MOJ—such was the position based on the assumption that the guiding principle for the treatment of detainees be their legal status. In particular, since detention of suspects in police cells was a substitute for MOJ detention, the rules governing suspects should therefore be derived from those applying to the proper place of detention—a MOJ detention centre. In particular, those viewing substitute prison as an exception would adopt this outlook, namely that a single MOJ bill would suffice for all prisoners.

On the other hand, appealing to the fact that substitute prison placed suspects under police administration, it would also be contended that there was justification for corresponding NPA legislation. According to this camp, since NPA facilities were arranged quite differently to MOJ ones, it was only natural that separate consideration be extended to them; it would be irregular for one administrative agency to be setting the rules for the staff of another. Furthermore, it would also be questioned whether the practice was really exceptional, since the Prison Law did not contain an explicit provision to this effect. On these grounds, it was reasoned that the NPA had a good claim to draft a second bill regarding treatment of suspects in their cells.

Which side the relevant actors fell on this issue is, of course, informative, but it is also possible to learn more by taking a detailed look at the justifications they gave for doing so. In particular, although the NPA and MOJ would end up taking the Two Detention Bills (*Kōkin ni hōan*) approach when drafting legislation, the explanations they gave for this were markedly different, with the NPA adopting a fundamental philosophical position on the matter and the MOJ a more pragmatic one. As for the JFBA, its position was also primarily one of principle at this point, and it would be the lawyers' clash with the NPA that would ultimately shape the discussions. Before describing the fate of these, as is done in the next section, it will be useful to collect in one place the core arguments made by the MOJ, the NPA, and the JFBA.

The NPA: Indispensability for effective investigation

The police strongly advocated retaining substitute prison, and proposed that it should be legislated for in a separate bill that related only to its detention facilities. Without substitute prison, it argued, expedient and accurate investigation would become difficult, thereby reducing the remarkable efficiency of the Japanese criminal justice system, to which it claimed the low crime rate could be attributed. A second bill was seen as necessary to make explicit the NPA's role in detaining suspects, and to eliminate the discrepancy between the treatment of arrestees and that of suspects.

This position of substitute prison retention was primarily justified by pointing to the superiority of the police's detention sites over the MOJ's, particularly for the purpose of investigating suspects. For a start, the NPA argued, whereas police premises were invariably equipped with important facilities, such as suspect interview, observation, and criminal identification rooms, the MOJ's detention centres could not always fulfil such investigatory requirements.[1] The question also existed of overcrowding of the MOJ's facilities, which meant that there was often little space to be used for the questioning of suspects, and sometimes staff shortages were a problem in arranging interviews. A third complaint the police had about the MOJ's detention centres was their accessibility. Being far fewer than police detention facilities (in 1993, for instance, there were 1,267 NPA detention facilities and only 154 MOJ detention centres) and mostly situated in remote areas outside of cities and towns, the NPA estimated that over 70 per cent of police officers would have to spend over an hour travelling to the closest MOJ detention centre, and in some cases the commute

[1] See, for example, the NPA's 1993 report to the UNHRC Committee on the ICCPR *Police Custodial Facilities in Japan—Outline of Our Effort to Ensure Fair Treat [sic] of Detainees*, or its response to the IBA study *The* Daiyō Kangoku *(Substitute Prison) System of Police Custody in Japan*, 1995.

time could be as much as two hours in each direction. Notwithstanding the financial cost of travel, it was argued that the geographical problem would make it difficult for investigating officers to interview suspects, take them to confirm the site of the crime, show them evidence objects, and let them be identified by witnesses within the twenty-three-day limit for pre-indictment investigation. Furthermore, it was reasoned that detention in far-off places would increase inconvenience for lawyers and family members wishing to visit. With these deficiencies in MOJ facilities, the police believed that if the existing system was changed so that suspects had to be held there, then they would no longer be able to preserve safety in Japanese society.

The NPA justified the drafting of a bill of its own on two grounds. Firstly, it contended that, since the current Prison Law provided for the detention of remand prisoners in police facilities and likely so would any legislation replacing it, any revision attempt should include the Agency's input. In particular, police officials stressed that with the NPA having, and continuing to have, a responsibility for detaining remand prisoners as a consequence of a substitute prison article, the character of this office needed to be enunciated in law.[2] To this end, the NPA thus viewed it as only natural that it should produce its own bill to accompany the MOJ's. Secondly, police representatives also developed the argument that a second bill coming from the Agency would allow a common standard to be established for the treatment of all those suspects held in their care—both arrestees and remand prisoners. The NPA saw it as absurd that detainees in police facilities would be regulated for in markedly different ways, under the Prison Law or merely internal police rules, depending on whether they had been seen by a judge or not. By establishing its own bill, the NPA contended that it would be able to provide legal guarantees for the rights of all its detainees, rather than leaving them to the discretion of the individual government employees. In particular, under a single law it would be possible to harmonize rights regarding: daily routine; sleeping conditions; the supply of stationery; personal religious beliefs; time for contact with news, such as listening to radio or reading newspapers; and opportunities to file complaints to the relevant department within the police whenever there was a grievance with regard to treatment.

[2] Kurosawa Masakazu, NPA Commissioner-General, *Asahi Shimbun*, 20 May 1995, p. 4.

Concerning the exceptionality of substitute prison, police officials contended that those arguing against their bill on these grounds were misguided. Concretely, they claimed that there was nothing in the word 'substitute' indicating that the system was 'exceptional' or 'temporary' (Oguri 1996: 47). As a matter of fact, the NPA would note that the Prison Law did not contain any hard-and-fast criteria as to where detention should take place. Instead, under the Code of Criminal Procedure, the decision about where a suspect should be detained, be it in MOJ or police facilities, lay with the judge, who was under no legal obligation to prefer one of the options over the other. Thus, for the NPA, suspect detention in police cells was nothing out of the ordinary, and for it not to be legislated for specifically would constitute an unacceptable oversight.

As for the conditions under which suspects were held within the existing system of police detention, the NPA maintained that some of the criticisms being levelled at it were unwarranted, pointing in defence to recent procedural improvements it had made. Although officials conceded that in pre-war Japan torture and violence was used against suspects to extract confessions, they maintained that the system of the time was quite a different animal—as in other modernized police administrations, officers in Japan would risk losing their job if they relied on abusive methods. In response to the particular concern that substitute prison did not adequately separate investigation and detention of suspects, the NPA emphasized the efforts it had made to ensure the two offices were not confused. Particular structural measures along these lines had been instituted in April 1980 through the Rules Concerning the Detention of Suspects (*Higisha ryūchi kisoku*), under which detention affairs had been transferred from the Detective Section (*Keiji bumon*) to the Administrative Management Section (*Gyōsei kanri bumon*).[3] This measure prevented investigating officers from accessing suspects without first gaining authorization from the Director of the Administrative Management Section, who was in charge of ensuring that the day-to-day routine of detainees met certain standards. It was also the case that entry and exit checks were performed by detention staff to note the length of interrogations and look for signs of suspect abuse, such as bruises. These improvements, along with the argument for the necessity of the system, would be publicized in a number of pamphlets over the decade.

[3] Interview with NPA Official A and NPA Official B, 8 August 2007.

Turning to the actual content of the police detention bill, beyond the actual treatment of suspects, this clearly indicated the NPA's intention to further expand the application of the substitute prison system and reduce administrative dependence on the MOJ. Specifically, concerning the conditions under which detainees in its cells would be held, apart from some minor allowances for differences in facilities, the NPA constructed its bill to be identical to the MOJ's. Where it noticeably departed from the existing regime was in its granting to the NPA permission to increase its detention capacity through the establishment and application of suspect detention facilities independent of police stations. Moreover, rather than the prefectural police being reimbursed for the substitute prison office by the MOJ as was currently the case, it was proposed that expenses for this be supplied to the NPA straight from the Treasury. The explanation given for this was that it would streamline the present system by removing what was, as the MOJ agreed at the time,[4] unnecessary bureaucratic hassle.[5]

Finally, the police underlined that, even if reduction of the use of substitute prison was sought as an ultimate goal of the Prison Law reform, it would not be possible to simply hand over control of police cells to the MOJ in order to achieve this. Apart from a transfer of existing facilities from the NPA to the MOJ not being realistic in the first place, as they would still be needed for arrestees, it was also noted that since many of the buildings had been paid for by prefectural authorities, rather than from the national purse, it would not be appropriate for the MOJ to make them its own. In light of such issues, the police suggested that opponents of substitute prison would be better served by helping to improve the existing practices rather than obstinately demanding what was not possible.

MOJ: Insurmountable logistical difficulties

Taking a different line to the NPA, the MOJ argued that there were financial and practical constraints to increasing the capacity of their detention centres to the point that substitute prison could be abolished in the near future. Not being able to guarantee the housing of all suspects, the MOJ provided for substitute prison in its

[4] Interview with MOJ Official A, 9 November 2007.

[5] Interview with NPA Official A and NPA Official B, 8 August 2007.

own bill, and was prepared to co-operate with the NPA in its submission. Nonetheless, the MOJ would consider the possibility of substitute prison attrition being included as a supplementary provision.

Even if there was motivation to change the current system to one whereby all suspects were transferred to detention centres after the third day, this was, from the MOJ's perspective, simply unfeasible. To demonstrate the prohibitive financial burden of making such a transition, the MOJ released a number of detailed estimates regarding the resources needed. For instance, in 1983, it calculated that to replace the corresponding police detention facilities, as many as 333 new detention sites of inmate capacity ten, and eighty-seven sites of inmate capacity fifty, would need to be built.[6] Moreover, there would have to be a personnel increase somewhere in the region of 6,600 to administer and staff the new facilities. In total, the purchase of land, buildings, and human capital would require a budget hike of 337 billion yen. Similar estimates for this deficiency in the number of MOJ detention centres and staff were quoted throughout the next decade,[7] with the budgetary requirements being updated accordingly to one trillion yen in 1993, which the Ministry viewed as a pie-in-the-sky figure that it could not be guaranteed to obtain from the Treasury. Indeed, as it rather understatedly explained to the UNHRC in a discussion on this point, '[e]ven though Japan is a rather wealthy country ... one trillion yen is still a very large sum of money'.

For the MOJ, the difficulty was not just an economic one, however, as reversing the growth of substitute prison would also depend on what would inevitably be an unpopular development of a huge expansion of its network of criminal facilities. Indeed, even if the astronomical budgetary requirements to do so could be met, the MOJ claimed that it would be almost impossible for it to secure enough suitable sites for constructing new detention centres. Again explaining to the UNHRC in 1993, for example, a MOJ

[6] *The Main Contentious Points Regarding the Substitute Prison System: Concerning the Establishment of More Detention Centres* (Daiyō kangoku *seido wo meguru omo-na ronten: Kōchisho no zōsetsu ni tsuite*), MOJ material, 23 May 1983.

[7] The number of necessary detention centres was viewed as unchanged, and the MOJ slightly raised the predicted number of new staff required to 7,200. For further details, see the record of the UNHRC meetings on the third periodic report of Japan on the implementation of the ICCPR, Article 638.

official stressed: 'we always face [strong opposition] from the residents in the [nearby] community [when seeking to build new detention centres]'—the reason for this being that very few people in the public would want to have such institutions, which will possibly be required to detain some highly dangerous individuals, in their backyard.[8]

As for the typical view of substitute prison amongst MOJ officials, while they did not deny that the system had its problems, they did not see that these were of a sufficiently fundamental nature to render it in need of termination. Indeed, when quizzed on the potential pitfalls of retaining substitute prison, under which detention and investigation were conducted by the NPA, MOJ officials generally sided with the police in arguing that a single organization undertaking both roles was not a problem for as long as the two were adequately separated.[9] Additionally, despite acknowledging that the system had resulted in some abuses of suspects involving the coercion of a confession, MOJ representatives, just like those of the NPA, strongly refuted that these were a logical consequence of substitute prison. Rather, these were instead attributed to individual investigators going too far, which in principle could happen in any kind of detention facility and would not be resolved by abolishing substitute prison.

MOJ officials did not deem it appropriate to try to characterize in law when the use of substitute prison should be prohibited. This would later be suggested as a way to reduce the risk of forced confessions, but for the Ministry, there was no way the decision of whether to use the system or not could be reduced to a formal rule—such as 'if a suspect claims innocence, he or she will not be placed in police detention'—since it depended on too many factors.[10] In the MOJ's eyes, it was better that the final judgment of where to detain a suspect be left to a judge, who could consider each case on its own merits, taking into account, for example, investigative requirements, the suspect and their family's wishes, the interest of the lawyer, and the location and capacity of the available facilities.

[8] Record of the UNHRC meetings on the third periodic report of Japan on the implementation of the ICCPR, 1993, Article 638. That this is indeed the general public sentiment was confirmed by Moritaka Kamoshita. Interview, 29 August 2007.

[9] Interview with MOJ Official B and MOJ Official C, 31 August 2007.

[10] Ibid.

On the basis of the above logistical concerns and its perception of the system as not being inherently flawed, the various draft versions of the MOJ's penal institutions bill each contained a clause permitting the continuation of substitute prison detention without limitations. With this being the case, the MOJ would agree to submit its bill in partnership with that of the NPA so as to achieve revision of the complete regulatory framework for suspects. It should be remarked, however, that although it would become a central issue in discussions, for the MOJ, substitute prison was only one part of the broader Prison Law reform project that it would become increasingly keen to conclude. Indeed, when substitute prison detention proved to be a stumbling block to amending the legislation for prisons, the MOJ was prepared to discuss its gradual reduction.

The JFBA: Substitute prison needed neither in practice nor in law

Highlighting the temporary and exceptional character of substitute prison detention in the Prison Law, the JFBA would remain staunchly set against this system. As well as deeming the NPA bill regulating for suspects in police jurisdiction unwarranted, the lawyers insisted that the MOJ's bill include a concrete proposal for the reduction of its use.

The JFBA underpinned its argument against substitute prison by pointing to concrete examples of misdoings under such detention, which it condemned as 'a hotbed for false convictions' (*enzai no onshō*). Citing a number of cases—even after the NPA's efforts to put greater separation between officers in charge of investigation and those responsible for detention—in which the voluntary character of the confession in substitute prison was in question, the lawyers argued that nothing other than the total abolition of this system would suffice to adequately safeguard against wrongful convictions.[11] For them, it was still too easy for detention officers

[11] This and other viewpoints of the JFBA can be found in the following documents: JFBA Resolution Demanding the Abolition of Substitute Prison (*Daiyō kangoku haishi wo motomeru ketsugi*), 31st Periodic Meeting, 24 May 1980; JFBA Resolution Opposing the Two Detention Bills (*Kōkin ni hōan ni hantai suru ketsugi*), 33rd Periodic Meeting, 29 May 1982; JFBA Resolution Opposing the Two Detention Bills and Anticipating the Realization of a True Revision of the Prison Law (*Kōkin ni hōan ni hantai shi, shin ni aru beki Kangoku hō no kaisei no jitsugen wo ki suru ketsugi*), 34th Periodic Meeting, 28 May 1983; JFBA Declaration

to accommodate the wishes of those in charge of investigation, and for as long as suspects were under police detention, their rights could not be properly protected (Igarashi 1991). Although they would report interrogation marathons taking place, whereby torture methods such as deprivation of sleep, food, and drink had provided a convenient way to circumvent the problem of leaving marks on the suspect's physique, the lawyers stressed that it was not necessarily physical maltreatment that was the problem in substitute prison detention. Instead, they asserted, there was a prevalence of application of psychologically abusive techniques, such as intimidation, shouting, brainwashing, and verbal assaults. In the JFBA's experience, with their daily life being controlled round the clock for twenty-three days by the investigators, even innocent people often gave in to investigators, confessing to crimes that they had not committed. The lawyers also pointed out that this was particularly problematic in Japan, since confession tended to be seen as indisputable evidence in courts there, and so, once obtained, a false confession would usually result in an unsafe conviction.[12]

Even putting its failures in practice to one side, the JFBA's position was that there was no legal justification for preserving substitute prison simply because the police required it for the sake of investigation (JFBA 1995: 76–8). The lawyers argued that the NPA's demand for easy access to suspects was based on the premise that the purpose of detention was the interrogation of suspects—a point that they were keen to stress was not recognized in any existing Japanese legislation. For them, the original purpose of suspect detention under the Code of Criminal Procedure was to prevent escape, or destruction or concealment of evidence; for these ends, detention in MOJ facilities was clearly sufficient, whatever inconvenience this might incur for investigators.[13]

In response to the MOJ's calculations about the cost of abolishing substitute prison, the JFBA provided its own figures, so as to demonstrate that such a step might not be as far-fetched as the bureaucrats had claimed. Indeed, from the lawyers' viewpoint, the MOJ had vastly overestimated the problem. To begin with, JFBA

Against the Resubmission of the Two Detention Bills (*Kōkin ni hōan no saisai teishutsu ni hantai suru ketsugi*), 28 September 1990; and Joint Committee of the Three Tōkyō Bar Associations for the Study of Substitute Prison report entitled *Forced Confessions—How the Japanese Police Forced 30 Innocent People to Confess*, 1988.

[12] Interview with Shin'ichirō Koike, 2 October 2007.

[13] Interview with Maiko Tagusari, 18 July 2007.

estimations in the early 1980s suggested that 20 per cent of the capacity of at least twenty-eight detention centres remained unused, and seventy facilities could accommodate more suspects than they currently did.[14] Later in the decade, when the lawyers gained access to more detailed government statistics,[15] they concluded that there were even more empty cells than they originally thought, with as little as 60 per cent of MOJ's detention centres capacity being used on average, and that especially the large-scale detention centres were left vacant to a great extent (Igarashi 1989). In addition to these statistics of under-use, and somewhat shockingly for those who had hitherto been working under the assumption of a dearth of detention centres, the JFBA highlighted that the same government source had also recommended that, in order to eliminate the budgetary waste, the smaller facilities should be closed. As for building new detention centres, the JFBA was of the opinion that much of the extra capacity needed could be found by expanding the facilities on existing sites. Moreover, it asserted that the MOJ had over-counted the number of new sites for detention centres required, as it was not essential for every single summary court to have its own cells. Finally, with regard to the MOJ's argument about the impossibility of making a sudden transition, the JFBA suggested it might still be possible to undertake a phased abolition, which for the lawyers was better than nothing.[16]

As for the NPA's proposal that a separate bill be drafted for the continuation of substitute prison, the JFBA deemed that creating such legislation was completely unnecessary. Even if it was decided in the Diet that substitute prison should continue for some period of time, the lawyers argued that the issue of the MOJ delegating authority to the NPA for undertaking detention was not as complicated as the police had argued; as in the existing Prison Law, it would suffice to include a clause stating that the treatment of

[14] *The Main Contentious Points Regarding the Substitute Prison System: Questions to MOJ—20 Points Regarding the Substitute Prison* (Daiyō kangoku *seido wo meguru omo-na ronten: Hōmushō he no shitsumon jikō—Daiyō kangoku ni kan suru nijyū mon*), JFBA, 21 June 1983.

[15] In particular, a 1971 report produced by the Administration and Management Agency (*Gyōsei kanri-chō*), now subsumed by the Management and Coordination Agency (*Sōmushō*).

[16] *The Main Contentious Points Regarding the Substitute Prison System: Questions to MOJ—20 Points Regarding the Substitute Prison* (Daiyō kangoku *seido wo meguru omo-na ronten: Hōmushō he no shitsumon jikō—Daiyō kangoku ni kan suru nijyū mon*), JFBA, 21 June 1983.

suspects in police cells should be the same as those in detention centres.[17] The JFBA contended that, simply because detention was sometimes conducted at prefectural police facilities, the fundamental character of the office of detention should not change and it should not cease to be the central government's responsibility, with police detention being supervised by the MOJ (at least in theory, even taking into account that this was already not happening in practice). Hence, the JFBA considered that the drafting of legislation regarding detention in police facilities should be entrusted to the MOJ alone (Oguri 1996: 50–2).

The JFBA further maintained that, were an NPA bill to pass, the exceptional character of police detention of suspects would be irrevocably lost. At the time of its inception in law, the lawyers argued, substitute prison was intended as an exceptional measure, to be used in lieu of the MOJ's detention system. Creating separate rules for the treatment of suspects in police cells would, for the JFBA, constitute a de facto upgrading of these facilities to a formal place of detention.[18] Moreover, the JFBA determined that the proposed legislation failed to clarify the character of substitute prison as a second option for detention, granting as it did an increase in the NPA's jurisdiction to include the detention of suspects, and incorporating a scheme of reimbursing local police authorities directly for detention in police facilities. This being the case, the lawyers feared that, were the two bills to pass, it would be near impossible to reverse the tide towards its eventual abolition—a consequence of which it was certain the NPA was not unaware.

To back up its position against substitute prison and the Two Detention Bills with realistic alternatives, the JFBA produced several templates for legislation during the course of the discussions, each including a concrete attrition plan. Intended to serve as a useful point of reference for opposition politicians in debates involving the government-sponsored bills, the first of these proposals was released in 1978, and this gradually evolved into the full-fledged JFBA Bill for the Treatment of Criminal Detainees (*Keiji hi-kōkinsha no shogū ni kan suru hōritsuan*) of 1992.[19]

[17] Interview with Yūichi Kaido, 18 July 2007.

[18] JFBA President Shigeru Kobori, *What's* Daiyō Kangoku*?!: Abolish* 'Daiyō Kangoku—*Japan Police Custody System' Now*, JFBA pamphlet, 1 August 1999, p. 2.

[19] An explanatory booklet, 'JFBA's Treatment of Criminal Detainees Law: A Humane System of Treating Prisoners', would also be produced in 1994.

Based on an expensive feasibility study conducted through local bar associations about the increase of the capacity of the detention facilities, the latter proposition contained a detailed ten-year abolition blueprint requiring a budget of only 30 billion yen—less than 10 per cent of that projected by the MOJ (Asahi 1992: 29–30). During the transitional period, the JFBA recommended that those in police cells be regulated for by MOJ legislation and paid for by the MOJ, as had hitherto been the case, and further insisted that MOJ staff should actually start to supervise police cells in practice.[20]

Another notable difference between the 1992 JFBA bill and those of the authorities was the requirement that police detention should not be used for certain particularly vulnerable suspects. This measure was included to safeguard against the investigation appealing a judge's decision to detain in detention centres individuals who had not yet been assigned professional counsel, those denying important facts regarding the criminal case, or those exercising their right to silence (Asahi 1992: 39–40). Under the existing system, along with requesting to the judge that the suspect be detained, a prosecutor could express the preference that this be in a police cell. Since it was generally accepted by judges that such a place of detention would be of benefit to the investigation, the prosecutor's wish was normally granted. The JFBA was concerned that, even if it was not, it was usually the case that the original decision was overturned on appeal to another judge, meaning that substitute prison detention was being used on close to every occasion. Without a provision of the type they had suggested being placed in law, the lawyers argued, it would be impossible to ensure adequate treatment for those most in need of protection of their rights.[21]

The above strong opposition to substitute prison, and particularly the Two Detention Bills being proposed by the authorities, was the official stance maintained by the JFBA throughout the 1980s and 1990s. Whilst it should be noted that already at the time there were some lawyers who expressed in private a difference in opinion, finding it much easier to visit their clients when they were held in police cells, this was not a vocal minority and did not significantly impact on the policy discussions of the day.

[20] Although this was meant to happen under the 1908 Prison Law, it was not the case in practice.

[21] Interview with Maiko Tagusari, 8 November 2007.

Monkey on the MOJ's Back

When the MOJ started to make plans to reform the Prison Law, its every move would be shadowed by the NPA, which would not let amendments be made without its own input. Incensed that the NPA was trying to further institute substitute prison, whose reduction in use had been agreed upon at the consultative phase, the JFBA successfully lobbied the opposition to block the Two Detention Bills presented by the MOJ and NPA on the three occasions that they reached the Diet, in 1982, 1987, and 1991. With the NPA's bill proving the obstacle for the MOJ's one to progress, commentators gave colourful characterizations of both the Agency, as 'the ghost clinging on [MOJ's] back' (*onbu obake*), and the whole situation, as 'a child-turtle being carried by a parent-turtle' (*oya-game no senaka ni ko-game*), where, when the latter falls over, the former is taken down too.[22]

Emergence and first submission of the Two Detention Bills

On the basis of a proposal produced by an advisory council (*shingikai*), the MOJ set about preparing a revised version of the Prison Law. Despite the proposal containing a clause recommending the attrition of substitute prison, there would be no trace of such a provision in the MOJ's bill, and moreover the existence of an NPA bill seemed to contradict it outright. This resulted in a movement against the bills that would prevent them from even being deliberated, let alone enacted.

Sensing that the MOJ's work behind closed doors might soon result in the production of new prison legislation, the JFBA decided to make a statement with a proposed new Prison Law of its own. Following the discussions of the Prison Law Revision Preparation Body, the MOJ had twice produced amendment bills, once in 1968 and once in 1972, albeit that these never reached the Diet. To the JFBA, this smacked of an attempt to reform the law without outside consultation. Since they were determined to have input into any revision, the lawyers decided to state their vision of the future law for prisons. To this end, in September 1975 the JFBA submitted to the incumbent Justice Minister a Proposal for a Criminal Detention Bill (*Nichibenren keiji kōkin hō yōkō teian*)

[22] The JFBA Vice President Araki Kuniichi. *Asahi Shimbun*, 27 March 1995, p. 4.

intended to supersede the Prison Law. In order that the name of the new law described the nature of the treatment rather than the facilities, the JFBA recommended that it should be called the Correctional Administration Law (*Gyōkei hō*). This law would clarify the rights and legal position of prisoners and institute a mechanism for filing complaints to a quasi-governmental organ, making it, in the words of the JFBA, the *Magna Carta* for prisoners. Most importantly, however, it provided a detailed five-year plan for the abolition of substitute prison.

In reaction to the JFBA's move, in March 1976 the MOJ requested that the Judicial Council parliamentary discussion group (*Hōsei shingikai*)[23] consider the issue of Prison Law reform. To meet the approval of external critics, incumbent Justice Minister Osamu Inaba appointed as the Chair an outspoken criminal justice commentator, Professor Ryūichi Hirano of the University of Tōkyō, who wrote frequently on ways of improving existing practices.[24] Along with Hirano, this body was composed of other scholars, those with experience of working within the prison system, and also representatives of the JFBA and the NPA. The deliberations of the Judicial Council were to be conducted under the three banners of 'modernization', 'internationalization', and 'legalization' (*kindaika, kokusaika*, and *hōritsuka*). Firstly, the call for 'modernization' signified the intensity of the demands to bring the Prison Law up to date in form and content, removing archaic language from its name and body. Secondly, 'internationalization' of the Prison Law was viewed as necessary to overcome the failure of the 1908 Prison Law to meet the UN Standard Minimum Rules for the Treatment of Prisoners, as well as its divergence from the trends in correctional administration expressed in the legislation of other nations at Japan's development status. Thirdly, through

[23] A panel of experts under the authority of the Justice Minister whose role it was to discuss penal and civil legislation. Specifically, the group entrusted with the task at hand was the Judicial Council Sub-committee on Prison Law (*Hōsei shingikai kangoku hō bukai*).

[24] Hirano is best known for arguing that the Japanese criminal justice system places too much weight on confessions. For instance, his most celebrated work laments 'the current criminal justice law [of Japan], when compared with its Western counterparts, is culturally troubled, and even quite sick ... To express this in a word, it could be said that whilst the Western courts decide guilt or innocence, their Japanese counterparts are places where the guilt is simply confirmed' (Hirano 1985; see also Hirano 1963 for writing of his on the treatment of prisoners in particular).

'legalization' of the Prison Law, it was intended that any new statute for prisons should be less reliant on auxiliary procedural instructions regarding the rights and duties of the imprisoned than its predecessor had become—for some critics, this dependence even constituted a breach of the *nullem crimen* principle, that is, punishment cannot be meted out where crime, as defined by the law, does not exist (for expansion on this point, see the later work of Akaike and Kusumoto 1996). Although the current prison legislation and regulations had been criticized from the outside on each of these three grounds, it should be noted that the MOJ too was anxious to update what was an embarrassingly old law.

During the Prison Law revision deliberations, substitute prison immediately emerged as a controversial issue, and would remain so until the very end of the discussions. Even the scholars on the Council, who were arguably the most removed from the issue, could not agree on how best to approach it (see the discussions between Hirano, Nakayama, Mitsui, and Ishihara, amongst others, in one of *Hōritsu jihō*'s special editions on the Prison Law Reform (1978: 8–43)). And, with the JFBA and government spokesmen clashing on the issue—the MOJ insisting on the impossibility of the system's abolition and the JFBA producing a five-year plan for doing so (for a commentary on this see Hirano 1976)—the talks soon stagnated (Asahi 1992: 27–8). As a result, the MOJ's plan for submitting draft legislation in April 1978 could not be fulfilled. In fact, it would not be until November 1980, after four and a half years of meetings, that the work of the committee was drawn to a close with the release of a proposal which represented the foundation on which revision was to be undertaken.

Unsurprisingly, given the unresolved dispute about substitute prison, no radical steps were taken with regards to the Proposal to Serve as a Framework for Amending the Prison Law (*Kangoku hō kaisei no kosshi to naru yōkō*, henceforth the 'Proposal'). Although the authorities' arguments for retaining substitute prison ensured that the system would be preserved,[25] the position taken in the Proposal was that, whilst it should be applied for the time being, 'the gradual reduction in the instances where substitute

[25] In the Proposal, 'substitute prison' was changed to 'substitute detention' (*daiyō shūyō*), but since it was essentially the same system, for reasons of clarity, I will continue to refer to it as 'substitute prison'.

prison is used should be sought in the future'[26]—an article that would come to be known as the 'attrition clause' (*zengenka jōkō*). This mutual compromise made in the Proposal was reminiscent of that made at the birth of the Prison Law: whilst the authorities had to promise a reduction in the use of substitute prison in the future, this promise was not accompanied by a concrete time frame for abolition. In such a way, the Proposal met each side's demands only halfway, and it is difficult to establish whether MOJ officials had any serious intention to follow up on their pledge, since the primary reason it had been included in the Proposal was to satisfy the JFBA so as to conclude the consultation process. Even without a firm plan towards abolition, however, the lawyers would point to the Proposal's attrition clause whenever draft legislation concerning substitute prison lacking a similar provision was debated.

Whilst the MOJ was working on turning the Proposal of the Prison Law reform body into a bill, the NPA showed signs of preparing a bill of its own to accompany this (Oguri 1996: 5). During the Proposal's drafting, preparations were initially made within the MOJ for a single bill. However, such plans met with strong resistance from the NPA—which was adamant that separate rules needed to be created for police facilities, over which the MOJ had no jurisdiction—and it was agreed between the two government institutions that two separate bills should be submitted. The first time that this was made public was in January 1982, with justification for the move being presented to the mass media in March, shortly before the process of the bills being passed for approval through the various sections of the Liberal Democratic Party (LDP) began.

The news that the NPA had decided to prepare an independent bill caused a furore within the ranks of the JFBA, which saw it as a ruse to perpetuate substitute prison. Apart from seeing no justification for a separate bill for remand prisoners detained in police facilities, the lawyers were incensed that the NPA had tried to override the Judicial Council. They claimed that, even if it was within the jurisdiction of the NPA to produce a bill that was applicable to arrestees, making decisions on the treatment of any detainees, especially remand prisoners, should not be carried out by the NPA alone, and the content for such a bill should have been more widely

[26] *'Kangoku hō kaisei no kosshi to naru yōkō' (Proposal to Serve as a Framework for Amending the Prison Law)*, Judicial Council, November 1980, *Sono Ta (Others)*, paragraph 2.

deliberated. The JFBA feared that the enactment of an NPA bill that entrenches existing police detention practices would '[turn back the hands of time] more than 200 years' in the protection of the basic rights of suspects,[27] returning the country to a system more reminiscent of pre-modern Japan, and the hope of attrition of the substitute prison system would be lost for the foreseeable future. For the lawyers, the NPA's bill was no more than a by-product of the Agency's sense of crisis that substitute prison might see its demise if no action was taken by it.

Co-ordinating their efforts, in April 1982 the MOJ and NPA eventually submitted to the Diet what would thereafter become known as the Two Detention Bills—the Penal Institutions Bill (*Keiji shisetsu hōan*) and the Police Detention Institutions Bill (*Ryūchi shisetsu hōan*). In line with the Proposal, the MOJ included the provision that 'suspects could be kept in custody in the detention facilities established at the prefectural police, as an alternative to [MOJ] facilities'.[28] Consequently, even though the MOJ's bill was not tied to the NPA's, the two were seen as a set, with the former allowing for the exceptional use of substitute prison and the latter providing rules that should be followed there. Controversially, the advisory committee's recommendation of future attrition of substitute prison was completely absent from the MOJ's bill. Although it was mooted by some officials that the MOJ intended to use the inclusion of an attrition clause in the form of a non-binding external resolution as a bargaining chip during the Diet deliberations (Hirano, Odanaga, and Fujimoto 1988), the JFBA were adamant that by 'taking out the bones' of the Proposal in this way, the MOJ had backtracked from the agreement that had been reached.[29]

Aside from this omission of the attrition clause and the existence of a separate NPA bill, the JFBA was also dissatisfied with what it saw to be retrogression in the MOJ's bill from the Proposal on more than 100 points, including a number of changes that would limit lawyers' access to suspects in MOJ facilities. In general, it seemed to the bar that the Ministry had put too much of its own spin on the framework that had been reached in the earlier

[27] *What's* Daiyō Kangoku*?!: Abolish* 'Daiyō Kangoku – *Japan Police Custody System' Now*, JFBA President Shigeru Kobori, pamphlet, 1 August 1999, p. 2.

[28] Article 166.

[29] Interview with Yūichi Kaido and Maiko Tagusari, 18 July 2007.

deliberations, deleting various provisions for ensuring fair proceedings and rights protection,[30] and adding clauses to reinforce the existing disciplinary regime.[31] However, the JFBA was particularly unhappy about the retention in the MOJ's bill of restriction of lawyers' visitations to the institution's working hours. This constraint was made on the grounds that visitations outside of these hours would 'obstruct the management of the facilities', but the lawyers argued that their other professional commitments made it difficult for them to provide services to their clients. Related to this, the daily limit placed on the number of visitations a lawyer was allowed to make to their client in detention, for the purpose of preventing the concealment of evidence, and the lack of any avenues for complaints by lawyers whose right to visitation had been arbitrarily curtailed also provoked outcry. Some lawyers even suggested that these restrictive measures formed part of a conspiracy of the authorities to make visiting MOJ facilities even less attractive than police cells, so as to decrease objections to substitute prison.

Ultimately, the subsequent campaign spearheaded by the JFBA against the Two Detention Bills proved to be successful in blocking their progression through the Diet. Immediately after the LDP's submission, the JFBA established a Countermeasure to the Two Detention Bills Headquarters (*Kōkin ni hōan taisaku honbu*) in Tōkyō, with a sub-office at each local bar association. Through this initiative, the lawyers also hoped to create a base of support for a wholesale revision of the MOJ's proposed Penal Institutions Bill, as well as completely abolishing the NPA-drafted Police Detention Institutions Bill. Moreover, in a resolution adopted at their annual general meeting in May 1982, the lawyers swore to do all that they could to make both bills drag, and to prevent any substantive deliberations of them in the Diet until they were dropped. To this end, the JFBA members lobbied each of the major opposition parties, and one after another these would also declare themselves in opposition to the Two Detention Bills. First was the

[30] Examples include such issues as training of staff, regulation of the use of restraining devices and solitary confinement, medical care, remuneration of prisoners' labour, the formation of an independent inspection committee, and a revised prisoners' complaints procedure.

[31] These covered the use of weapons and restraints, and increasing the discretion with which prison wardens could impose disciplinary measures to the end of maintaining order.

Japanese Communist Party (JCP) in April, followed by the Japan Socialist Party (JSP) in June, and then the Democratic Socialist Party and Kōmeitō in August. Objections lodged over the next few months by parliamentarians from these parties would stall discussions, forcing the LDP to shelve the Two Detention Bills in the autumn of 1982. They would finally be dropped with the dissolution of the 100th Diet Session of the House of Representatives in December 1983.

Two years of stalling

After the initial failure of the Two Detention Bills, the MOJ promptly returned to the drafting board, attempting to appease the JFBA by inviting it to discussions at which the Ministry conceded numerous points on its bill. The NPA, on the other hand, never sought to instigate such an inclusive approach in order to reduce opposition to its proposed legislation. As a consequence, realizing that the continuing strong opposition would make the promulgation of the bills (that still prescribed the continuation of substitute prison) unlikely, the NPA was left with no other option than asking the MOJ for the resubmission process to be put on hold. Following this step, and growing weary of supporting a doomed bill, the LDP commanded the police to reconsider its approach.

In a bid to ensure its next legislative attempt would be successful, in November 1982 the MOJ approached the lawyers with a request to conduct an 'exchange of views' so as to take on board some of their suggestions. Earlier, representatives from the JFBA had participated in the advisory council stage, but now the lawyers' organization was targeted on its own as the main barrier for the MOJ's long-cherished desire to amend the Prison Law. The Ministry's expression of willingness to accommodate the JFBA's demands convinced the lawyers to accept the invitation, and in February the following year a series of as many as twenty-two negotiation sessions began. In the course of the first few meetings, the MOJ brought the lawyers on side through a host of concessions regarding the treatment of convicted prisoners.[32] Reaching common ground on the substitute prison issue would again prove difficult, though, as both sides refused to budge from their original

32 Interview with Yūichi Kaido and Maiko Tagusari, 18 July 2007.

position in terms of the content of a new law. The only consolation which the MOJ offered the JFBA on this point was its open declaration that a substitute prison attrition clause be included at the parliamentary stage, either as an external resolution or as a legally binding supplementary provision to the law. Without having anything in black and white within the law, however, the JFBA feared that the MOJ would easily be able to renege on its promises.

As the end of the year approached, the negotiations took an acrimonious tone, as the MOJ—bent on not missing the window for bill submission in April 1984—sought to foreclose the meetings with the JFBA despite there being no agreement on substitute prison yet. Judging that it had made enough concessions to the JFBA over the preceding nine months to ensure the passing of the bills in the Diet, the MOJ announced its intent to post its updated bill at the next opportunity, and thereafter adopted a harder line with respect to police detention. The Ministry argued that since the abandonment of the previous legislation had happened in a natural way with the dissolution of the House, as opposed to its content being criticized as problematic, there was no reason to alter it beyond the modifications already made. To this, the JFBA reacted angrily with the remark that if this was the case then it would have to continue its opposition movement, and advised the MOJ to reconsider the issue of substitute prison within the bill before submitting it. The JFBA vowed that if two detention bills were again to be submitted to the Diet, it would make sure the revision of the Prison Law would only become more distant, whilst the MOJ responded in turn with the declaration that it would be difficult for the treatment of sentenced criminals and suspects to be collated in a single bill.

In contrast to the MOJ's efforts to interact constructively with the JFBA, the NPA had hardly any contact with the lawyers' organization. Although it might well have been the case that, as with the drafting process for the original proposed Police Detention Institutions Bill, the NPA did not deem it necessary for outside consultation to take place, its relationship with the JFBA was less straightforward than that between the MOJ and the JFBA. Specifically, the extra complication arose from the JFBA being opposed to the principle of the NPA's involvement in revising the Prison Law on the grounds that the proper jurisdiction for the detention of suspects should lie with the MOJ. In the only meeting that did take place between the JFBA and the NPA, in December 1983, the sole aim of the NPA was to explain its position that substitute prison was an indispensable tool for the Japanese criminal justice system and could not be abolished, even though the Agency was already aware that the JFBA would not sympathize with this argument (Oguri 1996: 52).

Despite the MOJ's eagerness to proceed, the April 1984 deadline would come and go with no resubmission, as the NPA pleaded for more time to prepare its bill. The NPA's request came at what were meant to be the final discussions regarding the alignment of the Two Detention Bills before they were presented again to the Diet, and although reluctant, the MOJ agreed to wait for another year.[33] The official reason given for this postponement was that more work needed to be done to appease critics such as the JFBA so that any new legislation would be widely accepted.[34] Reducing the JFBA objections to the Two Detention Bills, which was seen as an important step to lessening political opposition, was especially important in this period given the tenuous situation of the LDP in the Diet, whereby the party no longer wielded a majority and had been forced to form a coalition government with the breakaway New Liberal Club (*Shin jiyū kurabu*).[35]

Almost immediately after the decision to delay was taken, the MOJ and JFBA resumed negotiations that eventually resulted in yet more concessions being made in the lawyers' favour, but still the two parties remained at odds with each other. Determined not to miss another legislative opportunity, the MOJ was keen to make quick progress. Almost identically to the previous year, however, the talks reached deadlock over the substitute prison issue. When the dialogue broke off in November 1984, the JFBA described the MOJ's intent to resubmit after having made no substantive changes as 'regrettable', and stated that it would continue its movement to inhibit the submission of the Two Detention Bills.[36] In a last-ditch attempt to secure approval from its opponents, however, in late January 1985 MOJ officials sought the JFBA's approval for a draft Penal Institutions Bill in which nine of the articles had been amended from earlier versions in accordance

[33] *Nihon Keizai Shimbun*, 16 April 1984, p. 31.

[34] *Nihon Keizai Shimbun*, 19 May 1984, p. 2.

[35] In the 1983 general election, the LDP gained only 250 out of a possible 511 seats and were forced to collaborate with the New Liberal Club, which gained eight.

[36] *Nihon Keizai Shimbun*, 20 November 1984, p. 2.

with lawyers' demands.[37] Despite acknowledging the MOJ's efforts with regard to the changed articles, the JFBA assessed the bill as negative overall, requesting that the number of amended articles be increased to include the Proposal's recommendation for the gradual elimination of substitute prison in particular.[38] After the JFBA reaffirmed at a general meeting in February its opposition to the draft legislation, the MOJ wasted no time in amending another five articles of its bill, some of which were high up on the lawyers' agenda.[39] Furthermore, although, in answer to the JFBA's request that restrictions on visitations be eased, the MOJ did not make modifications to the proposed law, the Ministry promised that it would strive to meet this demand in practice. The JFBA, though, still considered the adjustments insufficient and continued its posture for developing a movement aimed at blocking the proposed legislation in the Diet.

Come April 1985, the Two Detention Bills were again stalled before reaching the Diet, but this year it would be the LDP that was responsible. Notwithstanding the JFBA's threat to incite political resistance to the bill, the MOJ did not want to wait another year, and was joined by the NPA in presenting its proposed legislation to the LDP for approval. Facing united opposition, however, the vulnerable LDP for the first time did something other than simply accepting the officials' proposals, and refused to sponsor the Two Detention Bills on this occasion. Moreover, the LDP suggested to the NPA that it discontinue its forceful pressing of the Police Detention Institutions Bill, and create an opportunity, as the MOJ had done, to exchange views with the JFBA (Oguri 1996: 57–9). Seeing that its plans to update the Prison Law were about to collapse again, the MOJ attempted to salvage the situation by finding a solution that the politicians could endorse immediately through

[37] Concrete amendments included a relaxation of the provision regarding lawyers' visitations of suspects, so that restrictions could only be imposed on the grounds of administration rather than the grounds of preventing the concealment of evidence. Further clarification of the difference in the legal positions of sentenced and suspects was also made.

[38] *Nihon Keizai Shimbun*, 30 January 1985, p. 2; *Asahi Shimbun*, 30 January 1985, p. 3.

[39] Amongst these was one that made it clear that the documents brought by a lawyer to a visitation would not be subject to scrutiny by the prison authorities, and one stating, according to some of the lawyers' stronger appeals, that a doctor should be consulted about the state of health of a prisoner when he/she is to be put in isolation as a measure to maintain order.

the unification of the two bills into a single MOJ proposal. This idea did not take root, however, as the MOJ was reluctant to include as much of the NPA's proposed legislation as the Agency desired in terms of specific provisions for its facilities, and the resubmission was thwarted for a second successive year.

Two more failed submissions

The NPA would eventually extend an offer to the JFBA to engage in talks regarding their bill. Despite no progress on substitute prison being made when these took place, the MOJ and NPA would go ahead with resubmission of the Two Detention Bills, only to see them fail twice more.

In November 1985, the NPA officially invited the JFBA to engage in dialogue, and after some initial caginess, the lawyers agreed. The NPA's approach, taken on the LDP's prompting, was an event that was seen by onlookers as a radical step, but it placed the JFBA in a dilemma: it seemed to the lawyers that whether they chose to accept or decline, it would not prevent an NPA bill being submitted. If the JFBA accepted, the way for submission of an amended bill would be paved, as the NPA would have fulfilled its duty to consult them; if they declined, on the other hand, this would give the NPA justification to resubmit the original bill. That it took the lawyers five months to make up their mind might not be a coincidence, given their fear that a quick acceptance would leave only a few weeks for discussion before the NPA used the pretext of closing the discussions in time for the coming spring's submission deadline. Reserving their ultimate decision for later, between November 1985 and April 1986 the JFBA conducted preliminary negotiations with the NPA, in which they obliged the police officials to agree to discuss all contentious points, including the necessity of the police legislating at all, the form of the legislation, and the Proposal's attrition clause. The JFBA also sought a guarantee that the sessions would not be prematurely foreclosed. Once this framework was in place, the JFBA's Countermeasure to the Two Detention Bills Headquarters organized a referendum in order to determine the organization's final response. After a close-run vote, the position that the JFBA adopted was to accept the NPA's offer with the intention that the exchange of views would be used as a forum for directly demanding the withdrawal of the NPA's bill as part of the lawyers' movement against the Two Detention Bills (FTBA 1985: 46–8, Oguri 1996: 17-22).

Unsurprisingly, when discussions between the NPA and the JFBA eventually commenced in July 1986, they did little to resolve the differences between the two organizations. During the ten meetings held prior to April 1987, both sides maintained the position that the other simply did not understand the issue at hand. At the outset, the NPA acknowledged the JFBA's anti-Two Detention Bills resolution, and the two bodies declared that they were sincere in their desire to reach agreement.[40] However, it was apparent that this would be difficult, as the NPA made it clear that one of its goals was to obtain an understanding from the lawyers about why substitute prison had to be maintained, whereas the JFBA commenced its arguments with the constitutional objection that forced confessions are illegal and, for as long as substitute prison continued to be used, there could be no adequate safeguards against these occurring. The impasse that the two parties soon reached would not be resolved, and, although the NPA made amendments to its draft bill, this did not deflect the JFBA's attention from the more fundamental issue of the very existence of substitute prison (and, anyway, what changes the NPA made were criticized by the JFBA as mere rewording).

In spring 1987 the MOJ and NPA announced that they were now ready to submit the Two Detention Bills for a second time, before trying to convince the JFBA of their merit once more. Since meetings between the NPA and the JFBA had by this time been conducted, in March 1987 the MOJ declared that there was no reason to delay any further the resubmission of its bill to the Diet, and, unsurprisingly, it was joined in doing so by the NPA. Then, in a final attempt to secure the JFBA's approval of their draft legislation, MOJ officials approached the JFBA for a second round of meetings, and over the month before its resubmission the two parties convened four times. The JFBA was criticized by the MOJ for its uncompromising approach, even after having obtained so many concessions in earlier talks. To this, the lawyers responded by distilling their demands to only two: abolition of substitute prison,

[40] *Ryūchi shisetsu wo meguru keisatsu-chō to no iken kōkan-kai chūkan hōkoku: Kaisai no keii to dai go-kai made no gaiyō* (An Interim Report on the Exchange of Views with the NPA regarding the Police Detention Facilities: The Sequence of Events up to the Beginning of the Meetings and a Synopsis of the First Five Meetings), JFBA, 20 January 1987.

and unrestricted access to clients in detention (Oguri 1996: 52). The NPA also met with the JFBA a further three times, but there would be no major breakthrough in either set of negotiations, and substitute prison remained contentious to the last.

In April 1987, the Two Detention Bills[41] were submitted to the Diet for a second time, but ultimately this legislative attempt was no more a success than the first one. During this period, parliamentary time was dominated by Prime Minister Nakasone's proposed tax reforms, which were severely criticized even within his own ruling party (the LDP), and so Prison Law reform went without discussion for nearly a year. Although the LDP politicians attempted to motivate substantive deliberations in March 1988 by referring to the age of the current Prison Law, attention to the Two Detention Bills was deflected again—this time as a result of the uproar caused by the ongoing revelations of the so-called 'Recruit Scandal', in which many prominent parliamentarians, mostly ruling LDP members, were forced to resign over allegations of insider trading and corruption.[42] With the LDP's ensuing loss of control of the House of Councillors and little support from opposition politicians for the Two Detention Bills, it was clear that passing them was unrealistic at this time, and so no vote was taken, leading to the inevitable conclusion of the bills being dropped for a second time with the dissolution of the House of Representatives at the end of the 117th Ordinary Diet Session in January 1990.

Blocking the detention bills twice had given the JFBA hope that the MOJ and NPA would be dissuaded from presenting them in the same form again, but it would not be long before this optimism was proved groundless. In an effort to convey its resolve to not tolerate the repeated submission of the Two Detention Bills, the JFBA sent the Justice Minister and the NPA's top-ranking

[41] In fact, there were actually four detention bills submitted on this occasion, the additions being a MOJ bill for the amendment of the Prison Law Enforcement Regulations and a bill (*Kaijō hōan-chō no ryūchi shisetsu ni kan suru hōan*) prepared by the Maritime Safety Agency (*Kaijō hōan-chō*) seeking to regulate the treatment of those held in the detention facilities administered by them.

[42] This scandal would reach as high as the Cabinet, and even the Prime Minister of the time, Noboru Takeshita, was compelled to stand down in June 1989. In the House of Councillors election the following month, the LDP witnessed its share of seats in the House of Councillors fall from 143 to 109 of the 252 available seats, thus seeing a commanding 57 per cent majority shrink to a mere 43 per cent, whilst in the same election the main gains were made by the JSP, who were strong opponents of the proposed detention bills.

officer, the Commissioner-General, a resolution that it had adopted against this course of action (Oguri 1996: 57–9). Nonetheless, with the MOJ remaining as determined as ever to achieve Prison Law revision and the NPA unwilling to let that happen without its own input, the Two Detention Bills soon resurfaced. The legislation whose promulgation the MOJ and NPA sought on this occasion was almost identical to the previous version, as this time there had not even been any outside consultations with a view to their revision. Within the LDP, concerns existed that political risks would be involved in attempting to enact the Two Detention Bills in a form that was close to that which had failed twice previously, especially given its current weakened position in the House of Councillors, but the proposals of the MOJ and NPA would eventually earn enough approval to warrant their resubmission in April 1991, only a few months after they were dropped.

When the Two Detention Bills were submitted for a third time in 1991, the LDP appealed that it was high time some compromises were made by its opponents on the issue of amending the Prison Law. Shortly after its submission, for example, senior LDP politician Ichirō Nakanishi told the Judicial Affairs Committee of the House of Councillors that, although the LDP recognized that on some issues the legislation it was sponsoring in the Diet did not meet the expectations of the JFBA[43] and opposition parties, the Two Detention Bills did contain as many improvements in parallel with the conclusion of the Judicial Council as could realistically be achieved, and that it was time for both sides to make concessions so that the stalemate could finally end.[44] In particular, on the issue of substitute prison, Nakanishi asked that, rather than insisting that the JFBA's proposition for its complete demise within ten years be included within the law, advocates of its abolition consider, as a starting point, that an external resolution for a five-year reduction of its use be attached instead. Going on to describe the political situation, Nakanishi noted that the passage of the bill through the House of Representatives would probably be straightforward given the LDP's majority there, but that to pass the House of Councillors it would be necessary for the opposition to vote with the government. He pleaded that his opponents appreciate

[43] By now, the JFBA's position had been further publicized through its own Prison Law reform proposal.

[44] 9 April 1991.

the forward steps that the new draft legislation contained and not let idealism block the progress that could be made now.

Opposition politicians were not swayed by such arguments, and the resulting stalemate led to the Two Detention Bills being dropped for a third consecutive time. The JSP, in particular, raised questions as to why the government was persisting with bills that had repeatedly been dropped, as well as with the system of substitute prison that had been so strongly criticized by the United Nations Human Rights Council (UNHRC) and international human rights non-governmental organizations (NGOs) such as Amnesty International.[45] Seeking to underline this final point, Tetsuo Kitamura from the JSP cited a long list of examples in which substitute prison had led to false convictions, even quoting from a verdict of the Tōkyō High Court that:

> Substitute prison . . . is a system which comes with much risk of producing forced confessions, and it is necessary to think seriously about its operation. The offices of detention and investigation of suspects, even if they are undertaken by the same agency—the police, are completely separate from each other and their operation should not be merged. It is necessary for the two duties to be undertaken independently of each other, and it should not be permitted that the detention is used for investigation.[46]

In response to these attacks, LDP members explained that the MOJ did understand the increased recognition of human rights expressed in the reports of the UNHRC and international NGOs, but maintained that, nevertheless, the practical reality of the situation meant that substitute prison could not be abolished immediately. In the bills' defence, they continued to point to measures in the proposed bills that did improve the protection of the human rights of detainees.[47] With it being clear that the LDP would not be able to convince the House of Councillors to vote for the enactment of the Two Detention Bills, however, no vote was ever taken

[45] Amongst the questions made were those of: Shinozaki Toshiko, JSP, Committee for Local Administration, House of Councillors, 25 April 1991; Kitamura Tetsuo, JSP, Judicial Affairs Committee, House of Councillors, 25 April 1991.

[46] Statement by Judge Shin'ichi Tateyama, Tōkyō High Court, with regard to the exoneration in a 1974 case of the killing of an office worker at Matsudo. Reported at the Judicial Affairs Committee, House of Councillors, 25 April 1991.

[47] For example, see the Justice Minister's response in an interview for the *Hōritsu zasshi*, 9 April 1991.

on them, and they would slip off the agenda, ultimately being dropped at the culmination of the 126th Diet Session in July 1993.

Phantom Fourth Amendment Bill

Throughout the rest of the 1990s and even beyond, no further moves to reform the Prison Law would be made by the MOJ and the NPA, at least in public. With the negotiations between the authorities and the JFBA ceasing, and neither party commanding enough power to force the issue, it seemed that the amendment of this law had reached deadlock. What would later emerge, however, is that during this period, the establishment of an instrument through which the long-standing wish of the JFBA for the abolition of substitute prison could be achieved might not have been out of sight.

Former Correction Bureau official Moritaka Kamoshita has publicly claimed that upon the bill's third failure in the Diet, the MOJ finally managed to obtain the NPA's agreement to include the Proposal's attrition clause within the text of their next draft bill, although no concrete proposals along these lines would ever appear in the open. Apparently, in 1992 Kamoshita had been personally in charge of securing the NPA's approval of such course of action, and his efforts at negotiating a deal had borne fruit. In particular, during a more recent debate on the future of substitute prison, he asserted in the Diet that for the first time an accord had then been reached between the MOJ and the NPA on a concrete proposal for reducing the use of substitute prison.[48] Although, in response to intense pressure by opposition politicians from the DPJ and the JSP to produce the draft bill in question, both Justice Minister Seiken Sugiura and Correction Bureau Director Yoshinobu Onuki denied its existence in the Diet—explaining that their senior colleague had most likely misunderstood the situation—Kamoshita has maintained his position in interviews published in the media.[49] The reported reason for this bill not reaching the Diet is the LDP's 1993 loss of power. More specifically, in the ensuing parliamentary disorder, in which three new Prime Ministers would take office within the year following the

[48] Diet testimony, Judicial Affairs Committee, House of Representatives, 11 and 12 April 2006. Also, interviews with Kamoshita, 29 August and 25 October 2007.

[49] *Mainichi Shimbun*, evening edition, 12 April 2006, p. 1; *Tōkyō Shimbun*, evening edition, 12 April 2006, p. 10.

1993 general election, the bill containing what the print media would later call the 'phantom attrition clause' disappeared, never to see the light of day.

Some Near-death Experiences

The lawyers' movement against the Two Detention Bills was bolstered by a sequence of widely publicized court decisions to acquit death-row inmates whose sentences had been based on confessions obtained after torture in substitute prison—including what are commonly referred to in Japanese legal circles as the 'Big Four' exonerations. These developments lent substance to the arguments of those seeking the abolition of substitute prison, and would gradually inspire broader interest in the issue.

The first exoneration of a death-row inmate to occur was the Supreme Court's acquittal in July 1983 of Sakae Menda, which represented a watershed in the JFBA's anti-Two Detention Bills campaign. Menda had originally been sentenced to death in 1951, charged with two murders and two assaults leading to injury and robbery. The case against him had depended on his self-incriminating confession, made on the fourth day of his detention under the police's authority during which he had not been allowed sleep, food, or rest and had been, in his own words, 'hassled with leading questions, torture and violence'.[50] In 1979, after six attempts, Menda was finally granted a retrial, and—on the grounds that he had an indisputable alibi—his sentence was overturned, making him the first person to be acquitted of the death penalty as a result of retrial in Japan. Although the JFBA had argued against substitute prison throughout the post-war period and had previously been able to point to less serious criminal cases where abuses had happened, the Menda verdict gave credence to the lawyers' claims in a way that had not been the case previously. Since his retrial had allowed Menda to so narrowly escape the ultimate punishment, it would dominate the media, and many in the public would for the first time become aware of the substitute prison issue that had been at the heart of the story.

Two more similar acquittals would soon follow, and each would add to the negative publicity surrounding the Two Detention Bills, with the first of these in particular arguably playing a part in the

50 Talk given by Menda, October 2007.

authorities' decision to put off the submission of their bills in 1984. In March of the preceding year, Shigeyoshi Taniguchi, who had been sentenced to death in 1952 for the alleged crime of robbery combined with murder, was cleared after retrial proceedings. The Court found that a false confession had been extracted from him whilst in substitute prison detention, where he had been detained for a total of nearly four months, after having been repeatedly arrested under unrelated charges of theft. This exoneration would have made it impossible for the Two Detention Bills to have a quiet ride through the Diet had they been submitted as the MOJ had planned to do in the spring of 1984, and no doubt cemented the authorities' decision to postpone them at that time. Later that year, in July, Yukio Saitō was exculpated for the crimes of murdering four family members and arson, and the grounds for acquittal were again linked to his coerced confession whilst in police detention. What was now a series of three death-row exonerations placed pressure on the incumbent Justice Minister, Sumie Isaku, in the form of questions raised by the opposition regarding the MOJ's resistance to take on board the JFBA's and wider concerns about substitute prison.

The number of verdicts calling into question the reliability of confessions obtained in substitute prison continued to increase throughout the second half of the 1980s. Indeed, two more death-row acquittals were made—the last of the Big Four in 1989, on the grounds of a confession that was not credible, and yet another in 1990, with the presiding judge declaring that 'the evidence [against the defendant] based on his accomplice's confession was untrustworthy'.[51] In the same period, several life sentences were overturned as well.[52] With these cases, a tendency became established for judges to highlight the need for strict separation between the offices of detention and investigation in their explanations of the verdict. Moreover, taken as a collection, they would reveal that it was not uncommon for a judge to be confronted with a lawsuit where there was a barren controversy (that is, with the suspect insisting that their confession had been given under duress, and the police and prosecution denying any coercion), but there being no way to ascertain the true facts of the matter, as no records of interviews would have been made.[53]

[51] Masao Akabori and Norio Shimogami were the respective defendants.
[52] For example, of Yoshimitsu Umeda in 1986.
[53] Interview with Judge A, 7 January 2008.

The JFBA did not miss the opportunity to publicize, both at home and abroad, this succession of miscarriages of justice, which, in its eyes, typified the underlying problems of the criminal justice system of Japan. Along with producing many pamphlets with its explanation of the procedural failures leading to guilty verdicts that would later be overturned, the JFBA also made efforts to ensure broader coverage of the events through popular media channels. For example, lawyers would contribute to the NHK's May 1989 documentary entitled 'Miscarriages of Justice: Can Wrongful Convictions Be Prevented? (Lessons from British and American Law)', in which there would be a serious treatment of the substitute prison issue, an introduction to the facts surrounding the exoneration cases, and explanations as to where the Japanese system of criminal suspect detention was deficient by comparison to those of other countries, in particular the UK and the USA. Combined with these domestic activities, the JFBA was also keen to promote its campaign against the Two Detention Bills in the international media. The lawyers' goal was to shame the Japanese government abroad by presenting Japan as an uncivilized country, and, to this end, information about the exoneration cases that had hitherto occurred was sent to both American broadcast and print media. The resulting television coverage included a seven-minute feature, shown twice in December 1988 on the national channel NBC, that was intended to inform the American public of the Two Detention Bills being repeatedly submitted to the Japanese Diet. Amongst the American newspaper reportage were articles in the *New York Times*[54] and the *International Herald Tribune*.[55] These endeavours aimed to ensure that the JFBA's movement against the two bills would not be forgotten amongst the wider public.

Apart from seeking media coverage, the JFBA also made efforts to develop a grassroots movement to support its cause. The groups created under its auspices took initiatives to broaden public awareness of the state of the Japanese criminal justice system even further. Symposiums and forums where lawyers or exonerated individuals were invited to talk of their experiences with substitute prison were organized not only in the big cities but also in residential suburbs, with most being scheduled for evenings, so that citizens' participation was not inhibited by their work commitments.

[54] 21 November 1988, p. 19.
[55] 3 March 1989.

At these meetings there would even be performances of the theme song of the movement against the Two Detention Bills, which had been commissioned by the JFBA in 1984, entitled 'One Day Suddenly ...' (*Aru hi totsuzen ni ...*).[56]

As each new acquittal involving substitute prison detention brought further attention to the system, it was only a matter of time before the JFBA was joined in its abolition campaign by writers, scholars, and various civil society groups. One notable example of an author keeping the issue in the public consciousness was Otohiko Kaga, whose fictional work 'The Marsh' (*Shitsugen*) was in 1985 serialized in the mainstream liberal paper *Asahi Shimbun*. It told the story of a man and a woman who, having been taken into custody one day out of the blue and subjected to physical and mental torture in substitute prison, go on to make confessions to the alleged crime that, despite subsequent denials in court, lead to guilty verdicts. Kaga, a prize-winning author[57] who had studied psychiatry and criminology at the University of Tōkyō's Medical School, decided to undertake the project after seeing the parallels between Japanese criminal justice practices and some of the more grotesque features of Kafka's classic work, *The Trial*. Despite being denied permission to view police detention cells before writing up his story, regardless of having approached the Tōkyō Metropolitan Police—invariably receiving the answer that the 'situation of substitute prison was something that was not open to the ordinary public'—Kaga was able to draw on his previous work as a psychiatrist for prisoners and his contacts with policemen, prosecutors, judges, lawyers, and various individuals who

[56] Composed by Shihei Umehara. Its lyrics can be translated as follows:

Who is the one that confiscates the simple happiness of my day?
Who is the one that uses the law, in spite of his role as its guardian, to put handcuffs on my tomorrow?
You cannot tie my heart with chains,
You cannot rob me of my freedom with your iron bars.
The truth is always only one—
The brotherhood of man.
Why does he slash my day that was full of smiles?
The voice screaming innocence in gaol is breaking through the wall and is calling you . . .

[57] Kaga's prizes included the 1968 Minister of Education Award for New Artists, the highly regarded Tanizaki Prize in 1974, and the Japan Literature Grand Prize in 1979. He would also win the Osaragi Jirō Prize in 1985, awarded to *Shitsugen* as the best popular social science work of the year.

had been acquitted in order to create a story that was considered realistic by many with first-hand experience of the system.

As for the scholarly community, parts of this would also be galvanized into action by the boom in publicity regarding the reappearance of the Two Detention Bills in the Diet. Throughout the 1980s, there was ongoing discussion in academic literature of the problems of reforming the prison legislation (see, for example, *Hōritsu jihō* 1983, 1988), and Japanese scholars gathered at some events to discuss in a formal manner the domestic criminal justice system (Murai 2003: 2–4). Due to the difficulties of amending the Prison Law and other related legislation, such as the Penal Code and the Juvenile Act (both of which had undergone revision attempts similar to that of the Prison Law), however, in 1987 some academics decided to go a step further and establish a Correctional Legislative Research Group (*Keiji rippō kenkyū kai*, hereafter the 'Research Group' and cited as 'KRKK')[58] (Murai 2003: 2-4). This group was keen to differentiate themselves from the so-called '*goyō gakusha*'—scholars, typically with conservative attitudes, often invited by the government to perform as expert witnesses in the Diet—and would analyse the treatment of prisoners from the point of view of international standards. In an attempt to form a comprehensive view of the Japanese system, the discussion panel of the Research Group would: hear from lawyers and people with experience of substitute prison; make inspections of police detention facilities, MOJ detention centres, and questioning rooms in summary courts; and seek explanations from the NPA, judges, and prosecutors. Its subsequent reports and books would call not only for the abolition of substitute prison, but also for the recording of interrogations and guarantee of the rights to silence and professional counsel (see, for instance, the various contributions by members of the Research Group to the special edition of *Hōritsu Jihō*, KRKK 1988). Perhaps its most significant output, published in 1991, was a provisional draft Prison Law revision bill, which had many features in common with the lawyers' proposal and, along with the accompanying notes, firmly established the Research Group's position against the Two Detention Bills (KRKK 1991).

[58] Apart from Ryūichi Hirano, who had previously served as the Chair of the Judicial Council, the Research Group also included Toshikuni Murai (Hitotsubashi University), Shin'ichi Ishizuka (Ryūkoku University), and Hiroyuki Kuzuno (Ritsumeikan University), amongst others.

Furthermore, stimulated by the exonerations, prisoners' rights civil society groups began to emerge. These pressed for overall prison reform, and would play an increasingly active role in the substitute prison abolition movement. Groups with an interest in suspects' rights had been in existence for some time already by the 1980s, including notably Japan's pre-eminent independent human rights organization, the Japan Civil Liberties Union (JCLU),[59] and the Relief Contact Centre (RCC), which ran a telephone line to distribute advice to those currently being held by the police.[60] These were now joined by several newer entities, such as the self-descriptive Civil Centre Demanding the Abolition of Substitute Prison and Opposing the Two Detention Bills (*Shimin sentā*, hereafter the 'Civil Centre'), which grew from 50 to 500 members in the year following its 1988 formation;[61] the similarly titled Group that Fights against the Retrogression of the Prison Law (*Kangoku hō kaiaku to tatakau gokuchūsha no kai*), which published detailed criticisms of Japan's prison system and police detention practices;[62] and the anti-death penalty Forum 90, which listed substitute prison as one of the problems of the Japanese criminal justice system that increases the incentive to put an end to executions.[63] Another group with a broader focus was the Centre for Prisoners' Rights (CPR), formed in 1995 by Yūichi Kaido, a particularly active prisoners' rights lawyer, and Kōichi Kikuta, who had recently retired from a Meiji University professorship of criminal law. These groups would continue to work towards their goals throughout the 1990s and beyond.

Overseas Interest

During this period, substitute prison also caught the attention of the international human rights community. As it did, the JFBA and

[59] Formed in 1947, see: <jclu.org/index_e.shtml>.

[60] Formed in 1969, see: <qc.sanpal.co.jp> This website seems to have been moved to <kyuen.jp>, so I would like to make this replacement if possible (Japanese only).

[61] *Kōkin ni hōan ni hantai shi, daiyō kangoku no haishi wo motomeru shimin sentā* (The Civil Centre Opposing Substitute Prison and Demanding the Abolition of the Two Detention Bills), Pamphlet published by the JFBA, June 1989, p. 32.

[62] See *Kangoku hō kaiaku to tatakau gokuchūsha no kai*, 1985, and more recent editions.

[63] For Forum 90 website, see: <www.jca.apc.org/stop-shikei/epamph/dpinjapan.html>, retrieved 10 May 2009.

its domestic allies received the support of the UNHRC, the Council of Europe (COE), and a host of global NGOs in their campaign against the system. These outside forces also raised a number of other concerns about the prison system more generally.

On examining, in July 1988, the Japanese government's second report on the implementation of the ICCPR, the UNHRC urged that substitute prison be abolished. Although it had previously expressed concerns about the system, this time the recommendation was made in a much more specific manner, perhaps as a result of the additional information provided by domestic NGOs, who would broadly publicize the outcome. In particular, the UNHRC's concluding observations plainly stated that substitute prison was in breach of the Convention, and heavily criticized the restrictions on the right to counsel of suspects whilst undergoing interrogations in detention and the lack of a pre-indictment bail system. In arriving at its conclusions, the UNHRC had at its disposal, along with the government report, alternative data provided by more than ten human rights groups, which included material delivered by the JFBA and the recently formed Civil Centre. As well as submitting counter-reports, in order to reflect the 'real' situation in Japan, the lawyers and the Civil Centre considered it necessary to dispatch their representatives to Geneva in advance of the examination to provide the UNHRC members with yet more details about the state of Japanese criminal justice and to try to persuade them to take a stern approach towards the establishment. Upon returning to Japan, representatives of the JFBA and the Civil Centre issued summaries of the events. Moreover, the mocking attitude that some of the members of the UNHRC had taken during the examination of Japan's official report and their financial justification for the retention of substitute prison was reproduced in pamphlets with such titles as 'The Great Economic Power—Japan, Lacks Budget for Building Detention Centres'. Similarly, *Asahi Shimbun* printed that the UNHRC report had given Japan the reputation internationally of a 'developing, backward country'.[64]

In the 1990s, the UNHRC returned concluding observations on a further two Japanese government ICCPR reports that were notably sharper in their appraisal of detention in Japan. Many comments about pre- and post-trial detention would recur, but a comparison between the wording of the Committee's 1993 and 1997 concluding remarks reveals the gradual strengthening of the

[64] 26 July 1988, p. 3.

UNHRC's anxiety with regard to Japan's failure to follow through with the UN recommendations. The 'concern' of 1993 that Japan's pre-trial detention system was not in accord with the ICCPR and 'recommendation' for its reform, for instance, became a 'deep concern' and 'strong recommendation' to reform with 'immediate effect', respectively. In 1997, the UNHRC also added the entire prison system to its list of principal concerns. The international body had 'serious questions of compliance' with regard to the harsh prison rules and punishment measures (including the frequent use of solitary confinement and restraining devices), a lack of transparent procedures for the disciplining of both prisoners and guards, and the inadequacy of the prisoners' complaints procedure, which they asserted did not currently align with the Paris Principles.[65] Moreover, the humanity of death-row conditions was questioned, with the 'concern' of 1993 becoming by 1997 another 'serious concern' of the UNHRC.

During this period, the UN was joined in its condemnation of aspects of Japan's criminal justice system by the COE.[66] Witnessing the increasing integration of the European bloc with the new trade arrangement agreed in Maastricht in 1992, the Japanese government realized the need to engage in diplomacy with the region as a whole, rather than merely with individual European states. In an attempt to develop deeper links with the continent, Tarō Nakayama, a former Minister of Foreign Affairs, promptly formed the Japan–Council of Europe Parliamentary League of Friendship, which would encourage the Diet to submit a formal request to join as an observer,[67] hot on the heels of a similar step taken by the USA. Even though Japan's retention of the death penalty was in conflict with one of the deeply entrenched guiding principles of the COE, its request was granted in 1996.[68] Hoping to persuade the

[65] The Paris Principles (formally known as the Principles relating to the Status of National Institutions) were adopted by the General Assembly in December 1993, and emphasize the independence of the institution from the government, the diversity of its membership composition, that the institution should have as broad a mandate as possible, that it be adequately funded, and that it is able to advise the government.

[66] The COE was formed in 1949 and represented an attempt to achieve harmonization of legal standards, the rule of law, and democracy across Europe. Perhaps the most famous of the COE bodies is the European Court of Human Rights.

[67] After the Maastricht Treaty was signed, on 14 May 1993 the COE Committee of Ministers adopted a statutory resolution permitting observer status (COE Statutory Resolution 93(26)).

[68] COE Committee of Ministers Resolution (96)37.

Japanese authorities to abandon this penalty and to investigate Japan's prison system, representatives of the COE would subsequently embark on a number of sorties there.[69] One early such visit was made in 1998 by Rapporteur Renate Wohlwend, whose report, along with the expected reminder to Japan that the COE 'has always taken a very firm position on the issue of the abolition of capital punishment', included concern at the post-arrest problems, such as limited access to a lawyer as well as the 'credible allegations of torture and forced confessions in [substitute prison]'.[70] With the latter problem, the COE Rapporteur reflected that 'it is possible that some of the current death-row inmates were convicted unfairly, and are indeed innocent'.[71]

As well as the official government interaction with the UN and the COE, the 1980s and 1990s would see two significant investigations focusing on substitute prison conducted by international NGOs. At the request of a group of Japanese lawyers,[72] the first of these was undertaken in January 1988 by the French lawyer Ettiene Jaudel, representing the International Federation of Human Rights, and Karen Parker, an American lawyer acting as a delegate of the Association of Humanitarian Lawyers. After interviewing detainees with experience of questioning in police detention, the two lawyers produced a report advocating forcefully that substitute prison be abolished (Jaudel and Parker 1989), and an annotated translation by Hirano was widely circulated within Japan (Hirano, Nagano, and Suzuki 1989). The Parker–Jaudel report started by criticizing the Japanese government's stance of maintaining the system for its efficiency, stating that human rights law requires the state to sacrifice efficiency, if necessary, in order to fulfil its higher duties. Moreover, it contended, even if the 'efficiency argument' was justified, with the number of overturned

[69] Interview with Mario Henrich, Secretary of the Standing Committee, Committee on Rules of Procedure and Immunities, Secretariat of the Parliamentary Assembly, COE, Strasbourg, 20 October 2008.

[70] *Abolition of the Death Penalty of the Council of Europe Observer States*, Renate Wohlwend, COE document 9115, 7 June 2001. See also *Abolition of the Death Penalty of the Council of Europe Observer States: Introductory Memorandum*, Renate Wohlwend, COE document AS/Jur (1998) 39, p. 7.

[71] *Abolition of the Death Penalty of the Council of Europe Observer States: Introductory Memorandum*, Renate Wohlwend, COE document AS/Jur (1998) 39, p. 7.

[72] Specifically, by the Committee for the Advancement of the Rights of Arrested to Assistance of Counsel, which had been created for precisely this purpose.

guilty verdicts occurring in recent years in Japan, it would be difficult to give it accolades on these grounds. The two authors went on to condemn the violation in Japan of the right to request a lawyer in substitute prison, explaining that, with this restriction, confessions drawn there would have to be presumed to have been coerced. Although one professor saw fit to comment that Jaudel and Parker's report '[misunderstood] the facts and [drew] rash conclusions' (Morishita 1989: 1302), the comparative study was broadly endorsed by Japanese scholars and lawyers and eagerly received by the domestic opponents to the Two Detention Bills whose fate was not yet determined.

The second major examination into substitute prison was that of the International Bar Association (IBA)—the Japanese lawyers' international counterpart and the world's largest legal organization comprising lawyers, judges, and prosecutors. This investigation consisted of two missions whose organization was aided by the JFBA, the first of which took place in September 1994 and was led by the association's vice president, Nicholas Cowdery. His goal was to form a balanced view about the situation in practice through interviewing prisoners, lawyers, police officers, government officials, and court officers, and also examining suspect detention facilities. The resulting report[73] made it clear that the IBA believed there was a link between abuse of substitute prison and forced confessions. Regarding this and other issues, in the second mission in February 1995, IBA president Ross Harper and Cowdery would conduct interviews with the relevant authorities, politicians from several parties, and academics. Although MOJ officials did agree to attend an interview, the IBA representatives described the 'tense and acrimonious' thirty-minute session as 'a thinly veiled rebuke and warning to keep out of Japanese criminal justice affairs', which, to the lawyers, was 'regrettable'. In order to give the bodies that had been surveyed a chance to react to the draft final report, in which similar recommendations were made as in Cowdery's preliminary one, advance copies with questionnaires inviting comments were sent to them. The responses were interesting, but not entirely surprising: the JCP responded by describing how its members had been subjected earlier in the century to 'torture and abuse under the substitute prison' and expressing that the

[73] *The* Daiyō Kangoku *(Substitute Prison) System of Police Custody in Japan*, IBA, September 1994. This report would be translated in Japanese and published by the Japanese bar (JFBA 1995).

system should be abolished with immediate effect; the ruling coalition member, New Party Sakigake, explained that, although substitute prison should be abolished 'in the long term', the difficulty of securing budgets and sites for new detention centres made accurate forecasts of when this could be achieved impossible; the NPA argued that the IBA had not considered the criminal justice circumstances of the individual country and expressed the hope that the IBA would 'examine [Japan's] whole system objectively with more sources again'; and the remaining questionnaires, including the ones sent to the MOJ and the LDP, were not returned.

Apart from placing yet more pressure on the government over substitute prison, the IBA report provided plenty of food for thought for the abolitionists. While recognizing the strong arguments made for the abolition of substitute prison, Cowdery suggested that 'there are other features of the criminal justice system that might usefully be modified so as to reduce the temptation to use substitute prison improperly',[74] thereby defeating the purpose of detaining suspects for prolonged periods under the police. He went on to make ten concrete suggestions to improve detention conditions, amongst which were changing the rules of interrogation to include compulsory recording of all questioning, and making taboo the interrogation of those declaring they would exercise their right to silence. This aspect of the IBA report would divide the JFBA and others campaigning on this cause into those maintaining that substitute prison abolition was the only option for real progress, and those advocating the strategy of institutionalized compulsory recording of interviews in order to achieve the same objective.[75] The latter group took the view that, since judges had an interest in ensuring that disputes over voluntariness of confession did not occur, convincing the courts to adopt a recording requirement—which would be a first step to abolishing substitute prison—was more realistic than trying to persuade the NPA directly. Long after Cowdery had left Japan, activists would continue to ponder which was the better course of action.

[74] Ibid., p. 23.

[75] For example, Kuniichi Araki, JFBA Vice President, *Asahi Shimbun*, 27 March 1995, p. 4.

Conclusion

Almost to the exclusion of all other aspects of the prison system, the Prison Law reform discussions of the 1980s and 1990s were dominated by how the substitute prison article in the original legislation should be amended. Throughout, the NPA actively pursued entrenchment of the system via persistent presentation of draft legislation, despite this being somewhat inconvenient for the MOJ as well as downright objectionable to the JFBA and other interested parties, both at home and abroad. Such findings provide a clear indication as to which of the key actors was the driving force behind substitute prison's expansion prior to the start of the debate, and why ultimately no changes of statute were made as a result of the extensive discussions that took place.

The NPA's participation in the decision-making process was not universally accepted, but nonetheless the Agency did play a central role in shaping the deliberations, with its sole goal being to maintain its authority over suspects. Without question, for the NPA, that there was a legal basis for the prolonged detention of suspects in its facilities had been something of a gift left by the American occupiers. Indeed, as the Agency would reiterate time and time again, substitute prison had, by the 1980s, evolved into an essential part of its investigative armoury—a situation that readily explains why it was being utilized to such a degree that detention in police custody was already the norm. That the NPA would not let its claim to detain suspects just slip away in the face of domestic and international criticism of the substitute prison system was clearly demonstrated in the creation of its own detention bill, which was repeatedly submitted, even after it became clear that it stood no chance of passing and would only serve to stall the reform process.

Whilst it would not be entirely accurate to describe the MOJ as neutral on substitute prison—with its erring on the side of caution about making a radical change—of all the three major actors in the discussions, it was arguably the most prepared to compromise. Starting off by declaring the unfeasibility of substitute prison abolition during the early consultations, the Ministry eventually accepted an attrition clause in the Proposal, and would go so far as to offer such a measure as a legally binding supplementary provision in the hope that this would secure its coveted revision of the Prison Law. Despite the shrouding in mystery of exactly what events unfolded within the Ministry after the third abandonment of the bills, there were hints that plans had even been made to follow through with the latter option. For the NPA and the JFBA, however, there was no middle ground, and it was this stand-off that meant the MOJ's willingness to bend was never truly tested.

Apart from its obvious opposition to the substitute prison policy, what the events of this chapter demonstrate about the JFBA is that, during the period under study, it played a critical role in determining the future of suspect detention policy in Japan. It is true that the JFBA was not able to lobby ruling party politicians to pressure the bureaucrats to adopt any of its central demands on the substitute prison issue, particularly its abolition. Nonetheless, the MOJ did invite the lawyers to the initial consultations regarding the Prison Law reform, and when the passage of the Ministry's bill became uncertain due to the lawyers' stance against substitute prison, it yielded to the JFBA on a number of points, including the inclusion of an attrition provision. Apart from the MOJ's actions, the importance of the lawyers in instigating the opposition to vote against the government's proposals is evident from the LDP suggesting to the NPA that it engage in dialogue with it. It is because the NPA was not subsequently able to come to an agreement with the JFBA that the amendment project stagnated.

Domestic civil society groups more generally did not play a significant part in the blocking of the Two Detention Bills, but rather than this being due to general public support for the authorities' proposed legislation, more likely it was because of a lack of awareness about the issues involved. To expand on this, during the early part of the Prison Law reform, there were very few people engaged in civil society activities on any scale relevant to police detention, and so those that were had very little influence on policy development. After the death-row inmate exonerations hit the headlines and it became clear that substitute prison had led to a number of serious failures, however, interest in the subject led to the formation of several organizations that supported the JFBA in its anti-Two Detention Bills campaign. Although these mostly only became active towards the end of the 1980s, by which time the parliamentary debate had already reached an impasse, their formation highlights that the domestic detractors of Japan's system of prolonged police detention did extend beyond the liberal legal elite.

With the exonerations being publicized abroad by the JFBA, the substitute prison system also rose up the list of concerns of international human rights advocates, but it is questionable how much this impacted the policy debate domestically. Despite outside pressure on the Japanese government to reform its police detention practices beginning to grow, by placing efficiency over all other factors in its rhetoric, the NPA in particular seemed to deny that international law was of a higher consideration. The MOJ's reaction to the IBA and HRW representatives, too, suggested that the Ministry saw the missions of these groups as unjustified interference in its activities. Perhaps the most notable contribution of the international community to the substitute prison debate was in its provision of ideas and support to the JFBA and other indigenous groups advocating its abolition. This combination of international and domestic opposition to the prolonged police detention permitted by the substitute prison system quite possibly contributed to the continued stalling of the amendment process in the 1990s.

Finally, as has already been noted, it was the deadlock on the substitute prison issue that prevented the Prison Law being reformed—an outcome which meant that the human rights protection of prisoners suffered. The MOJ certainly wanted to update the Prison Law, which it saw as having become, by the end of the 1970s, no longer fit for purpose. When in 1976 it put together a committee to deliberate changes necessary for the treatment of convicted criminals, nothing less than a scheme for new legislation was enough, even though this required several years of discussions for the negotiating parties to settle on a proposal with which each was satisfied. The Ministry's persistence in submitting the resulting draft bill to the Diet on three occasions over the next decade attests to its desire to follow through with this project, and thereby bring the law governing the administration of detention facilities up to date. What put a spanner in the works of the MOJ's plan were the irreconcilable differences between the NPA and the JFBA on what would turn out to be the decisive substitute prison issue. Indeed, the JFBA and MOJ generally agreed on how prison management should be revised—with the MOJ making a lot of concessions to the JFBA on this front, and the latter having no major objections to the former's bill with regard to the treatment of convicted inmates. However, the lack of agreement between the lawyers and the NPA on substitute prison had a spillover effect, causing the whole reform process to grind to a halt.

4

Two-step Amendment Compromise

> If the soul is left in darkness, sins will be committed. The guilty one is not he who commits the sin, but the one who causes the darkness.
>
> Victor Hugo, Les Miserables

> One of the many lessons that one learns in prison is, that things are what they are and will be what they will be.
>
> Oscar Wilde, De Profundis

The lull in the debate concerning the Prison Law amendment was shattered by the storm that erupted from media coverage, starting in late 2002, of a sequence of abuses leading to inmate injury and death by guards at Nagoya Prison. However, it was not the incidents per se, but rather the way in which they came to light and the flaws in the system they revealed, that triggered an outburst within the Diet in which the whole of the penal administration within Japan was called into question. Following these events, the Ministry of Justice (MOJ) was more motivated than ever to achieve revision of the Prison Law. So as to avoid the situation of the 1980s and 1990s, whereby the debate over the substitute prison system had brought the reform process to a standstill, a decision was made between the MOJ, the National Police Agency (NPA), and the Japan Federation of Bar Associations (JFBA) to delay the amendment of the part of the law relating to suspects until new legislation for sentenced detainees had been passed. Both the format and content of the subsequent two amendment stages received markedly contrasting reactions.

Scrutinizing these events has clear benefits for understanding the current police detention policy-making landscape of Japan. Firstly, apart from enriching the evidence regarding the institutional positions of and relationships between the MOJ, the NPA, and the JFBA, as well as other relevant actors, it also allows these to be brought up to date. Moreover, considering how this picture might differ from that of the earlier reform period enables a stronger conclusion to be drawn about the trajectory of the substitute prison system than would be possible by looking at a single static time. In particular, assessing how the various players' support or opposition to this policy evolved in the intervening years will help gauge its present level of entrenchment.

The Nagoya Saga

Six Nagoya Prison guards were arrested in November 2002 for their alleged perpetration of two separate assaults of inmates at Nagoya Prison involving the use of leather restraining devices (*kawa tejō*) and padded protection cells (*hogo-bō*), one of which resulted in death. Ever since the news of the prosecution's investigation into these incidents had been made public two months earlier, the opposition had expressed suspicions that such abuse might be widespread, but, even after the arrests, the MOJ strenuously denied that the events were typical. Despite this, revelations about problems with the prison system quickly started to snowball, and the Ministry was left with no choice but to admit its failings and return to the Prison Law reform project it had abandoned a decade earlier.

The smoke before the fire

The first case of abuse at Nagoya Prison emerged after accusations were made by an inmate of that institution against his guards. The thirty-four-year-old Hideki Yamashita had, on 25 September 2002, reportedly been subdued with a leather restraining device consisting of handcuffs attached to a belt in such a way as to cause internal bleeding, before being placed into a protection cell.[1] Consequently, seventy days of recovery time were necessary. Allegedly, the abuse had been inflicted as a result of the inmate's refusal to withdraw a grievance filed directly with the incumbent Justice Minister, Mayumi Moriyama, as was permitted under the Ministerial petition (*jōgan*) system recognized in the Prison Law. This

[1] *Guardian* (online edition), 15 November 2002; *Japan Times*, 17 November 2002, p. 12, 28 November 2002, p. 2, 12 March 2003, p. 2, and 2 October 2003, p. 3; *Yomiuri Shimbun*, 30 March 2007, p. 27.

complaint had also been copied to the local bar association, who were scheduled to meet him the next day.[2]

With this incident casting doubt over the cause of a death in similar circumstances in the same institution, the MOJ decided that it would be in its best interest to confirm that the claimed injuries and the fatality had indeed occurred, as well as declare what steps they were taking to deal with these cases. At a press conference held on 4 October 2002 by Nagoya Prison authorities to answer concerns about the reports of abuse, however, scant detail was given about the case bar that the injuries actually existed and that it was now in the hands of the Nagoya District Public Prosecutors Office (hereafter the 'Nagoya Prosecution') (Yokoyama 2004: 254). The Prison Warden did, however, note that the guards were within their rights to subdue the inmate, as per the Rules for the Implementation of the Prison Law (*Kangoku hō shikkō kisoku*).[3] At the same event, the MOJ also fielded questions from the local media about the unexpectedly premature death earlier that year, in May, of a forty-nine-year-old male prisoner who had been found on the floor of a protection cell in which he had been placed after behaving violently.[4] The prison officials answered such inquiries by explaining that at the time of the incident, as in the latter case, the appropriate procedures were adhered to by the guards,[5] with the family being informed of the cause of death—which, according to the autopsy, was 'acute heart failure' (*kyūsei shinfuzen*). They went on to explain that, although no complaints had been made against this ruling, the Nagoya Prosecution was now investigating further.[6]

When quizzed later about her knowledge of these happenings, Moriyama would declare that the first time she was briefed about the events at Nagoya Prison referred to the May incident at the end of May, but it would only be the second case that prompted her concern. In May, the Head of the Correction Bureau, Kenji Nakai, had reported to her that a prisoner who was detained in a

[2] Mizuho Fukushima, Judicial Affairs Committee, House of Councillors, 31 October 2002; *Guardian* (online edition), 15 November 2002.

[3] Mizuho Fukushima, Judicial Affairs Committee, House of Councillors, 10 December 2002.

[4] Mizuho Fukushima, Judicial Affairs Committee, House of Councillors, 31 October 2002.

[5] Mizuho Fukushima, Judicial Affairs Committee, House of Councillors, 10 December 2002.

[6] *Japan Times*, 10 November 2002, p. 2.

protection cell and on whom a leather restraining device had been used had died, and that, in order to find out what had happened, it had been requested of the Nagoya Prosecution to investigate (Moriyama 2004: 140–1). At this stage, Moriyama asserted, there was no reason to think that the prison authorities were guilty, and it did not occur to her that the leather restraining device may have been tightened to a point where it caused death (Moriyama 2004: 140–1). For that reason, she considered that the prosecution investigation would be sufficient to determine the facts of the case (Moriyama 2004: 140–1). When details of the September case, which featured the application of the same punishment techniques, had been presented to Moriyama at the end of that month, however, both Nakai and Moriyama started to consider broader action and agreed that the subsequent investigation should be made public, resulting in the aforementioned press conference (Moriyama 2004: 140–1).

In the first session in which the occurrences at Nagoya were discussed in the Diet, at the end of October, the MOJ was keen to reassert that the appropriate actions had been taken and that there was no reason to have been suspicious earlier, despite it transpiring that there had been yet another fatality in a Nagoya Prison protection cell the previous December. At the start of the proceedings, Mizuho Fukushima, the leader of the Social Democratic Party (SDP),[7] challenged Nakai as to why the prison authorities had been reticent to release the findings of their internal inquiries regarding the May and September cases at Nagoya. During this cross-examination, Nakai repeated that the correct procedure had been followed, with all the relevant information being handed to the local prosecution, and that it was up to them to determine what further action was necessary.[8] Fukushima also brought up how, in the weeks following the September incident, she had conducted a rapid investigation of deaths in protection cells, including at Nagoya. It had been this effort that proved the May 2002 incident was not an isolated event, with its uncovering of the December 2001 death. At this stage, even though the details of the December case were with the prosecution, Moriyama believed that it was not in the same category as the other two instances, as she had apparently been informed previously by Nakai that the prisoner's death had resulted from injuries to the anus caused by his own hand and

[7] The Japan Socialist Party (JSP) renamed their party 'SDP' in 1996.
[8] Judicial Affairs Committee, House of Councillors, 31 October 2002.

that this was not the first time the specific prisoner had mutilated himself (Moriyama 2004: 143).

Fukushima would also raise a query as to why it had been so difficult for her to access data about suspicious deaths in prisons, but was told that information about such cases was both limited for administrative purposes and restricted on the grounds of data protection. Through her research into fatalities similar to those at Nagoya Prison, she had discovered that a total of five deaths involving protection cells had occurred over the past three years, including the two at Nagoya. Frustratingly for her, however, three years was as far back as she could trace, as the Correction Bureau claimed it could only provide records of deaths in prisons that occurred after 1999.[9] When asked what the reason for this was, Correction Bureau chief Nakai declared that for 'practical reasons' only three years of data was kept, and that, in general, information about deaths was not released due to concerns about the privacy of the inmates' families.[10]

The next month saw arrests of guards involved in the May and September Nagoya Prison incidents, with the prosecutors revealing several potentially important facts about the May death that had not been reported to relatives when it occurred. In connection with the first revelation, in November 2002, five guards, including Head Guard Takashi Watanabe, were arrested under Article 195 of the Penal Code, namely Assault and Cruelty by Special Public Officers (*Tokubetsu kōmuin bōkō ryōgyaku chisshi*), indicating that the Nagoya Prosecution considered the allegations of abuse made in September by the inmate Yamashita were not without substance.[11] Soon afterwards, in their investigation of the May case, the same prosecution service collected enough evidence to suggest that Fukushima's claims in the Diet about how the death in question could have occurred due to the way in which the prisoner had been subdued with a leather restraining device, similarly to the September case,[12] were not unfounded.[13] Notably, the fact that the prisoner had been restrained shortly before his death had been omitted in the explanation provided to the family earlier that year

[9] Ibid.
[10] Ibid.
[11] *Japan Times*, 10 November 2002, p. 2.
[12] Mizuho Fukushima, Judicial Affairs Committee, House of Councillors, 31 October 2002.
[13] *Yomiuri Shimbun*, 30 November 2002, p. 37.

by the prison authorities,[14] even though it had been included in the report given by the Correction Bureau to Moriyama (Moriyama 2004: 140–1). Furthermore, although a legally ordered autopsy had been made immediately after the incident, in which it was demonstrated that the heart failure had actually resulted from pressure on the stomach leading to a damaged diaphragm, the inmate's family was also not informed of this fact at the time, and would only discover these details later through the media.[15] With this information, the prosecution's suspicions were raised that the improper use of physical restraints had directly contributed to the fatality, and they issued further arrest warrants for the same charge as in the September case for three guards, two of whom were amongst the five already arrested.[16]

These moves forced the Justice Minister to issue the statement that 'the brutality at Nagoya was regrettable, but only as a case of maltreatment by individual guards rather than as a problem for the prison system as a whole' and that she '[had] not heard of any similar cases at other prisons'.[17]

Quis custodiet ipsos custodes? *Maybe not the Justice Minister*

The Justice Minister's point of view on the cases of alleged abuse at Nagoya Prison was quickly opposed by various NGOs, and the ensuing debate would reveal that perhaps she herself was not completely on top of what had transpired there. Amnesty International Japan, for instance, declared that 'we don't agree that [Nagoya Prison] is an exceptional case ... the use of leather restraining devices and the abuse of solitary confinement can be seen at any prison. The normal practices of Japanese prisons violate international standards'.[18] Similar concerns were raised domestically, too, with the Centre for Prisoners' Rights (CPR) in particular claiming that most human rights abuses in prisons went unreported, as prisoners' complaints were usually subjected to censorship by the authorities, and often prison staff would aggressively discourage

[14] Ibid.; *Japan Times*, 10 November 2002, p. 2.
[15] *Yomiuri Shimbun*, 30 November 2002, p. 37.
[16] Ibid.; *Japan Times*, 28 November 2002, p. 2.
[17] *Guardian* (online edition), 15 November 2002.
[18] Ibid.

their being made in the first place.[19] It listed several cases in which inmates had experienced problems with contacting them—in one a guard had supposedly torn up the letter of an inmate before his very eyes—and also cases involving abuse in protection cells and using leather restraining devices. The CPR would even suggest that if reports of such allegations had reached them at the time when the inmates had originally tried to send them, maybe the May and September incidents at Nagoya Prison might never have happened.

The anecdotal evidence presented by non-governmental organizations (NGOs) that the complaints mechanism for prisoners was not operating as it should by law was confirmed when the Justice Minister admitted in the Diet that the flow of prisoners' grievances had hitherto been processed routinely at the level of bureaucracy. Pointing to the fact that, as well as the two deaths known to have occurred in Nagoya Prison's protection cells—one involving a leather restraining device—there had been a nearly threefold year-on-year increase in the use of leather restraining devices there—most of which coincided with detention in a protection cell[20]—in early November 2002, Fukushima sought reassurance that, in the case of such disciplinary measures being abused, inmates had an adequate means of recourse.[21] Over the coming weeks, Fukushima and other members of the opposition would question Moriyama as to how, in particular, inmates' appeals for help to the Justice Minister were handled upon arriving at the MOJ,[22] and what improvements she had thought necessary on reading the thirty such applications from Nagoya Prison sent before the end of October 2002.[23] Moriyama explained that a large number of prisoner complaints were sent to the Justice Minister (approximately 2,400 in 2001). Due to this and the fact that many of the issues they raised did not fall into any of the four categories of 'punishment', 'medical care', 'visitations', and

[19] See CPR founder Kaido's *Kangoku to Jinken (2): Gendai no gōmon·Nagoya Keimusho jiken wa naze okita ka (The Prison and Human Rights (2): Modern Day Torture and Why the Nagoya Incidents Occurred)* (2004). Tōkyō, Akashi Shoten.

[20] Fukushima cited the following: for the period from 1 January to 30 September 2002, in Nagoya Prison there had been 158 applications of leather restraining devices, 148 of which took place inside a protection cell. This compared to sixty-one applications in the whole of the previous year at Nagoya Prison. Judicial Committee, House of Councillors, 31 October and 12 November 2002.

[21] Judicial Affairs Committee, House of Councillors, 12 November 2002.

[22] Ibid.

[23] Judicial Affairs Committee, House of Councillors, 10 December 2002.

'correspondence' about which grievances were permitted to be filed under the relevant statute of the Prison Law, a screening process managed by Correction Bureau staff was first undertaken before the content of any important letters was reported to her.[24] Although this first step was not immediately controversial, the opposition was scandalized when Moriyama was forced to confess that this had meant that, in practice, she had not seen a single complaint from a prisoner in her eighteen-month tenure, including those sent by Nagoya Prison.[25] Further probing into the management of prisoners' medical complaints also took place, but at the time the MOJ brushed off these concerns with an explanation that, although there was still room for its enrichment, there already existed an extensive framework for treating medical conditions and procedures to be followed upon the reporting of an illness.

During further inquiries into the incidents at Nagoya Prison, the Nagoya Prosecution had their suspicions raised that an additional, third case of abuse in a protection cell had occurred, leading to the apprehension of yet more of the personnel there in February 2003.[26] When it became clear that MOJ staff had made false statements to the public and the Justice Minister about their awareness of this case, the slow-brewing 'prison problem' of the previous few months suddenly erupted in the Diet. Specifically, after seeking further explanation about the newly uncovered events, which had taken place in December 2001, the opposition received responses that left them stunned at the standard of the reporting from the Correction Bureau to the higher echelons of the MOJ. Indeed, when questioned as to whether the situation was

[24] For example, see dialogue involving Nobuto Hosaka, Judicial Affairs Committee—Health Welfare and Labour Committee Joint Session, House of Representatives, 27 November 2002, and Fukushima, Judicial Affairs Committee, House of Councillors, 10 December 2002.

[25] Ibid.

[26] The conclusion was initially drawn that the prisoner in question, who had a history of self-abuse, had mortally damaged himself. However, on studying the autopsy results in detail, the Nagoya Prosecution inferred that maltreatment was a real possibility given the extent of the injuries, and, upon testing their conjectures of criminality on two anaesthetized pigs, instigated a third set of guard arrests. For further details, see Toshiaki Hiwatari, Director, Criminal Affairs Bureau, Budget Committee, House of Representatives, 21 February 2003; Dialogue between Fukushima and Nakai, Budget Committee, House of Councillors, 6 March 2003; and *Yomiuri Shimbun*, 2 November 2005, p. 36 and 5 November 2005, p. 28.

indicative of a deep-rooted propensity within the MOJ to bury unwelcome facts,[27] Nakai explained that he did not think it strange that the information received in the Correction Bureau had not been passed to the Director of General Affairs or the Justice Minister earlier than the arrests. When pushed on this matter, he would reiterate even more strongly that 'it is my personal belief that [the sensitive information] should definitely not have been reported to the Justice Minister'.[28] This statement caused uproar and even compelled the Judicial Affairs Committee's Chair to reprimand Nakai for his 'flippant attitude'. Moriyama only poured oil onto the fire when answering the charge that she was not sufficiently angered by Nakai's answers suggesting that the Justice Minister was unreliable in managing top-secret information with the seemingly nonchalant response that 'there is no need for me to be told each and every detail [from within the MOJ]'.[29] The furore in the Diet would last the entire session, as opposition politicians continued on the offensive by subjecting Moriyama to the accusation that not keeping track of the activities of her subordinates was a dereliction of her duties relating to prisons—a criticism that would be repeatedly levelled at her over the following months as further details of the scandal were revealed.

It would not be until the whole story of what had happened at Nagoya was uncovered, though, that the full impact of the events would be felt by the government, as on the day following Nakai and Moriyama's cross-examination in the Diet, the issue would go as far as halting the all-important budgetary debate.[30] The specific cause of this delay of two and a half hours was an ultimatum presented by the Democratic Party of Japan (DPJ), the SDP, the Liberal Party, and the Japanese Communist Party (JCP). These opposition parties were resolved not to let the issue slip into the background, given the major flaws and deceitfulness in the communication within the MOJ that they believed had been revealed.[31] Thus, at the meeting of the chairmen of the Diet Policy Committees, they warned the ruling Liberal Democratic Party (LDP)-led coalition that unless the Justice Minister could be seen

[27] Ikuo Yamahana, DPJ, Judicial Affairs Committee, House of Representatives, 18 February 2003.

[28] Judicial Affairs Committee, House of Representatives, 18 February 2003.

[29] Ibid.

[30] *Nihon Keizai*, 20 February 2003, p. 2.

[31] Interview with MOJ Official B and MOJ Official C, 31 August 2007.

to be taking responsibility for the deaths by resigning after intensive examination of the matter, the four parties would boycott any further deliberations in the Diet.[32] Although LDP politicians claimed that the opposition bloc could not adopt the strategy of rejecting deliberations, and that the incident's influence on the ongoing budget discussions would be small, they nonetheless agreed to give Diet time to rigorous debate of the issue within the next few days.[33] This duly took place, with an extensive number of hours in the next week being devoted to discussing the flaws in the administration of prisons, both at Nagoya and more broadly, and yet more disclosures being made about the way in which the Ministerial petition mechanism operated.

The prison system of Japan moved one step closer to becoming a national disgrace when, in March 2003, yet another controversy broke out—this time involving the MOJ's restriction of information not only to the Justice Minister, but also to the Diet. In particular, the Ministry would be proven by the opposition to be obstructing knowledge about the records of deaths in penal institutions, which was an area that had been probed by Fukushima close to the outbreak of the scandal. When the MOJ finally released the requested information through a collection of so-called 'Death Registers' (*shibō-chō*), the poor quality of the data proved something of an obstacle to those hoping the full facts would be revealed.[34] In particular, from amongst the 238 unnatural deaths the registers described, there would be vastly differing interpretations of how many of these could be deemed suspicious—for the MOJ, only fifteen were possibly suspicious and eighteen implicated poor medical treatment, whereas the CPR's investigation of the same data suggested figures of twenty-nine and seventy or more, respectively.[35] Whatever the true figures were, the revelations certainly justified the fears of NGOs and the opposition that the suspicious deaths surfacing at Nagoya Prison were only the tip of the iceberg, and that the problems of

[32] *Nihon Keizai*, 20 February 2003, p. 2.

[33] Ibid.

[34] Interview with Nobuto Hosaka and perusal of Death Register copies, 23 August 2007. See also Chiba Keiko, Judicial Affairs Committee, House of Councillors, 20 March 2003.

[35] '*Nagoya Keimusho jiken no gen'in to gyōkei un'ei no mondaiten*' (The Causes for the Nagoya Prison Incidents and the Problems with the Penal Administration), MOJ interim report, 31 March 2003; *Japan Times*, 9 July 2003, p. 3. Also, interview with Yūichi Kaido and Maiko Tagusari, 18 July 2007.

unexplained deaths and poor medical care in prisons were endemic.

The Death Register exposé—which had demonstrated that, once again, information had been wilfully concealed by the bureaucracy—proved to be the final straw. The MOJ acknowledged that many of its prison staff had insufficient awareness of human rights issues regarding prisoners and handed sanctions to several for their part in the story, suspending three of the senior prison officials in the chain of supervision at Nagoya Prison[36] for three months each.[37] Not satisfied with these measures, members of the opposition were keen to hear how the responsibility of MOJ employees for their flawed management of the Ministerial petition system, their failure to disclose the details of the December 2001 death to Moriyama, and their masking of the Death Registers had been recognized.[38] They would be disappointed with the response—5 per cent of one month's salary had been deducted from two Nagoya District Correction officials, the Director of Nagoya District Correction had been reprimanded, and four officials working in the central MOJ offices, including Nakai, had received either cautions or admonishments.[39] Moriyama herself would make no public criticism of Nakai. It is, though, noteworthy that the next week just happened to see a new Correction Bureau Director.[40]

Although there was little the opposition could do to pin any further blame on the bureaucrats, it is perhaps surprising that the persistent calls for Moriyama's resignation since the outbreak of the Nagoya Prison crisis, including the four-party budget deliberation block threat, allowed her to emerge, while not unscathed, still in her position at the end of the episode. Later, Moriyama would write that at the time, she did consider the possibility of resignation, but decided that it would be better to grin and bear it in the hope that she would eventually be in a position to apply the

[36] The individuals were, at the time of the incidents, the Warden of Nagoya Prison (*Keimusho shochō*), the Director of the Treatment Division (*Shogū buchō*), and the Chief Correctional Treatment Officer (*Shuseki kyōsei shogū kan*).

[37] Kenji Nakai, Budget Committee, House of Councillors, 17 March 2003.

[38] For example, see the questioning of Nakai by Giichi Tsunoda, DPJ, Judicial Affairs Committee, House of Councillors, 20 March 2003.

[39] Giichi Tsunoda, DPJ, Judicial Affairs Committee, House of Councillors, 20 March 2003.

[40] DPJ news release, 25 March 2003. Retrieved from <www.dpj.or.jp> on 19 May 2009.

valuable lessons she had learnt about the philosophy of rehabilitation during this difficult time to make a difference to the prison system of Japan, the problems of which she had considered to have been brewing since well before her watch (Moriyama 2004: 146–7). In this resolution, Moriyama was supported by Prime Minister Jun'ichirō Koizumi, who, on being asked in the Diet why he had not dismissed her, replied that 'the responsibility of the Justice Minister is to self-examine herself in light of the points made [by the opposition] with a view to correcting them'.[41] So it was that, during the remainder of her term as the chief correction administrator of Japan, Moriyama would embark upon a wholescale reform of penal administration, including commanding the commencement of the process that would eventually lead to the long-anticipated revision of the Prison Law.

Time to Go to Work

The events of the preceding few months had led the Justice Minister to recognize that the world within the walls of prisons in Japan had been very tightly closed, and that the system had become urgently in need of updating. Moriyama and other bureaucrats at the MOJ acknowledged that, even if the guards involved turned out to be personally responsible for the deaths of the inmates at Nagoya Prison, the worsening situation of overcrowding had led to a poor living environment for prisoners and highly stressful working conditions for prison staff.[42] To overcome what she perceived as the lagging behind of Japan's correctional administration and to put right the problems she believed had been lying dormant for a long time (Moriyama 2004: 146), in March 2003 the Justice Minister announced the convening of an advisory organ.[43] The recommendations of this body would form the basis of the following partial amendment of the prison legislation, from which substitute prison was excluded.

The diverse composition of the panel established by Moriyama, which was given the title of the Correctional Administration Reform Council (*Gyōkei kaikaku kaigi*, hereafter the 'Council'),

[41] Budget Committee, House of Representatives, 3 March 2003.

[42] Judicial Affairs Committee, House of Councillors, 20 March 2003. Also, interviews with MOJ Official B and MOJ Official C, 31 August 2007, and Moriyama, 17 December 2007.

[43] Judicial Affairs Committee, House of Councillors, 20 and 27 March 2003.

would win the approval of even the MOJ's regular critics, including the JFBA. Wanting to avoid a narrow debate between legal experts bringing their own prejudices to the deliberation room, the MOJ launched its reform initiative under the slogan 'Prisons that Gain the Understanding and Support of the Citizens' (Moriyama 2004: 148–54). To incorporate the 'common sense' that was necessary for this goal to be achieved, its membership was drawn from a wide pool, including lawyers (one of which was a former JFBA president), a former Supreme Court Judge, a former director of a High Court, a bureaucrat, a university president and several university professors, a journalist, the executive director of *Yomiuri Shimbun*, the director of Asahi Television, and the director of a large company.[44] Knowing that gaining the acceptance of the opposition and groups such as the JFBA would be vital to the success of the programme, the MOJ had also made sure that the Council incorporated a larger proportion of individuals known to have made criticisms of the administration of justice in the past than had hitherto been the case. Indeed, some members of the panel themselves expressed surprise at receiving the call from the MOJ, with, for example, Kōichi Kikuta of the CPR commenting that the only reason he and those around him could think of for his invitation was merely as a 'front [for the authorities] to legitimise [the subsequent discussions]' (*kakuremino*).[45] Nonetheless, the balanced composition of the Council was acknowledged by the JFBA to be generally satisfactory and by Amnesty International Japan as having the potential to realize, at long last, actual progress on penal reform.[46]

[44] The chairman of the Council of fourteen members was Hiroshi Miyazawa, former Justice Minister (1995–6). The other members were: Masaharu Gotoda, former advisor to the Deputy Prime Minister; Yutaka Narita, Dentsū director; Kazutomo Ijima, lawyer and former Supreme Court judge; Shōko Egawa, journalist; Kazumasa Kuboi, lawyer and former JFBA chairman; Akira Segawa, Dōshisha University professor; Ayako Sono, writer; Fumimarō Takahisa, Jichi Medical University president; Takuo Takihana, *Yomiuri Shimbun* Tōkyō Headquarters executive director; Yukio Nozaki, lawyer and former Nagoya High Court director; Michisada Hirose, Asahi Television director; Hiromasa Minami, Hitotsubashi University professor emeritus; Kōichi Miyazawa, Keiyō Gijuku University professor emeritus.

[45] CPR Newsletter, No. 36, 3 February 2004, p. 1.

[46] Interview with Makoto Teranaka, 28 August 2007. Also, Moriyama herself would take pride in this outcome as one of her major accomplishments in her unusually long, but not always enjoyable, term of two years as a Justice Minister. Interview with Mayumi Moriyama, 17 December 2007.

With the still-controversial substitute prison system not part of its remit, the Council could devote all of its time to the task of discussing prison conditions, which it did with great zeal. In her first speech to the Council, Moriyama made it clear that there was no sacred ground the members should refrain from touching upon, and that she would remain hands-off so they could hold uninhibited discussions (Moriyama 2004: 151). Arguably the most significant factor in why the talks did not stall on this occasion, though, was that only the treatment of convicted prisoners was on the agenda. This meant that the substitute prison issue did not take over the sessions as it had done in the meetings of the Judicial Council in the late 1970s, when the tensions between those advocating its continued use and those calling for its abolition had dominated proceedings. Over the next nine months the group would hold regular meetings, and made a substantial effort to survey a large number of both guards and inmates, interview leading prison experts, and study the prison reform attempts of other countries, most notably those in the UK in the early 1990s.[47] Many of the members would also find time in their busy professional schedules to make trips to prisons in Japan and overseas, including to the UK, France, and Germany.[48] Furthermore, Moriyama herself would in February 2003 present a report to the Council of her observations made whilst earlier visiting American penal institutions (Moriyama 2004: 152). Although the Council would continue in an advisory capacity in the future (see, for example, GKK 2004), the bulk of their work was completed in December 2003 with the release of a proposal for a new law.

The Council's final recommendations were broadly welcomed, particularly as they suggested the creation of third-party monitoring bodies for prisons. Indeed, whilst there were criticisms that the Council had failed to put forward concrete measures to reduce the use of lengthy solitary confinement and to make prisoner medical care independent of the MOJ, overall its suggestions were widely

[47] This had been encouraged in the Diet by the opposition. See, for example, Giichi Tsunoda from the DPJ referring to the Woolf Report, released on 25 February 1991, which summarized the results of an inquiry following a twenty-five-day riot at Strangeways Prison, Manchester, as part of the research of which every single prison guard and prisoner was invited to provide feedback on the penal system of the UK. Judicial Affairs Committee, House of Councillors, 20 March 2003.

[48] Correctional Administration Reform Council (*Gyōkei kaikaku kaigi*), Minutes of the three sub-committees, First Tōkyō Lawyers Association, December 2003.

seen as improving the lives of prisoners and increasing the transparency in the administration of prisons.[49] Since much of the content of the proposal echoed the JFBA ideas, overall the Council's work was given a positive evaluation by the lawyers, who saw it as '[confirming] that the basic idea of prisoners' treatment is the respect of their humanity'.[50] One measure that was particularly lauded by the JFBA and other prisoners' rights campaigners was the Council's advice to establish Boards of Visitors for Inspection of Penal Institutions (*Keiji shisetsu shisatsu iinkai*, henceforth the 'Prison Boards') to independently inspect facilities, so as to discern systematic failures in prisoners' rights protection.

The Council's work would serve as the foundation of a new law for prisons, but before designing its new legislation, the MOJ set about increasing the resources available to support its amendment project. Specifically, in the same month as the Council's report was published, it was announced that an extra 451 prison staff would be employed—the largest ever annual increase in personnel.[51] This step would be combined with an increase in the prison budget of 4.3 billion yen, along with 459 million yen extra for medical care of prisoners.[52] The main goal of these actions was to lower the burden of individual officers and ease overcrowding, which had been seen as the underlying cause for the problems at Nagoya Prison, and indeed the prison system as a whole. With this boost in human and financial capital, the Ministry could start the drafting process on the right foot.

Why Do Today What You Can Put Off Until Tomorrow

In order to maintain the positive momentum that the Council's deliberations had generated, it was agreed that the best strategy would be to revise the part of the Prison Law relating to the safe area of sentenced inmates, which the Council had discussed, and

[49] Interview with Makoto Teranaka, 28 August 2007, Yūichi Kaido, 18 July 2007, and Aya Kuwayama, 3 December 2007. See also *The Alternative Report on the Japanese Government's Report of CAT*, CAT Network, March 2007, p. 4.

[50] *Report on the Japanese Government's Implementation of CAT*, JFBA, 18 January 2007, p. 6.

[51] This increase was to a force of approximately 17,000 members, and was especially notable since the majority of the civil service were seeing cuts. Interview with Kōji Sakata, 18 October 2007.

[52] *Japan Times*, 23 December 2003, p. 2.

leave the more sticky issue of suspects for later. Although some members of the opposition expressed their fear that the draft bill eventually prepared by the MOJ contained measures that would bias the future discussions on suspects, in the Diet it would receive unanimous support and would soon be promulgated.

To rebuild the MOJ's reputation after the Nagoya Prison crisis, the Ministry's bureaucrats understood that they would have to be more receptive to the demands of the JFBA in preparing a bill to amend the Prison Law. With the MOJ having been put under fire for its prison practices by the UN Human Rights Council (UNHRC) at the 1997 examination of Japan's report on the implementation of the ICCPR, the Correction Bureau approached the JFBA with a view to resuming the deliberations on the treatment of convicts that had broken down in 1987.[53] As a starting point, it was decided that the two parties should work through their proposed amendments, selecting those that both agreed upon and taking the draft of a new law from there. With both sides being rather cagey, however, progress was slow. This situation changed after the Nagoya scandal,[54] as the humiliation suffered by the MOJ generated a greater sense of urgency within the Ministry for attaining Prison Law revision.[55] The effects of this were immediately noticeable to the lawyers in that, in terms of openly discussing and considering options from outside of its camp, the 'MOJ became considerably friendlier'.[56] Furthermore, after accepting the proposal of the Council, when the MOJ began preparation of the Prison Law reform this was done in close consultation with the representatives of the JFBA's Headquarters for the Realization of a Reform of the Criminal Detention System (*Keiji kōkin seido kaikaku jitsugen honbu*).[57]

Wanting a full reform of the Prison Law, the MOJ invited the NPA to take part in talks regarding substitute prison, but the JFBA raised objections about legislating for suspects and death-row inmates without them having been discussed—at least not explicitly, in the case of the latter—by the Council. In June 2004, at the

[53] Personal communication with Yūichi Kaido, 12 August 2009.

[54] Interview with Yūichi Kaido, 18 July 2007.

[55] Minutes of a round-table discussion (Kitajima, Yamashita, and Kawaide 2006: 54). Also, interview with MOJ Official B and MOJ Official C, 31 August 2007.

[56] Interview with Yūichi Kaido, 18 July 2007.

[57] This body had grown out of the Countermeasure to the Two Detention Bills Headquarters, and at this time consisted of approximately 100 lawyers. Interview with Katsuhiko Nishijima, 31 October 2007.

MOJ's instigation, what were actually the first three-party talks between the MOJ, the NPA, and the JFBA commenced with the hope that an agreement could finally be fashioned on substitute prison. In these sessions, the JFBA adamantly insisted that this issue was separate altogether from the treatment of convicted inmates, and that if suspects were to be regulated for, a separate advisory body, similar in composition to the Council, should be set up for this explicit purpose.[58] The lawyers also used this opportunity to assert their belief that even though death-row inmates were convicts, they deserved special consideration, recognizing their position as being different from that of ordinary prisoners.[59] More precisely, the JFBA's position was that death-row inmates should be guaranteed the same standard of treatment as suspects and held in detention centres on the grounds that they were simply awaiting the execution of their penalty, rather than being punished by penal servitude or made the subject of rehabilitation.[60] In support of this argument, the lawyers not only explained how this principle had guided those drafting Japan's first prison legislation[61] (Ōno and Asakura 1966: 86, Ogawa 1976: 95), but also cited several more recent Japanese court precedents and UN instruments.[62]

Rather reluctantly, the authorities conceded that the Prison Law should be updated in two steps, with the part of the amendment process relating to suspects and death-row inmates being postponed for the time being. The MOJ attempted to portray the JFBA's demands as problematic from a technical point of view, claiming that it would be highly irregular to make amendments only for sentenced inmates not on death row when the Prison Law actually provides for death-row inmates and suspects as well, and would thereby create a gap between the treatments of those regulated for by a revised law and those left at the mercy of the 1908

58 Yūichi Kaido, CPR Newsletter, No. 37, 3 June 2004, pp. 5–9.

59 Kōichi Kikuta, CPR Newsletter, No. 37, 3 June 2004, pp. 1–4.

60 '*Miketsu nado kōkin seido no komponteki kaikaku wo mezasu*' (Aiming at the Radical Amendment of the System for Suspects), JFBA, 16 September 2005, p. 43. Retrieved from <www.nichibenren.or.jp/library/ja/opinion/report/data/2005_55.pdf>.

61 In fact, it is for this reason that death-row inmates are granted the same status as suspects and are placed in detention centres rather than prisons.

62 '*Miketsu nado kōkin seido no komponteki kaikaku wo mezasu*' (Aiming at the Radical Amendment of the System for Suspects), JFBA, 16 September 2005, p. 43. Retrieved from <www.nichibenren.or.jp/library/ja/opinion/report/data/2005_55.pdf>.

law.[63] Similarly, echoing its arguments from the earlier Two Detention Bills dispute, the NPA protested that it would be inconsistent to only revise half of a law and retain the century-old provisions for suspects, and reasserted its position that, if the MOJ submitted a bill that included the treatment of suspects, it would submit a second bill that regulated the treatment of suspects in police custody.[64] Moreover, as had also been the case in earlier reform discussions, the police were keen to create provisions regarding arrestees, for which no statute currently existed (Iwase 2006: 54–5). After wrangling on this point for six months, in December 2004 the three parties eventually arrived at the conclusion that the best trade-off would be to complete the revision of the part of the law concerning sentenced inmates, apart from those on death row, and then immediately create a panel on whose recommendations the remaining part of the law would be reformed (KRKK 2005: 254, Kitamura 2005: 46).

In early 2005 the MOJ completed the drafting of its bill, which the JFBA was overall satisfied to endorse. Following the agreement between the MOJ, the NPA, and the JFBA, discussions between the Ministry and the lawyers continued relatively smoothly, with both sides prepared to yield some ground to achieve progress. The MOJ was happy that it looked like it would be able to finally shake off the outdated terminology of the old Prison Law, especially in the title of the law, with designations such as '*kangoku*'—a word that is roughly equivalent to the English 'gaol'—being replaced by '*keiji shisetsu*', which translates as 'penal institutions'. The JFBA, too, was satisfied to accept the big picture as well reflecting the report of the Council.[65] For the lawyers, one of the most significant steps forward was the inclusion in the law of the Prison Boards that the Council had recommended, which would consist of at least one lawyer, doctor, and public official each amongst other experts, and would be able to examine prison conditions, interview inmates, and have their opinions read by the prison authorities and the Justice Minister.[66]

63 Yūichi Kaido, CPR Newsletter, No. 38, 10 August 2004, pp. 6–7.
64 Ibid.
65 '*Prison Law Revised First in Century [sic]*', JFBA press release, 1 June 2005.
66 For further details of activities, see Penal Institutions in Japan, Correction Bureau pamphlet, MOJ, retrieved from <www.moj.go.jp/content/000079580.pdf>.

After less than two months in the Diet, and some minor amendments, the MOJ's bill was enacted as the Act on Penal Institutions and the Treatment of Sentenced Inmates (*Keiji shisetsu oyobi jukeisha no shogū nado ni kan suru hōritsu*). Unlike the Two Detention Bills of the 1980s and 1990s, this time the draft legislation was deliberated immediately on its arrival in the House of Representatives in April 2005. After only a week in this House, the bill was accepted unanimously, with only four modifications that had been agreed upon by both ruling and opposition parties being made.[67] These adjustments included a guarantee that the Justice Minister would make available to the public the content of the reports made by the Prison Boards and the inclusion of a clause stipulating a compulsory review of the new law's implementation in five years' time.[68] The progress would be equally rapid in the House of Councillors, with its promulgation being confirmed in the following month.[69]

Despite substitute prison not having been considered during the preparatory work towards this amendment, there were concerns over the neutrality of the new legislation with regards to the system, and the JCP in particular sought to make corresponding changes. At the earlier three-party talks, an accord had been struck between the MOJ, the NPA, and the JFBA that, under the revised legislation, the provisions of the 1908 Prison Law would remain in force for suspects, including in the substitute prison system, to allow separate revision of this piece of legislation. However, because the MOJ's bill had contained explicit references to police detention, it was seen by the JCP as prejudicing the direction of the planned second stage of reform by already establishing a basis for a police bill. In particular, Inoue Satoshi of this party asserted that to leave any reference to the existing pre-trial detention system within a new law was pre-emptive and created a 'danger of placing binding restrictions on the expected consultations for the treatment of suspects'.[70] For this reason, before the voting for the original draft bill, the House of Councillors was asked to vote on an amendment bill proposed by Inoue on behalf of his party. The main demand in the JCP's proposition was the deletion of all the

[67] The LDP, the DPJ, and New Kōmeitō.

[68] The other two changes regarded the training of the prison guards and some slight rewording.

[69] Judicial Affairs Committee, House of Councillors, 17 May 2005.

[70] Ibid.

clauses relating to substitute prison and inspection of police cells, and there was also a specific request that the application of gags (*bōsei-gu*) and restrictive clothing (*chinsei-i*) in police detention be formally abolished—this final step had already been taken in detention centres, and the NPA had temporarily suspended the practice following the fatal suffocation of a suspect under police detention in Wakayama prefecture in April 2004 as a result of his inability to communicate his suffering to the guarding officers when a gag was used in conjunction with restrictive clothing.[71] Despite Inoue's pleas, this motion was not passed, as the House was satisfied that serious discussions regarding the part of the law concerning substitute prison would take place henceforth.

To ensure that the reform of the prison system would not stop at convicted inmates, each of the parties expressed in the Diet their commitment to not waste time in moving on to the next stage. Specifically, in both houses, a multiparty proposal—supported by members of the LDP, the DPJ, New Kōmeitō, and the JCP—for adding external resolutions to the new legislation was unanimously adopted.[72] The future goals outlined in these external resolutions included many of the points that the JFBA and opposition parties would have preferred to have been actually incorporated into the law, but most importantly stated: 'on the issue of suspects, including the existence of the substitute prison, there should be swift consultations with the JFBA, and efforts should be made for the early establishment of legal provisions for these prisoners'.[73]

With the acceptance of these resolutions, the business of promulgating the Act on Penal Institutions and the Treatment of Sentenced Inmates (*Keiji shisetsu oyobi jukeisha no shogū nado ni kan suru hōritsu*) was complete. It would come into force exactly one year later as the first concrete step of the correctional administration reform, which, as Moriyama would later comment, would probably not have happened had the Nagoya Prison scandal not occurred.[74]

[71] CPR Newsletter, No. 38, 10 August 2004, p. 15 and also Katagiri 2006.

[72] Proposed by the DPJ's Shōgo Tsugawa, Judicial Affairs Committee, House of Representatives, 8 April 2005. Also, the DPJ's Keiko Chiba, Judicial Affairs Committee, House of Councillors, 17 May 2005.

[73] Judicial Affairs Committee, House of Representatives, 8 April 2005; Judicial Affairs Committee, House of Councillors, 17 May 2005.

[74] Interview with Mayumi Moriyama, 17 December 2007.

Outstanding Business

After the relative success of the first part of the reform of the Prison Law, the consultation process for completing the project began. In contrast to the broad approval enjoyed by the Council set up to discuss issues relating to sentenced inmates, however, the new advisory committee would be criticized by the JFBA in particular for having too narrow a brief and not enough time to consider the subject properly, and for producing a timid proposal.

Amongst the first activities undertaken by the MOJ, the NPA, and the JFBA following the promulgation of the 2005 law was their joint preliminary fact-finding mission to Europe. More specifically, in July 2005 representatives from each of the organizations undertook a research trip to the Austrian Federal Detention Centre in Josefstadt, Vienna, and Rebbibia Prison in Rome for the purpose of studying the situation of pre-trial detention in both police and non-police detention facilities outside of Japan. The choice of Italy and Austria was made because it was thought that this would represent a typical European standard for the treatment of pre-trial detainees, and also because the pre-trial systems of the other large Western European countries (that is, the UK, Germany, and France), were already reasonably well understood.[75] In addition to inspecting the facilities themselves, the three parties met with local authorities, who explained their procedures for ensuring that suspects would not have to be returned to police detention after being brought before a judge.[76] Furthermore, with the Prison Boards already legislated for in Japan, it was on the cards that a similar mechanism would be created for examining the facilities of suspects, and the trip provided a good chance for the MOJ, NPA, and JFBA representatives to familiarize themselves

[75] CPR Newsletter, No. 42, 5 September 2005, p. 2.

[76] In Austria, to ensure that police detention of longer than the allowed forty-eight hours would not occur, in the Federal Detention Centre sentenced inmates were sometimes transferred to other facilities to free space for suspects, and the Centre would accept suspects even when functioning over capacity. In Italy, where initial police detention lasted twenty-four hours only (and the public prosecutor was then required to charge or release suspects within four days of their arrest), to manage prisoner numbers, alternative measures for dealing with those in suspect detention—such as house arrests and overseas travel bans—were also used. *Newsletter of the Headquarters for the Realisation of a Reform of the Criminal Detention System*, No. 5, 1 September 2005.

with the local systems for inspection.[77] Reports of the observations made upon this trip would be presented at the triumvirate's meetings in August 2005,[78] to which the JFBA would bring information about two other European countries where significant reforms had recently been made with regard to the police pre-trial detention systems—Hungary and Turkey.[79]

Once the dust had settled from this overseas adventure, the serious discussions between the MOJ, NPA, and JFBA would begin, with the authorities meeting the lawyers' desire for a single bill for suspects coming from the Ministry. As well as discussing the research trip findings, the three-party talks were continued in the hope that some early agreements could be made on the content of the planned bill for those detainees yet to be legislated for. Many of the important issues for the JFBA were similar to those it had demanded for convicted prisoners, and included improved rights for the suspect to communicate with their lawyer and the transfer of the jurisdiction of medical healthcare from the detention authorities to the Ministry of Health, Labour, and Welfare. The JFBA's primary request, though, in keeping with the spirit of its movement against the Two Detention Bills, was that the treatment of suspects in both detention centres and police cells be governed by the same regulatory regime, and that draft legislation, such as the former Police Detention Institutions Bill or any equivalent, would not be proposed.[80] This time, unlike in the 1980s and 1990s, the two government departments obliged.

Whilst the MOJ and NPA were prepared to work together to produce just one draft bill between them, as the JFBA had requested, the differences between the sides would soon resurface. Specifically, the bureaucrats were less accommodating in response to other JFBA demands, presenting a number of detailed papers objecting to many of the lawyers' arguments, including about the ever-contentious substitute prison. Some JFBA recommendations,

[77] In Austria this consisted of a Human Rights Inspection Council whose twelve members incorporated three bureaucrats, and in Italy it involved monitoring by politicians and NGOs.

[78] '*Miketsu kōkin shisetsu ni kan suru kaigai chōsa hōkoku: Ōsutoria, Itaria*' (Report on the Investigation Abroad Regarding the Suspects' Detention Facilities: Austria and Italy), Countermeasure to the Two Detention Bills Headquarters, JFBA, July 2005.

[79] Hiroaki Jin and Yūichi Kaido, CPR Newsletter, No. 42, 5 September 2005, pp. 2–7.

[80] Maiko Tagusari, CPR Newsletter, 5 September 2005, No. 42, pp. 8–9.

such as its proposal to introduce a pre-indictment bail bond system, were rejected as simply inappropriate, on the grounds that they related to the Code Criminal Procedure.[81] Others, including the suggestion to discontinue physical restraints for suspects—devices which the JFBA felt were currently being used as disciplinary measures in breach of the 'presumed innocent until proven guilty' principle—were resisted for practical reasons. Yet more recommendations were simply opposed, including the radical suggestion to transfer the jurisdiction of various detention-specializing police facilities under construction throughout the country, such as the 300-inmate capacity establishment in Harajuku, from the NPA to the MOJ.[82] On this latter point in particular the authorities raised a technical objection about how doing so would mean the inappropriate shift of a resource established using prefectural funds to central government control.

In the course of the three-party talks, moves were made to establish a panel of experts that would focus on the treatment of suspects. With the MOJ and NPA anxious to meet the legislation deadline for spring 2006, the debate swiftly turned to the formation of an advisory committee, whose role would be analogous to that of the council that had been set up to deliberate topics involving convicted inmates before the drafting of the first amendment bill. Despite the disagreements on some of the fundamental issues at stake, the JFBA was hopeful that both groups of detainees that had been covered in the preliminary talks—suspects and death-row inmates—would be part of the planned committee's remit. However, since the treatment of those on death row was outside of the NPA's jurisdiction, the authorities did not think it was the appropriate venue to consider how these inmates should be regulated for.[83] Despite the lawyers' request for a third advisory body to be set up for this purpose under the MOJ, no action along these lines would ever materialize, and the Ministry would simply draft this part of the bill alone.

Notably, even though the previous council had started their meetings nearly a year before the first possible bill submission

[81] Interview with Maiko Tagusari, 18 July 2007.

[82] '*Miketsu nado kōkin seido no komponteki kaikaku wo mezasu*' (Aiming at the Radical Amendment of the System for Suspects), JFBA, 16 September 2005. Retrieved from <www.nichibenren.or.jp/library/ja/opinion/report/data/2005_55.pdf>.

[83] Interview with Kōichi Kikuta, 29 October 2007.

date, the Council Concerning the Treatment of Suspects (*Miketsu kōkinsha no shogū nado ni kan suru yūshikisha kaigi*, henceforth the 'New Council') had only half this time to deliberate. In meeting to discuss the first part of the Prison Law reform, the Council for sentenced inmates met well over twenty times between May and December 2003, as well as visiting prisons in Japan and abroad. Even if the MOJ had originally desired that a proposal for a new law be presented in March 2004, this schedule would have allowed three further months of deliberations. By contrast, after the bill resulting from this first Council's work passed in May 2005, and after the MOJ, the NPA, and the JFBA had been on their research trip and held their preliminary talks, the New Council would be formed in September 2005.[84] This meant there was only a six-month period for the sessions of the New Council and the drafting process to be completed before the next submission deadline, which the authorities did not want to miss. Indeed, with the external resolutions attached to the first part of the legislation, there was political pressure for them to achieve this goal. This time frame—which would allow only six meetings to take place, including the inspections of police cells and detention centres in Tōkyō—was considered by the JFBA as inadequate (Takesako 2006: 80–1). The lawyers did not believe there would be enough time for the New Council to hear from experts with knowledge of the Code of Criminal Procedure or the basic idea of the modern criminal law and international human rights standards. On the other hand, since many of the former Council's members who were by now familiar with the issues surrounding the treatment of convicted inmates had been recruited again to the New Council,[85] the MOJ and NPA argued that this shorter period would be sufficient, as there were many common themes between suspects and convicted prisoners.[86]

[84] Kōichi Kikuta, CPR Newsletter, No. 37, 3 June 2004, pp. 1–4.

[85] The New Council consisted of five fewer members than the first Council, six of whom were selected from those who had served before: Kazumasa Kuboi, Kōichi Kikuta, Shōko Egawa, Kazutomo Ijima, Akira Segawa, and Hiromasa Minami. There were also three new NPA-nominated experts: Satō Hidehiko, former NPA Commissioner-General; Narita Yoriaki, Yokohama National University professor emeritus in administrative law (*Gyōseihō*); and Kasai Takayuki, Tōkai Japan Railways president.

[86] Interview with Kōichi Kikuta, 29 October 2007.

Not surprisingly, given the stances of the opposing camps, the existence of the substitute prison system again emerged as a sensitive issue at the gatherings of the New Council. At the very first meeting, the authorities reiterated their point of view that it was infeasible to abolish substitute prison immediately. On this basis, and also pointing to the large number of suspects held in police detention, the MOJ and NPA proposed that the debate be conducted on the premise that the system would be retained for the time being.[87] The JFBA had hoped that, as with the first Council, the new advisory committee would be given free rein in their deliberations and, with regard to substitute prison, be allowed to engage in a frank discussion of its abolition. With the discrepancy between their expectation and the reality, the JFBA members of the New Council were split as to the best tactic to adopt: should they withdraw themselves from the process in protest, or stay and fight for whatever improvements could be achieved?[88] In the end, the latter course of action was taken, which would in the future allow the establishment to claim unanimity on the issue.[89]

When the proposal of the New Council was released in February 2006, it contained no radical reform suggestions. In line with the authorities' position on substitute prison, the report of the New Council started with the declaration that:

> In attempting to legislate for the treatment of remand prisoners, and working under the premise that substitute prison be retained for the time being, [the New Council] is of the opinion that the best way to deal with the responsibility the public has entrusted on it is the consideration of concrete mechanisms about how the problems that could arise as a result of [substitute prison] could be avoided, as well as how to obtain a treatment of suspects that better matches the standard required internationally, and through this to try to achieve harmonization between correctly implemented investigation and the guarantee of suspects' rights.[90]

[87] Ibid.

[88] Kōichi Kikuta, CPR Newsletter, 1 March 2006, No. 44, pp. 4–6.

[89] Interview with Kōichi Kikuta, 29 October 2007. Kikuta of the JFBA and the CPR would rue that by not making a stand at this point for substitute prison abolition, the lawyers had lost the most important opportunity to do so.

[90] '*Miketsu kōkinsha no shogū nado ni kan suru teigen: Chian to jinken, sono chōwa to kinkō wo mezashite*' (Proposal on the Treatment of Remand Prisoners: Aiming towards Harmony and Balance between Order and Human Rights), the New Council, 2 February 2006.

However, even some of the specific changes to the system campaigned for by human rights advocates in the Diet in the discussions surrounding the bill passed in 2005 were not wholeheartedly picked up. For example, the New Council decided, on NPA advice, that the application of gags in police detention was important for the maintenance of order—especially in managing disorderly detainees—and that their continued use should be permitted, albeit with an improvement in the design of the gag itself, with videotaping of its use, and not when other means, such as protection cells, were available to officers (Katagiri 2006: 30, Takesako 2006: 91).

For more sceptical observers it was to be expected that the New Council had not brought as many new ideas to the table as its predecessor, given that there had been no triggering event, such as Nagoya, to highlight the flaws of the existing system.[91] Moreover, the New Council's non-committal hint towards substitute prison attrition,

> because the strong opinion also exists that substitute prison needs to be abolished in the future, and because an era has come for a criminal justice system overhaul, when next considering the criminal justice procedure, efforts should not be spared to examine . . . the place of substitute prison within the broader criminal justice system,[92]

was seen as ducking the most crucial issue, and only included so as to go some way to appeasing its critics.

Diet: No Alternatives

Built on the proposal of the New Council, a bill to complete the updating of the Prison Law was submitted in March 2006, but its passage through the Diet would not be an easy ride. In addition to overcoming an alternative proposal, it also had to withstand several developments rather adverse to its promulgation.

On its arrival in the Diet, the LDP–New Kōmeitō-sponsored Bill for Partial Revision of the Act on Penal Institutions and the Treatment of Sentenced Inmates (*Keiji shisetsu oyobi jukeisha no shogū*

[91] Interview with Yūichi Kaido, 18 July 2007.

[92] '*Miketsu kōkinsha no shogū nado ni kan suru teigen: Chian to jinken, sono chōwa to kinkō wo mezashite*' (Proposal on the Treatment of Remand Prisoners: Aiming towards Harmony and Balance between Order and Human Rights), the New Council, 2 February 2006.

nado ni kan suru hōritsu no ichibu wo kaisei suru hōritsuan) contained no big surprises. In particular, it closely reflected the proposal of the New Council, and so proposed maintaining substitute prison in close to its current form—notably this meant that, unlike the authorities' legislative attempts during the 1980s and 1990s, the 2006 bill incorporated the funding arrangement whereby the NPA was reimbursed by the MOJ for undertaking detention duties. One change that it did advance with regard to this particular article, though, was ending the use of police facilities for the detention of convicted inmates, which was still permitted by the substitute prison article and applied in practice.[93] Another headline change was that, similarly to the earlier amendment, the second bill included a measure for Boards of Visitors for Inspection of Police Custody (*Keisatsu ryūchi shisetsu shisatsu iinkai*, henceforth the 'Police Boards') to be set up to perform similar duties for police cells as the Prison Boards did for penal institutions. This measure was not combined, however, with a corresponding mechanism for the complaints of suspects to be reviewed by a third party,[94] as had been created for prisons in the earlier piece of legislation.[95] The justification given for this was that complaints about police cells were managed by prefectural Public Safety Commissions rather than police officials,[96] which the NPA argued meant there was already sufficient independence.[97]

Given that few of their objections to the New Council's recommendations had been heeded, the opposition made it clear that they would not give support to the bill, and put their own draft legislation up for discussion. Specifically, with the government bill's

[93] In 2004, for example, approximately 6,600 convicts were held in this way, albeit generally for short times whilst waiting for a prison cell to become available (Katagiri 2006: 13).

[94] *Report on the Japanese Government's Implementation of CAT*, JFBA, 18 January 2007, p. 3. See also the related *JFBA Update Report in response to the List of Issues to be Taken Up in Connection with the Consideration of the Fifth Periodic Report of Japan*, p. 19.

[95] Specifically, under the 2005 law, anonymous suggestion boxes for prisoners' complaints (*teian-bako*) were to be placed in prisons. The prison authorities would not have access to these, and only Prison Board members would be able to collect complaints from them.

[96] For further details of the procedure, see Fukuda 2006.

[97] Police Detention Administration in Japan, NPA pamphlet, 29 October 2008.

potential institutionalization of the substitute prison,[98] the JFBA and the CPR presented petitions against it to leading politicians of all parties and in both Houses. This lobbying was partially successful, with significant elements of the DPJ and the SDP indicating their willingness to present an amendment bill containing an attrition clause, along with six other key changes recommended by the JFBA.[99] Politicians from these parties would also take forward various JFBA proposals, including the transfer of some detention facilities from the NPA to the MOJ, which led to many of the same arguments from the earlier talks being repeated in the Diet.[100] Producing an amendment bill and raising such points in the Diet was perhaps as big a step as could have been taken by the opposition to derail the LDP's efforts, since, as the DPJ members themselves would concede, 'opposition parties in Japan do not have the resources to initiate their own draft bills and instead contribute to the legislation process at a point of consultation, where they can recommend concrete changes to the leadership's proposals'.[101]

Whilst the bills were being deliberated, the substitute prison abolitionists' cause was given an unexpected fillip by an April 2006 admission of a government witness. At the centre of this incident was the former MOJ official Moritaka Kamoshita.[102] In his Diet testimony, he described his surprise at finding that the new draft legislation did not include an attrition clause, which he believed his work of the early 1990s in liaising between the MOJ and the NPA had secured.[103] This would be the first time that knowledge of the 'phantom attrition clause' reached the public

[98] As with the 1980s draft legislation, the 2006 bill would rename the substitute prison system, but the practice of keeping suspects under police detention was to be preserved.

[99] These included expressions that further clarify that suspects are to be treated as innocent, the addition of a clause to guarantee absolute adherence to the sleep and meal times of the suspects, and better assurances that access to lawyers would not be subject to censure.

[100] For example, the DPJ's Chiba Keiko and Tōru Matsuoka, House of Councillors, Deliberative Assembly, 17 May 2006, and Judicial Committee, House of Councillors, 23 May 2006 respectively.

[101] Interview with Hideo Hiraoka, 31 August 2007.

[102] Now serving at the Correctional Association, as well as lecturing as a visiting professor at Chūō University and Ryūkoku University.

[103] Diet testimony, Judicial Affairs Committee, House of Representatives, 11 and 12 April 2006. Also, interviews with Kamoshita, 29 August and 25 October 2007.

domain,[104] and the JFBA immediately, but unsuccessfully, attempted to verify this.[105] The following day in the Diet, the SDP's Nobuto Hosaka and the DPJ's Hideo Hiraoka jumped at the chance to demand an explanation of what had happened to Kamoshita's hard-won agreement. Particularly targeted by these politicians was Justice Minister Seiken Sugiura, who had in his days as the Vice Chairman of the Tōkyō Bar Association campaigned on the streets for the abolition of the substitute prison, in the vanguard of the movement against the Two Detention Bills of the 1980s. However, Sugiura and Correction Bureau Director Yoshinobu Onuki refused to acknowledge that any such deal had been made between the MOJ and the NPA, and since Kamoshita had failed to provide documentary evidence, there was no way for the opposition to push this point further.

The second revelation to emerge whilst the government bill was still in the Diet was the existence of an NPA manual giving officers Guidelines for the Interrogation of Suspects, which would be strongly criticized by the JFBA and their allies as contradicting international standards. The media exposé of the internal agency document, published in 2001, occurred when the personal computer of a police officer in Ehime Prefecture was infected by a virus and the data on his hard drive drained on to the internet. Included in it were such instructions as:

Keep the suspect in the interrogation room as much as possible;
Do not leave the interrogation room until you obtain a confession;
If the suspect denies the charges, keep him in the interrogation room from morning till night (this also weakens the suspect).

Furthermore, its approach to questioning was openly combative, with its inclusion of such phrases as:

It is a one-to-one contest;
If you get into the suspect's head quickly, your victory will be that much sooner;

[104] In fact, in anticipation of the content of the bill, Kamoshita had even published an article that asserted the same views a year before his Diet appearance, but these had not caught the attention of the abolitionists (Kamoshita 2005: 32–5).

[105] Discussion with Kaido at his partner Fukushima's reception, 23 October 2007.

If you start wondering that the suspect's claim is true or if the investigation is getting nowhere, you will want to call it quits, but if you leave the room then, you will have lost.[106]

For the JFBA, these pieces of advice were in clear breach of a number of UN instruments, and exemplified why the substitute prison system had to be dismantled. When the issue was brought to the Diet by the opposition, the NPA spokesmen remarked that they would like to refrain from discussing it, since to do so would result in an even broader spread of the information.[107] Even though it was insisted that, as a general rule, interrogation manuals were produced neither by the NPA nor by prefectural police, the NPA representatives' failure to officially deny the authenticity of the leaked document was taken by their opponents as affirmation of its accuracy.

Despite the opposition being able to assume the upper hand in the debates regarding these unforeseen developments, it was still unable to introduce amendments to the government's bill, which was passed by the House of Representatives in May 2006 in its original form. Over the six sessions at the Judicial Affairs Committee,[108] the pieces of legislation proposed by the government and opposition were hotly debated. No doubt the JCP would have joined forces with the DPJ and the SDP in opposing the ruling LDP and New Kōmeitō coalition's bill, but it could not do so, as it was not represented in the Judicial Affairs Committee of the House of Representatives at this time.[109] Despite the opposition's endeavours, with only two members of the Board of Directors of the Judicial Affairs Committee of the House of Representatives remaining on its side following Prime Minister Koizumi's landslide general election victory of September 2005—a significant drop from the six present at the 2005 revision stage—its bill was to make no headway, being voted down in mid-April.[110] Moreover, on the same day, the DPJ and the SDP were unable to prevent the ruling

[106] *Shūkan asahi zōkan*, 12 April 2006. See also *Report on the Japanese Government's Implementation of CAT*, JFBA, 18 January 2007, pp. 32, 80.

[107] Dialogue between DPJ's Masatoshi Takayama and NPA's Commissioner-General, Takashi Andō, Judicial Affairs Committee, House of Representatives, 12 April 2006; also dialogue between DPJ's Takashi Ishizeki and the Director of NPA's Criminal Affairs Bureau, Osamu Nawata, Judicial Affairs Committee, House of Representatives, 18 April 2006.

[108] On 31 March and 4, 5, 11, 12, and 14 April 2006.

[109] Interview with Seiken Sugiura, 18 October 2007.

[110] Interview with Emi Akiyama, 24 August 2007.

coalition, which was now dominant in the House of Representatives,[111] from forcing their original draft legislation through this House.

In the House of Councillors, despite an NPA admission about manipulation of the substitute prison system for the sake of investigation, the progress of the bill was not derailed and, in June 2006, it was again accepted unchanged to become the Act on Penal Detention Facilities and Treatment of Inmates and Detainees (*Keiji shūyō shisetsu oyobi hi-shūyōsha nado no shogū ni kan suru hōritsu*). Disappointed with the fact that the bill had overcome the first hurdle to promulgation, the JFBA and CPR turned to the House of Councillors in an attempt to have as many as possible of their recommended seven changes incorporated into law.[112] As before, the substitute prison issue was at the heart of the discussions, and both the JFBA and the CPR sought to disprove the NPA's assertion that investigation and detention had already been separated by internal police regulations. To this end, the JFBA provided opposition politicians with information about cases where confessions had been extracted not only through poor treatment but also through favourable treatment, such as suspects being allowed to smoke in the questioning room, place horse-racing bets, be treated to sushi and whiskey, and even have sex with prostitutes.[113] In the Diet, when responding to claims that the proposed legislation did little more to separate the two roles than regurgitate existing internal police regulations, the NPA Commissioner-General Takaharu Andō described any further steps as being unnecessary.[114] However, under cross-examination, he would go on to—embarrassingly for the NPA—admit that detention had been taken advantage of by police officers, with meals being taken to suspects in the questioning room against the internal rules. Regardless, the bill's opposition party objectors were not able to prevent its promulgation. With the enactment of this new piece of legislation, the 1908 Prison Law had met its end, once and for all.

[111] Following the September 2005 election, the LDP–New Kōmeitō partnership held 327 out of 480 seats in the House of Representatives.

[112] Interview with Emi Akiyama, 24 August 2007.

[113] This information was supported by a CPR survey of former police cell suspects, entitled *Questionnaire on the Reality of the Substitute Prison*, which indicated that suspects who deny charges are handled inhospitably compared with those confessing, who receive treats. Interview with Yūichi Kaido, 18 July 2007.

[114] See questioning of Andō by the DPJ's Chiba Keiko and Kentarō Koba, Judicial Affairs Committee, House of Councillors, 23 May 2006.

With the opposition's alternative proposal having been rejected earlier, the only crumbs of comfort for critics of the government's bill were the external resolutions that kept the door open for further discussion on the attrition of substitute prison, and some of the other more contentious issues. Adopted unanimously in each House along with the passing of the bill, these cross-party motions[115] contained a number of aspirations concerning the direction in which the criminal detention system of Japan should be headed, many of which were along the lines of the JFBA and opposition's suggested amendments.[116] Most importantly, on the substitute prison issue, the government pledged that 'the relevant authorities would not spare efforts to reform [the system]' and also that 'when [they] consider the future of the criminal justice system, [they] should examine the use of substitute detention facilities in relation to the Code of Criminal Procedure'. Given that the 1908 law had also come with similar promises in the Diet, these hardly marked a major compromise on the part of the establishment.

The Aftermath

The first part of the revision of the Prison Law was welcomed, not only within the Diet, but also by domestic and international human rights advocates who were keen to see the legal changes implemented, albeit with the hope that this would not be the end of the improvement process. A rather more frosty reception was given by these groups to the 2006 amendment, which, by preserving the status quo for the substitute prison system, did nothing to move the arguments on from those being made before the passage of the bill.

Concerning the 2005 updating, the pros of the new legislation for prisons were judged to outweigh the cons. The JFBA, for example, considered 'the stage [as] clearly set for improvement',[117] and was joined in this assessment by domestic human rights NGOs, who also listed a number of positive aspects of the

[115] Proposed by the LDP, the DPJ, Kōmeitō, the SDP, and the People's New Party (*Kokumin shintō*).

[116] These included improvement of detainees' private communication with their lawyers, a budget increase to allow for female guards to be in charge of female detainees, the abolition of gags in police cells, better treatment of death-row inmates, and improved monitoring of suspect interrogation.

[117] *Report on the Japanese Government's Implementation of CAT*, JFBA, 18 January 2007, p. 6.

reform.[118] Similarly, the UN 'welcomed the adoption of the 2005 law on penal institutions and the treatment of convicted prisoners as an important sign of the State party's commitment to improving prison conditions'.[119] As previously noted, the Prison Boards were generally seen as the most significant of the new measures, but besides these, approval was also given for changes to the complaints system and increased opportunities granted to inmates for contacting those on the outside. NGOs were quick to take advantage of some of the relaxations of the regulations in practice. For some observers, there were still some outstanding issues, such as excessive use of solitary confinement, a need to reform medical care in prisons, and overly restrictive conditions on death row,[120] but these did not detract from the overall positive impression.

Later, in assessing the work of the Prison Boards, the extent of their powers and the transparency of their membership selection were questioned by the JFBA, but nonetheless it was consented that their monitoring capability did mark real progress for the prison system of Japan. In particular, the Prison Boards commenced their monitoring duties in June 2006 with the enactment of the first amendment. Rather than being expected to manage cases of individual abuse, following each of their four annual facility inspections, they were given the chance to formulate proposals for specific alteration to prison administration in general. Typically these would focus on ways in which to reduce risks of maltreatment by, for example, making it easier for inmates to identify guards, and also improving the standard of their medical care.[121] At a JFBA debriefing event, dismay was expressed that the Prison Boards were not being allowed full access to all the data that they requested on visits, were sometimes supervised too closely by prison management, and did not have their suggested changes put into effect often enough.[122] The lawyers' main worry, though, was

[118] For further details see *The Alternative Report on the Japanese Government's Report of CAT*, CAT Network, March 2007, pp. 4–5.

[119] *Consideration of Reports Submitted by States Parties under Article 19 of the Convention: Initial Report of Japan*, UN document CAT/C/SR.767, 16 May 2007, p. 5.

[120] Interview with Emi Akiyama, 24 August 2007. This point is also discussed further in Croydon (2014).

[121] Information obtained during attendance at the meeting of the lawyer representatives of the Boards of Visitors at the Tōkyō Headquarters of the JFBA, 13 November 2007.

[122] Ibid.

that the selection of the Prison Boards did not meet the government's criteria that members should be people who 'are enthusiastic about improving the operation of penal institutions'.[123] For the JFBA, this situation was a result of 'Board members ... [being] determined solely on the basis of selection by penal institutions'[124]—a point that would be reiterated by the UN. Notwithstanding these flaws, the JFBA was overall appreciative of the chance to obtain extensive information about the treatment of prisoners in each of the nation's prisons on a regular basis through the new monitoring system, rather than having to rely on isolated allegations of abuse.

One other corollary to the Nagoya scandal with regard to prisons that is worth noting, albeit not a part of the new legislation, was the MOJ's increased activity in dealing with the problem of overcrowding that had been steadily growing for a number of years. For the Ministry, many of the criticisms of the Prison Boards, the JFBA, and the CPR following the passing of the new law were unwarranted, but it did acknowledge that their prison facilities were in need of increases in size to handle the overcrowding problem and that upgrading was necessary for many of the existing institutions to ensure better protection of prisoners' rights (Shimato 2007). With such changes in facilities, it claimed, it would be possible for the full impact of the legislative adjustments to be seen, and since moves in this direction were already being made, it was only a matter of time before improvements in prison conditions would occur. In particular, with the incidents at Nagoya having been seen by the MOJ as an indirect consequence of the situation of prisons running at 106 per cent capacity, it was felt that the construction of new facilities was urgent. Knowing that it would be difficult to obtain more funding directly, in 2003 the MOJ placed a number of prison-building projects on a government list of Private Finance Initiatives (PFI).[125] That better, and less harsh, conditions for the inmates who would be held in these so-called Social Restoration Promotion Centres (*Shakai fukki suishin sentā*)[126] would no doubt result was underscored by

[123] Ibid.

[124] This quote, the point of which was repeated at the meeting, is taken from *Report on the Japanese Government's Implementation of CAT*, JFBA, 18 January 2007, p. 8.

[125] *Japan Times* (online edition), 28 January 2004.

[126] Ibid.

Justice Minister Kunio Hatoyama's questioning of whether the meaning of punishment would be lost for prisoners detained there.[127]

Turning to the 2006 amendment, for NGOs who viewed the substitute prison system as problematic, the only question was just how detrimental to their cause this new part of the law was, with some seeing it as maintaining the current state of affairs and others contending that it did more than that and actually enhanced the system's legal status. The JFBA members taking the former, more optimistic, position considered it a success of their campaign that the NPA had not been able to secure direct funding for the suspect detention system—instead continuing to be refunded by the MOJ for undertaking detention duties—nor been successful in its attempt to remove the word 'substitute' from the law. Moreover, lawyers in this camp considered that, with the inclusion of an attrition clause as an external resolution, '[they] had at least managed to save the situation, and prevent retrogression'.[128] Conversely, there were those who viewed such a position as merely a cover for the disappointment of not having been able to guarantee a radical change to the regulations, including more stringent provisions about the conditions under which suspects could be detained in police cells. Indeed, since the substitute prison facilities were previously used on the basis of a single clause, the very creation of detailed and concrete regulations for treatment of detainees there was seen by this section of the JFBA as a step back.[129] These disgruntled lawyers also pointed to the fact that the NPA had managed to retain the legal right to such measures as the application of gags in police cells with what they thought were even fewer restrictions than the New Council had suggested.[130] The CPR joined those taking the view that the 2006 legislation was retrogressive in

[127] *Weekly Asahi*, 26 October 2007.

[128] Interview with Katsuhiko Nishijima, 31 October 2007. Nishijima previously served as the Secretary-General of JFBA's Countermeasure to the Two Detention Bills Headquarters for eighteen years and at the time of the interview was Director Emeritus of the Headquarters for the Realization of a Reform of the Criminal Detention System.

[129] Interview with Maiko Tagusari, 18 July 2007.

[130] Interview with Yūichi Kaido and Maiko Tagusari, 18 July 2007. As a matter of fact, following the passing of the law, the NPA would immediately end their temporary suspension of this practice (see Katagiri 2006: 30).

terms of protecting the human rights of suspects with its declaration that the new law 'seems to promote detaining most suspects and defendants in police cells'.[131]

Not only did the JFBA and CPR argue that the law regarding treatment of suspects was not an improvement; they also sought to demonstrate that there had not been an operational improvement either. For a start, as well as not being coupled with an adequate complaints mechanism, in the eyes of the JFBA it was a serious failing that Police Boards did not have to accept bar association-recommended lawyers as members, as was the case for Prison Boards. With this legal difference, the JFBA were far from enthusiastic about the potential of the Police Boards to exert serious influence, and believed that the problem of selection of members would be even greater than those of the Prison Boards. As proof that the discrepancy was not only legal, in the first few months following the enactment of the law, the JFBA noted that as many as eighteen out of fifty-one candidates put forward by bar associations had been rejected, with the Public Safety Commission preferring either to make its own selection of a lawyer or simply not include one.[132] Furthermore, although they were not aware of any examples of abuses occurring in substitute prison after the new law for suspects was enacted in 2007 when they made their first post-change reports to the UN, the JFBA and the CPR claimed it was inevitable that such cases would eventually emerge. The two organizations argued that, since the law had hardly changed the situation, they could not see an end to the continuing stream of incidents of misuse of police detention being proved in the courts.[133]

Moreover, in determination not to let the substitute prison issue slip given that it was no longer in the Diet, the JFBA continued in its efforts to publicize the possibility of rights' abuse within police-detention. For instance, supplementary to its previous campaign techniques, the JFBA aided the production of several widely

[131] *The Alternative Report on the Japanese Government's Report of CAT*, CAT Network, March 2007.

[132] *JFBA Update Report in Response to the List of Issues to be Taken Up in Connection with the Consideration of the Fifth Periodic Report of Japan*, p. 19.

[133] Communication with JFBA and CPR members in Geneva at the 94th UNHRC Session, October 2008, at which Japan's Fifth ICCPR report was examined. For examples of cases, see also *Report on the Japanese Government's Implementation of CAT*, JFBA, 18 January 2007, pp. 33–6.

broadcast films about it. These included a forty-five-minute documentary film entitled '*Jihaku wa kōshite tsukurareta: Shibushi jiken no higeki*' (Creating Confessions: The Tragedy of the Shibushi Case), which had reportedly cost the association 100 million yen.[134] The lawyers also contributed guidance to the movie 'I Just Didn't Do It' (*Sore de mo boku wa yatte nai*), which has since been widely broadcast in Japan and screened abroad. The latter was directed by Masayuki Suo and inspired by a real case in which a suspect, detained for allegedly groping a woman on the underground, undergoes detention in substitute prison and an extended trial resulting in a guilty verdict, despite the scarcity of hard evidence. Whilst 'I Just Didn't Do It' was fictional, events of the kind it portrayed are a growing issue in Japan, with lawyers reportedly having had to defend their clients against spurious claims made by purported victims for a variety of reasons, including gaining out-of-court settlement money, creating drama in their lives, and avoiding work commitments (Araki 2006). Moreover, the psychological pressure on suspects to confess during the extended period of police detention, as investigators allegedly use the prospects of the suspect losing their job as leverage to make them submit to the 'victim's' version of events even though there is no chance of further evidence being collected against them during this time, is viewed as crucial in increasing the potential for resulting miscarriages of justice (Araki 2004). For the JFBA, involvement in the project consequently provided an excellent opportunity to highlight possible problems with the substitute prison system.

For the MOJ and NPA, by focusing on the question of its abolition, critics of the current legal provision for suspects were not recognizing the rights safeguards that had been made with the new law. The MOJ, for example, pointed to the better access to their clients in detention centres that lawyers now enjoyed, with the closure of such institutions having been pushed back from 5pm to 8pm, and Sunday visiting now possible.[135] The bureaucrats also stressed that with regard to lawyers keeping in contact with their clients, several other improvements that had been demanded by the JFBA and the external resolutions to the 2006 law had also

[134] Discussion in Geneva with Shin'ichirō Koike, Secretary-General, Headquarters for the Realisation of a Reform of the Criminal Detention System, 16 October 2008. Further details about the case in question were also published in a JFBA-edited booklet released at the same time (JFBA 2008).

[135] Interview with MOJ Official A, 9 November 2007.

recently been instituted, such as the broadening of telephone rights and introduction of faxes (Shimato 2007). As for the substitute prison article itself, although the NPA recognized that the JFBA's strong institutional objection to this remained and pledged to continue working with the lawyers to improve suspect treatment, the authorities' arguments for the article's retention had not budged—with the MOJ declaring it necessary on financial grounds and the NPA on practical ones.[136] Furthermore, now that its internal separation regulations were embedded in law, the NPA claimed cases of abuse in practice were 'impossible', since 'individual officers would not be prepared to face the sanction of losing their job over using detention for the sake of investigation'.[137]

Finally, the authorities' justification for the retention of substitute prison was accepted neither by the UN Committee against Torture nor by the UNHRC, which began to express its frustration with the lack of change. In the case of the former body, its concluding observations on Japan's initial report to the UN Committee against Torture (CAT) report in 2007 stated that detention of suspects in police custody 'increases the possibilities of abuse of rights, and may lead to a *de facto* failure to respect the principles of presumption of innocence, right to silence and right of defence'. The same committee went on to present the Japanese government with eleven 'grave concerns' with the substitute prison system, and recommended that the law adopted only one year earlier should be amended 'to limit the use of police cells during pre-trial detention' and 'ensure complete separation between the functions of investigation and detention'.[138] This final point must have been hard to take for the MOJ and NPA, which had earlier appealed that one of the strengths of the law just promulgated was the guarantees it provided to split these two offices. When, the next year, Japan was placed under the microscope again and gave the same responses to questions about substitute prison, the UNHRC members were not shy in reprimanding those representing Japan for its seemingly nil regard for UN advice.

[136] The NPA's viewpoint on the legislative reform was elucidated in a special edition of *Keisatsu-gaku ronshū* published immediately after the passage of the bill, prior to its implementation (National Police Academy 2006). The Agency's and MOJ's positions were further expounded in other venues too, such as by the Japanese government delegation at the 94th UNHRC Session, October 2008.

[137] Interview with NPA Official A and NPA Official B, 8 August 2007.

[138] Conclusions and Recommendations of the Committee against Torture: Japan, UN document CAT/C/JPN/CO/1, 3 August 2007.

Conclusion

As a consequence of the Nagoya Prison crisis, the political momentum for achieving a new law for prisons was significantly greater than it had been at any earlier point in the history of the 1908 Prison Law, and this served to catalyze the amendment process. The first part of the reform, which regarded the treatment of convicted prisoners, was completed on the basis of a relatively constructive MOJ–JFBA relationship. The antagonism between the NPA and the JFBA during the negotiations concerning the second part of the reform, on the other hand, replicated almost identically that of the earlier legislative attempts of the former to perpetuate substitute prison. The interactions of the MOJ and the NPA, however, suggest that the situation was not completely as it had been before.

Unlike the 1980s and 1990s, when the reform had not been a high priority for the ruling politicians, in the spring of 2003, with the opposition trying to gain political ground on this issue of prisons, it was essential that the LDP was seen to be taking action. The urgency of the Justice Minister to this end and the effectiveness of her command were readily apparent from the rapid steps taken by the MOJ to improve the situation in practice. Moreover, with the Justice Minister taking a personal interest in the first reform Council, the MOJ was under heightened political pressure to ensure the successful passage of the resulting legislation.

The drive within the MOJ to see the Prison Law updated was manifest in its increased receptiveness to external input, at least in the first stage of the reform. Coupled with its desire to cast aside the Meiji prison legislation, the political encouragement to do so led the bureaucracy to adopt an even more open position than it had done hitherto. Not only was the Council that the MOJ selected broadly acclaimed, but so too were its recommendations. In addition, whereas before the Ministry had been accused of backtracking on some points between the consultative phase and the submission of its draft legislation, now it was acknowledged by even the most critical of observers that its bill was in the same spirit as the Council had proposed. Finally, despite aspiring to a one-step overhaul of the system, the MOJ bowed to the demand that suspects, together with death-row inmates, be considered separately, demonstrating that it was prepared to make concessions so as to not jeopardize the project at this stage.

Perhaps the major beneficiary of the MOJ's amenable approach on prisons was the JFBA, which was much incorporated during the policy formation phase, and was also able to prevent the un-discussed revision of the part of the law concerning substitute prison. Since convicted prisoners, over which there was less fundamental disagreement than was the case with suspects, were the sole focus of the 2003 Council, and it was essential for the MOJ to appease the lawyers, the content of the subsequent proposal and bill took on board many JFBA suggestions, which the lawyers would publicly recognize. Moreover, that the JFBA was seen as an important actor with the potential to derail the authorities' progress is evident from its success in preventing the full reform in one go, and blocking an exclusive NPA bill full stop.

Although willing to wait for the second stage of the amendment, the NPA gave almost no ground in the discussions, and was able to retain its much prized substitute prison system. In contrast to the attitude adopted by the MOJ in the previous years' deliberations, the NPA showed no compunction in demanding jurisdiction over suspects with the same conditions as already existed. The NPA did not concede to Police Boards with as wide-ranging a remit as had been created for prisons, for example. Even the emergence in the Diet of some discomforting information during the final deliberations of the suspects bill did not prevent it reasserting its turf. Substitute prison was re-legislated for now, whereas it probably would have failed earlier, not because the NPA had convinced its critics of the advantages of the system, but rather due to the simple numerical advantage of the LDP in the Diet.

As for the JFBA, the two-stage reform had caused something of a quandary. Whilst the JFBA, whose overarching organizational position on substitute prison had not essentially changed since the 1990s, had initially been satisfied for the revision to be split into two stages, it would later realize that by agreeing to this it had given away some of its negotiating power. In particular, since, by the time new legislation for suspect detention was being proposed, the MOJ had already secured its much sought-after change of prison regulation, the JFBA did not, as it had in the 1980s, have the option of setting out an ultimatum to the authorities that it would do all it could to block their bill if they did not include a substitute prison outright abolition, or at least attrition, clause. Although, given the make-up of the Diet when the second bill was presented, it is unlikely that the lawyers would have been successful had they pursued such a strategy anyway, this point caused division amongst the JFBA regarding whether or not it had played its cards as well as it could have done.

Finally, in comparison with the earlier decision-making process, not much had changed—the NPA again provided the driving force for the continuation of substitute prison, and the JFBA resumed the fight against it from where this had been left off. However, the relationship between the MOJ and the NPA during the discussions suggests that substitute prison had become even more embedded than it was during the 1980s. Specifically, from the very start, the two governmental departments worked closely together in the production of legislation, with the MOJ happy to let the NPA play the role of an equal partner. This stood as a noticeable contrast from before, when for the MOJ the involvement of the NPA had been something of a nuisance. Such willingness to work together indicates that the MOJ was content with the status quo, and was certainly not prepared to move without the police on board, as it had been before. Moreover, some observers have even made the point that the authorities' splitting of the substitute prison issue from the main prison reform could have been an ingenious *jujutsu* tactic against their main opponents—with the MOJ calculating that it could formulate a bill for prisons that would meet the JFBA's requirements, but once this had passed the lawyers would find it hard to block the completion of the amendment process, even if they objected to its contents.

5

Deconstructing the Substitute Prison Landscape

> Every body persists in its state of rest or uniform motion straight ahead, except in so far as it be compelled to change that state by forces impressed upon it.
>
> Isaac Newton, Principia Mathematica

> There are not enough jails, not enough police, not enough courts to enforce a law not supported by the people.
>
> Hubert H Humphrey (former USA vice president)

To pull together the observations made hitherto, this chapter presents a crystallized version of the nature of the relationships between the key governmental actors and other parties with an interest in the treatment of suspects. To begin with, the intertwined positions of the National Police Agency (NPA) and Ministry of Justice (MOJ) are recaptured, and fleshed out with further commentary from officials and onlookers. This makes clear how the substitute prison policy was a reciprocally advantageous arrangement for both departments, and each played a part in the system becoming as prevalent as it now is. Of course, the NPA and MOJ were not acting in isolation, and to complete the picture, the remaining participants' contributions to the associated political processes will be elucidated, again appealing to additional evidence and insights to enrich the material presented in previous chapters. Finally, space is devoted to connecting these strings together in order to explain the positive feedback towards entrenchment of substitute prison. Specifically, the chapter will make the case that the more substitute prison was used, the greater the divergence became between the facilities in existence and those that would be needed to do without it. Thus, from a financial point of view, it was difficult to reverse course. It would be erroneous to conclude that this situation arose simply as a result of the NPA and MOJ being given *carte blanche* on suspect detention, however.

Rather, the weakness in the positions or indifference to the matter of the other stakeholders played a crucial enabling role.

Substitute Jurisdiction: The Mutually Symbiotic NPA–MOJ Relationship

Given the events described so far, the NPA's determination to retain the substitute prison system hardly needs spelling out again. Nor does the fact that this unyielding line on the substitute prison issue throughout the entire post-war period was borne of its belief that the system was an essential means of fulfilling its role as the guardian of the public. For the police, having regular contact with the suspect for the full twenty-three-day period allowed for an effective investigation, whereby officers could question closely and thoroughly the individual detained so as to secure evidence vital for understanding the true facts of the case. Without this access, the investigative authorities feared that the quality of the criminal inquiry would suffer, as they would struggle to collect enough evidence to establish guilt beyond reasonable doubt, leaving culpable people free to roam the streets and commit other crimes. For police investigators, and also those of the prosecution, Japan's low crime rate and high conviction rate were direct consequences of police detention practices. Thus, from the NPA's perspective, there was no question that substitute prison was absolutely necessary—a point that it made sure was widely publicized (see Figure 5.1, for example).

Given the NPA's desire to fully exploit the legal opportunity to detain suspects that had been granted it by the substitute prison article, it is not surprising that it has continually expanded its portfolio of detention facilities across the country, and makes extensive use of this. Data from 2004 reveals the existence of 11,000 NPA questioning rooms located within 1,286 widely dispersed police detention facilities—to give an indication of their prevalence, Figure 5.2 shows the locations of the approximately 100 facilities in the Tōkyō prefecture, and similar coverage is seen in other areas of the country (see Figure 5.3). By developing such an extensive network, the NPA has given itself the capacity to detain the majority of Japan's suspects, which it duly does. On any given day in 2004, for example, as many as 98 per cent of the approximately 5,500-strong population of suspects were being detained in police cells (this rate has grown steadily over the past thirty years

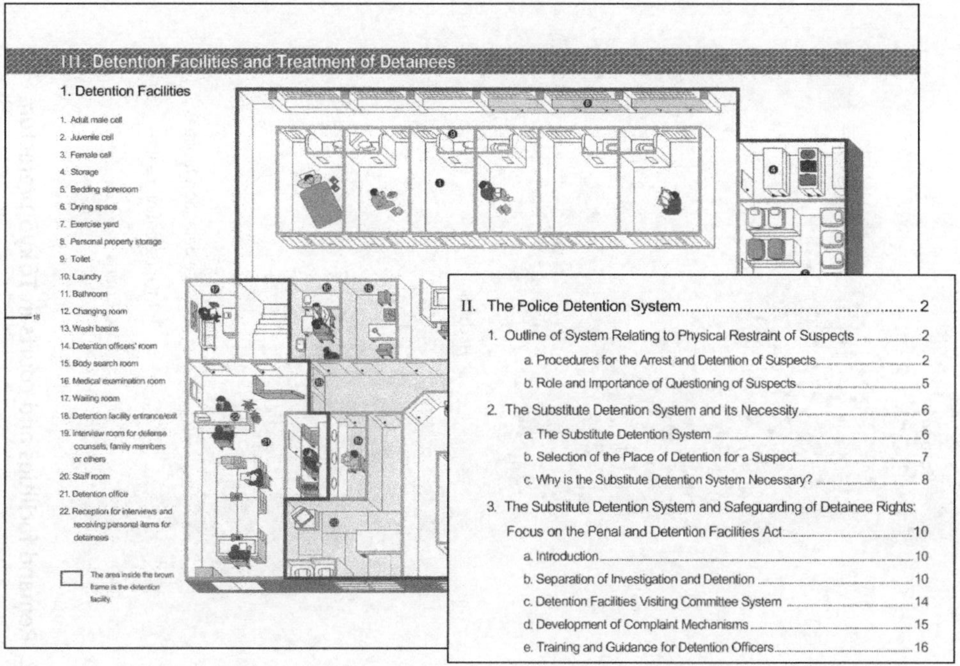

Figure 5.1. **Excerpts from NPA pamphlet regarding substitute prison**

Source: *Police Detention Administration in Japan*, NPA, 29 October 2008.

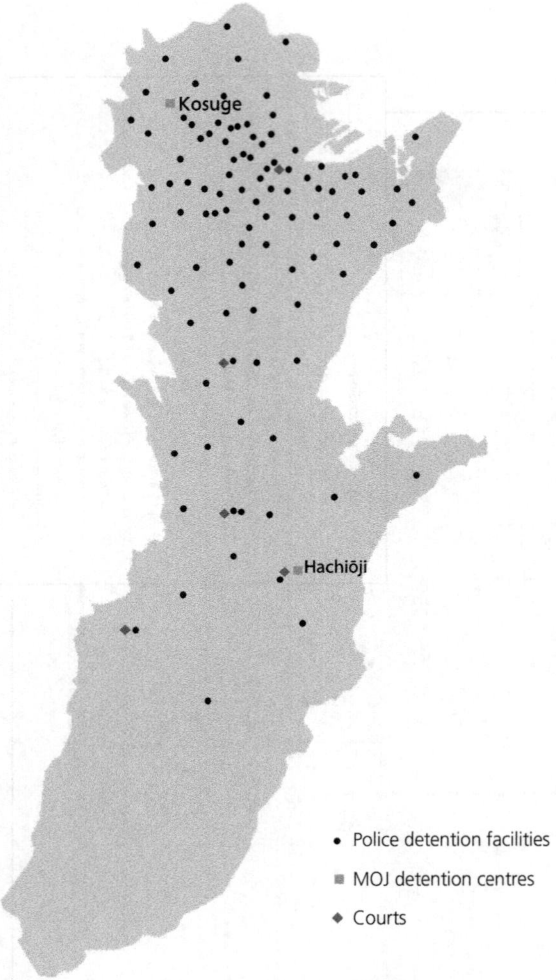

Figure 5.2. Remand facilities and courts in Tōkyō prefecture

Source: Material submitted by MOJ, Judicial Affairs Committee, House of Representatives, 6 December 2005

from approximately 3,000: see Figure 5.4). Moreover, whilst arrestees are held in police cells as a matter of course, on a suspect's presentation to a judge, the investigative authorities request in 93 per cent of cases that the suspect be returned to police detention facilities afterwards. This request is almost always granted so that suspects are detained beyond the initial three-day period into

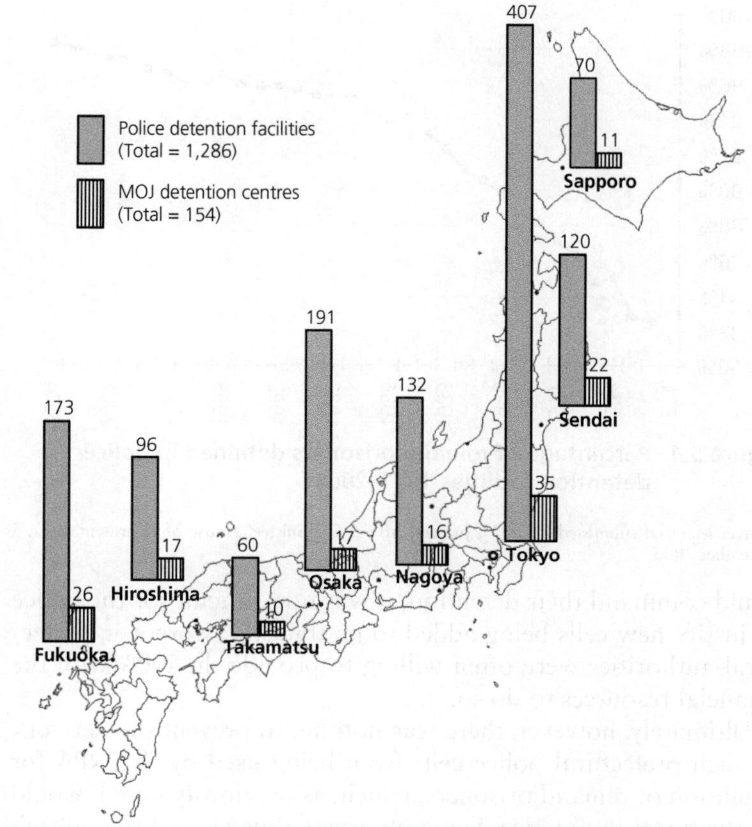

Figure 5.3. Number of police and MOJ detention facilities by high court jurisdiction

Source: Material submitted by MOJ, Judicial Affairs Committee, House of Representatives, 6 December 2005.

the first period of extension, and in 54 per cent of cases there is a further extension into the second.[1]

As a source of legitimacy for this expansion in its capability to undertake substitute prison duties, the NPA could point to its office of detaining arrestees. With the day-to-day duties of police officers involving such tasks as keeping drunkards and other anti-social individuals away from harm—either to themselves or others—as well as taking potentially dangerous criminals off the streets quickly, sometimes in the middle of the night when no court

[1] *Police Detention Administration in Japan*, NPA pamphlet, 29 October 2008.

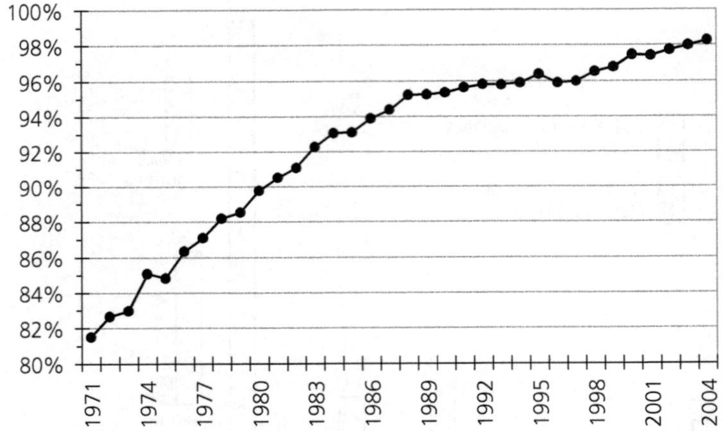

Figure 5.4. Percentage of remand prisoners detained in police detention facilities 1971–2004

Source: Material submitted by MOJ, Judicial Affairs Committee, House of Representatives, 6 December 2005

could command their detention, it was not difficult for the police to justify new cells being added to its stations. Moreover, prefectural authorities were often willing to provide the NPA with the financial resources to do so.

Ultimately, however, there was nothing to prevent the network of such prefectural police cells from being used by the NPA for detention of remand prisoners, which, as previously noted, would be the norm in practice. Some observers thus viewed the police's continual development of detention facilities as part of a deliberate ploy to embed the substitute prison within the Japanese criminal justice system. Indeed, to put the figures presented above for NPA suspect detention facilities into perspective, note that the same data shows the MOJ can boast only as many as 650 questioning rooms at 154 sites. Figure 5.2 shows the mere two MOJ sites in the Tōkyō prefecture, from which it is clear that the NPA's arguments of better accessibility for investigators, lawyers, and suspects' family members to its network is justified, at least in the capital. That the pattern is similar elsewhere is corroborated by Figure 5.3, which demonstrates that the same imbalance between NPA and MOJ facilities is repeated uniformly across the whole of Japan. Critics of the substitute prison system claim that this has not happened by accident, and that creating this disparity actually represents a conscious campaign by the NPA to put the MOJ's detention houses out of business:

> The NPA has been a little cheeky in developing so many of its own facilities, and because of this there is a danger that MOJ detention centres will become obsolete. Indeed, maintaining separate MOJ facilities is expensive compared to using police cells, which are anyway needed for detaining arrestees, and it has reached the point where it is not clear that doing so is necessary any more. After all, the criminal justice system of Japan would continue to function as usual if police facilities were the only ones used for the detention of suspects.[2]

For such observers, it is not only the creation of facilities that has formed part of this strategy, but also the improvement in the conditions of detention by the NPA. As a Director of the Board of the Japan Civil Liberties Union (JCLU), Jun'ichirō Hironaka, notes, this has meant that even suspects prefer to be held there:

> The police have money to spend on making their detention facilities much more attractive than those of MOJ—in terms of the food, the cleanliness, etc. Moreover, if suspects provide their own money, for example, they can eat what they want or smoke if they like. The end result is that even the suspects prefer to be detained under their jurisdiction.[3]

(The plan in Figure 5.1, taken from the NPA's own pamphlet, is intended to show how the police have created a good living environment for detainees in their facilities.) Whether the NPA planned to completely dominate the MOJ in terms of its detention provision from the time the American occupiers left, or whether this outcome naturally transpired as a consequence of its desire to fulfil its duties of investigation, is to some degree immaterial. A more important question is how the decision-making environment allowed the suspect detention situation to evolve in this way.

To begin by describing the NPA's place in this, it is clear that the Agency was highly autonomous politically. Specifically, the MOJ could do nothing about the NPA drafting its own bill, even during the period of the 1980s when the Ministry would clearly have preferred it to take a back seat. The LDP too was reluctant to meddle in the affairs of the NPA directly. This freedom of the police, which has been observed more generally, is commonly attributed to the relative lack of oversight that it enjoys. In particular, the Public

[2] Interview with Aya Kuwayama, 3 December 2008.

[3] Discussion with Jun'ichirō Hironaka, 7 November 2007. This situation was confirmed by policeman-scholar Isao Watanabe, 11 January 2008.

Safety Committees, which administer the NPA, 'almost always defer to police decisions' (Finch 1999: 496). Moreover, talking about its relationship with the prosecution, former judge Harumi Hori presents an argument for this independence in terms of the Occupation reforms:

> If the police decides to ignore what the prosecution says, then the latter cannot take a move. Whenever a relevant policy is being debated, the NPA invariably sticks its nose in, and there is no way to do anything about this. One can attribute this to being a remnant of power from the era when the police was part of the omnipotent Home Ministry.[4]

The NPA, whatever power it might have wielded, was however not a lone wolf. There was another major government department with a stake in suspect detention—the MOJ. And, although the Ministry was not the driving force behind the expansion of the application of substitute prison, it certainly did not fight it. Indeed, after tentatively discussing a substitute prison attrition clause in the 1980s as a bargaining chip, its legislative actions then, as well as the unified front it formed with the police in the recent Prison Law amendment, suggest that it is not something that the Ministry ever really sought.

For some observers, the Ministry's lack of a desire for change was a key factor in why the system has persisted to the present day. Had the Ministry fulfilled its obligation to supply an adequate volume of facilities for suspect detention, the argument goes, there would have not been a need for police cells to be used instead. Even NPA officials claim to have 'urged the MOJ on numerous occasions to enhance its suspects detention capacity',[5] and thus imply that the Ministry left them with no option than to develop their own alternative detention facilities. This lack of momentum for change from the MOJ has also been highlighted by SDP politician Nobuto Hosaka, who argues that if the MOJ really wanted to abolish substitute prison, then it could:

> It is not an issue of whether the human rights problems of substitute prison detention are understood. I mean to say, it is not a question of knowing right from wrong. [When it comes to the question of abolition,] the issue is whether MOJ ever comes round to the mindset of [doing so].[6]

4 Interview with Harumi Hori, 23 August 2007.
5 Interview with NPA Official A and NPA Official B, 8 August 2007.
6 Interview with Nobuto Hosaka, 23 August 2007.

MOJ officials, however, are quick to dispute accusations that the Ministry is to blame for current suspect detention practices, maintaining that it is not their responsibility to be making the call to abolish substitute prison. Although such a line appears to somewhat contradict the Ministry's earlier willingness to talk about substitute prison attrition with the Japan Federation of Bar Associations (JFBA), they suggest that it is for the policy-makers in the Diet to take such decisions. Moreover, for as long as the law does permit the practice, they maintain, the MOJ should not be criticized for the system's continuation. In the words of a Correction Bureau official,

> [i]t is not part of our job as civil servants to be deciding on the fundamentals of the criminal justice system; our role is simply to execute the law, including for substitute prison. If a political proposal comes up to review this, then of course we will do so.[7]

Arguably, this subdued approach of the MOJ towards substitute prison stems from the fact that discussions regarding the issue inevitably involve the NPA. More concretely, it has been suggested by some that the Ministry takes the stance that it does primarily to avoid the trouble that would result from standing up to the police. Talking specifically about the 2006 amendment, former Justice Minister Seiken Sugiura explains:

> MOJ [could not] do anything about demanding budget for the detention facilities in the Diet, because it would have [had] to go against the force of the 260,000-man police, which has a huge political clout, and the Ministry would [have suffered] severe consequences if it [did].[8]

The less cynical version of this argument is that it has never been within the MOJ's power to ensure suspects are placed in its facilities rather than police cells. For whatever it did with regard to its own detention facilities, it could not prevent the NPA from developing its own and encouraging the use of these, since such a step would involve the Ministry placing restrictions outside of its territory on the activities of the NPA—indeed, as claimed by the JFBA, many of the MOJ's existing detention centres often stood empty, whereas police cells were full to the brim with remand suspects, and also the MOJ were even decommissioning cells for remand

[7] MOJ Official B, interview with MOJ Official B and MOJ Official C, 31 August 2007.

[8] Interview with Seiken Sugiura, 18 October 2007.

detention. Legal scholar Masako Kamiya summarizes this point as follows:

> MOJ cannot trespass into the authority of the police, as in Japan there is the tacit principle that one governmental department does not barge into another department's work. Indeed, even though the NPA tells MOJ 'we don't mind at all you trying to enhance your detention capacity', the NPA would not allow the use of its own facilities to be reduced and there is no way for MOJ to oblige it to do so.[9]

In particular, the NPA's refusal to co-operate with a substitute prison attrition plan by agreeing to limit the use of its cells for the detention of remand prisoners reduced the MOJ's options to simply offering a plan for expanding its own facilities. As the Ministry deemed such to be unrealistic, it could be said that its hands were tied.

Whatever the underlying reason is for the MOJ's inaction on substitute prison, it would be a mistake to conclude that the Ministry is unhappy with the current state of affairs—for, by remaining in theory the department designated with authority over remand prisoners, the MOJ has the entire prison system within its domain. However, by relinquishing this part of its duties in practice, the Ministry is both eased of some of its burden and avoids the potential for bad publicity that comes with remanding suspects. As Kamiya again elucidates:

> It might sound strange why MOJ would not want to defend its turf of detaining those suspects, which rightfully belong to it—after all, the office of detaining suspects is one of the justifications for its existence! However, from MOJ's point of view, it is actually quite convenient that the NPA is to take this duty off its hands. For a start, MOJ has to cope with the huge problem of prison overcrowding, and so if NPA takes over the suspect detention system that is a relief for MOJ. Plus, suspect detention involves the dark and dirty job of dealing with those against whom there might not be enough hard evidence. MOJ is the focus of criticism often in society, and might not be able to manage events like the exonerations. On the other hand, it is much easier for the NPA, as the maintainer of public safety, to defend itself against the occasional criticism when a rare incident of exoneration occurs. As a result, the benefits for MOJ of letting the NPA do this job far outweigh the disadvantages, and so it is more than willing to pass it over.[10]

With such definite advantages for the MOJ in having the NPA substitute its jurisdiction over remand prisoners, it is easy to

[9] Discussion with Masako Kamiya, 7 November 2007.

[10] Ibid.

understand why the Ministry was so accommodating to the police in the Prison Law reform project.

The case has further been made that, to this end, the MOJ's rigidity in terms of the conditions it places on remand prisoners in its facilities is part of an effort to ensure the preservation of the status quo. The Ministry itself explains heightened disciplinary measures in its detention-specializing facilities, as compared to the more flexible arrangements of the NPA's suspect detention conditions, as a result of it being too problematic to create two regimes in the same institution. Moreover, although both the MOJ and NPA originally restricted lawyers' visitations to working hours, over the years the NPA became more flexible, so that in 2005, for instance, as many as 50 per cent of visits to its facilities took place at evenings and weekends (Katagiri 2006: 36). The MOJ, by contrast, maintained limited access to suspects, with its officials explaining this position in terms of staff shortages—arguing that placing an increased burden on the small number of guards available would result in security becoming looser. On both of these points, critics question the MOJ's motivation. Reflecting the observations made above about the circumstances of suspect detention in police facilities and underlining why suspects might themselves prefer to be held there, former Secretary-General of the JFBA's Countermeasure to the Two Detention Bills Headquarters, Katsuhiko Nishijima, explains:

> Detention centres are so strict—MOJ does not even let them relax their posture! Plus, it is very difficult for family and friends to visit them there during the times that MOJ permits. (Reception hours end at 3:30pm on working days, and visitation times are limited to 15–20 minutes.) By making only small changes and without tapping into its financial resources, the MOJ could easily address many of these issues.[11]

Thus it is that the MOJ's inflexibility regarding its regime for remand prisoners is widely seen by substitute prison abolitionists as part of a cunning stratagem by the authorities to promote the view that the existing system is better.

To summarize, there were shared benefits for the NPA and MOJ in the substitute prison arrangement. Despite their different objectives, the system suited both their needs, and was convenient for both: whereas the NPA was eager to take from the MOJ responsibility over remand prisoners so that it could use this for its investigative purposes, the latter was by no means averse to the idea

[11] Interview with Katsuhiko Nishijima, 31 October 2007.

of relinquishing this particular duty. To this end, the NPA pursued a strategy of developing its detention capacity, and made efforts to ensure that it would not only be investigators that preferred for its cells to be used for remand prisoners. As for the MOJ, despite it arguing that deciding the future of substitute prison was outside its remit, its willingness to accommodate the police throughout the legislative reform process, as well as its seeming lack of drive to compete in terms of developing its own facilities, suggested that it was quite satisfied with the current suspect detention situation. With such an understanding of this mutual symbiosis, it is easy to appreciate which were the forces behind substitute prison becoming the norm.

Supporting Actors

Why was it, though, that the authorities got their way on the substitute prison issue? In order to answer such a question, it is important to contextualize the NPA and MOJ's actions. Who was supporting these two governmental actors, and what opposition did they face? Moreover, why was it that those who did not see eye-to-eye with them were not able to turn the tide? This section examines these issues, explaining the roles of lawyers, politicians, the wider public, and judges in the decision-making process.

A divided bar

From its formation in the early post-war period until the present day, the JFBA retained an official line in opposition to substitute prison, and stood as the principal adversary of the NPA on this issue. Indeed, it was the efforts of the lawyers' organization that prevented the police from having its separate bill for detention passed in the earlier reform attempts, and stopped it from obtaining direct funding for the substitute prison system in 2006. (See Figure 5.5 for an example of one of the pamphlets that the lawyers have produced on this issue.) This being the case, it would be fair to conclude that, although the JFBA was certainly not powerful enough to be the lead influencer of policy, its political and financial clout did help shape the course of the discussions. In light of this observation, in explaining the persistence of substitute prison, one could thus not argue that this was due to a lack of any domestic opposition to the policy.

Figure 5.5. Excerpt from JFBA pamphlet regarding substitute prison

Source: Japan's 'Substitute Prison' System Shocks the World: Daiyō Kangoku *and the UN Committee against Torture's Recommendations*, JFBA, September 2008.

What does not become readily apparent from the above picture, however, is that the official JFBA line by no means represented the unanimous voice of the profession. Indeed, the picture on the finer scale is more complex than this, and also starts to hint that the current state of police detention in Japan might not only be due to the NPA, the MOJ, and the mutually symbiotic relationship between these two actors. In particular, many lawyers personally diverge from their professional association's stance on suspect detention, claiming that the merits of police detention can outweigh its disadvantages. To give just one, albeit significant, example, Hironaka of the JCLU argues that:

> It is, in some cases, much better for both me and my client if their detention takes place in one of the police facilities instead of a MOJ detention centre. This way I can visit them more often, which helps keep their spirits up, and aids our case because it enables me to keep telling them to persevere against pressure to confess. Detention centres are normally located quite far away, you see. So, if my clients are kept there, my busy schedule means I cannot visit them regularly and provide a good level of support. Plus, apart from the issue of distance with detention centres, there is the question of their visitation rules, which are very restrictive; I cannot go to see my client late at night and during weekends and holidays, for example, which is not true for police cells.
>
> Anyway, I have won in court after my client had been held by the police, and there are only a handful of cases where suspects have been tortured to confess. So I do not think there is a need to change the system and to move all suspects to MOJ facilities. I would think if anything is to be done in this regard, only the suspects for whom there is no hard evidence and for which the investigation would rely on confession should be taken out of police cells and moved somewhere more independent of the investigation.[12]

This point is echoed by scholar-cum-lawyer Nobuyoshi Araki, who argues that, although defence lawyers have as a rule a duty to request that suspects are removed from police detention, in practice this is not the most significant issue. Rather, for him, it is more important that lawyers meet suspects early on in the period of detention and frequently thereafter in order to highlight how crucial it is for them not to unduly confess, and for this it can be the case that police cells are more convenient (Araki 2006: 115–16). These views are expressed despite the warnings of lawyers with

[12] Interview with Jun'ichirō Hironaka, 7 November 2007.

more bitter experiences of substitute prison, who constantly seek to re-educate colleagues of theirs who hold these views about the pitfalls of being seduced by the short-term benefits of substitute prison. For instance, Maiko Tagusari, a lawyer and activist, is concerned that:

> Some lawyers, particularly young and inexperienced ones, can be unaware of or ignore the hazards of substitute prison. Mostly, these have not been on the scene when big exonerations have happened and thus do not know about the abuses that have taken place within the system. All too easily have they been convinced about its merits; you might say they have been blinded by its convenience.[13]

Although, as a large-scale organization, it is perhaps inevitable that there has been a certain amount of division on an issue that affects the everyday life of lawyers, such lack of unanimity could only have weakened the JFBA's position in its interactions with the authorities. Indeed, the establishment was well aware of this discord and did not shy away from exploiting it to its own advantage, pointing to the pragmatic position on substitute prison taken by some lawyers to deflect criticism of the system. In the 1993 UNHRC meeting examining Japan's third periodic report on the implementation of the ICCPR, an NPA official explained:

> Although this may have a personal note, I would like to mention that when I have a conversation with attorneys, some [of them] say that police custodial facility is better for the suspect or detainees. And some attorneys did say to me that it is easier to conduct interviews with their clients at the police custodial facility . . .[14]

Given that these words so closely mirror Hironaka's above rhetoric, it is clear that the claim was not a hollow one, and this gave the authorities a certain amount of leverage over the JFBA in negotiations. MOJ official Kamoshita even goes so far as to speculate that the difference in views amongst its membership led to the JFBA having trouble in unifying its position on substitute prison, and it was this that led to the leadership accepting the continuation of the system. According to him, they saw no way to obtain the backing of its membership for abolition, and so settled for seeking improvements in conditions for police detention as the more

[13] Interview with Maiko Tagusari, 8 November 2007.
[14] Record of the meetings, Article 646.

democratic option.[15] Former prosecutor Tsuneyasu Ozaki shares the opinion that the schism within the JFBA was somewhat to blame for the outcome, reflecting that '[i]f the JFBA had been like a monolith, it would have not been so easy to pass a law that retains the system'.[16]

Although it is easy to be sceptical about these outsiders' viewpoints, the claim that the JFBA was disadvantaged in the negotiations by the fact that it could not secure the support of all of its members could also be heard directly from the horse's mouth. Kōichi Kikuta, one of the JFBA representatives in the New Council, for instance, relays that when it came to the meetings, the top brass of the lawyers' organization did not take as hard a line on the substitute prison as had previously been the case. Principally, he claims, this was precisely because they knew that the majority of the lawyers in this big organization actually supported the retention of substitute prison. For Kikuta, who still saw abolition of substitute prison as a goal of the negotiations, this was somewhat disappointing, and he concluded that 'whilst it was earlier the case that securing concrete steps towards [this end] had been a fundamental goal of the JFBA—to the point that it was prepared to put this as an ultimatum—attrition was now nothing more than a slogan'.[17]

Hands-off legislature

Throughout the decades in which the MOJ was pushing for Prison Law reform, the ruling Liberal Democratic Party (LDP) exhibited little assertion with regard to the project. The events in the Diet following the abuses at Nagoya Prison demonstrated that there was potential for the rights of detainees in general to become a concern of the conservative leadership. However, apart from this period of political turbulence, when the opposition sought to gain advantage from the failures in the administration of prisons, the LDP was satisfied to follow the MOJ's lead on the matter. Moreover, the LDP did not at any point play an active role towards resolving the conflict over the substitute prison issue in particular, beyond urging the NPA to set up a consultation process with the JFBA before

[15] Interview with Moritaka Kamoshita, 29 August 2007.
[16] Interview with Tsuneyasu Ozaki, 8 August 2007.
[17] Interview with Kōichi Kikuta, 29 October 2007.

the second submission of the Two Detention Bills. The party neither attempted to point the bureaucracy in a direction that would satisfy the opposition, nor sought to force through the Two Detention Bills through backstage deals with its political rivals. Instead, it was content to leave the MOJ and NPA to work on reconciling their differences with the JFBA and their allies on the opposition benches by themselves.

This reluctance of ruling politicians to become embroiled in the substitute prison debate is perhaps not a surprise, given the electoral disincentives for doing so. On the one hand, abolishing substitute prison would involve the MOJ being granted extra resources, or at the very least being reallocated resources at the expense of the NPA, for creating further detention facilities—a move that politicians anticipated would be unpopular with not only the police, but also voters. Indeed, the view amongst legislators in the LDP with expertise on MOJ affairs was that money given to the MOJ for detention would invariably be seen by the public as money wasted on criminals. The LDP's Sugiura, Justice Minister at the time of the second amendment, highlights that the MOJ's consequent difficulty in securing funds was especially acute in the case of substitute prison, since it would potentially affect the NPA:

> [To understand why politicians cannot do something more about substitute prison,] you have to realise that nobody takes side with MOJ—nobody likes them! The country now is short of finances, and, even at the best of times, it is difficult for MOJ to secure budget in Diet. On the other hand, it is easy for the NPA to do so—because they are the guardians of the country, of course![18]

On the other hand, giving substitute prison backing other than simply on logistical grounds would have opened up the LDP to a wider possibility of attacks from those wanting to see its demise. Since there was no corresponding domestic political advantage for doing so, this was never likely to happen, and nor did it.

Uninterested populace

Despite campaign groups' efforts to educate people about the human rights issues involved, the public did not play a significant role in the substitute prison story. Indeed, the only time public

[18] Interview with Seiken Sugiura, 18 October 2007.

opinion was ever invoked in the political discussions was in objection to MOJ facilities being established. Moreover, it is not difficult to find cases in which the Ministry had encountered such a hurdle, to illustrate that legislators were on the mark in assessing this as a critical issue for ordinary citizens. A notable recent example is the Forum for Akishima City Creation (*Akishima machi-dzukuri fōramu*), which has fought for years with the local authorities over the planned construction of a MOJ International Justice Synthesized Centre (*Kokusai hōmu sōgō sentā*)[19]—a large-scale institution that would gather in one place various MOJ correctional facilities studded throughout Tōkyō. In particular, following a ten-year consultation period, the MOJ announced the construction publicly in 2007, with the local Mayor Jōichi Kitagawa officially accepting this in 2012. During the intervening years, the residents' group proactively sought to block this outcome—organizing a petition enlisting the names of 27,000 out of the population of approximately 110,000, and even commissioning an architect to produce an alternative proposal for developing their locality as an eco-city on the specific model of Freiburg in Germany. Although this group has not achieved its objective, that such a movement is typical is corroborated by MOJ official Moritaka, who also recalls an earlier case where the resistance had rather more success:

> Detention centres are often attached to prisons, and since this kind of facility is commonly associated in the public mind with criminals, escapes and other security problems, their construction is normally opposed by the public. You just have to look at how they have been driven out of towns and cities, so that there are almost none left close to built-up areas as there are in European countries, to understand just quite how unpopular these facilities are in Japan. Even here in Nakano, very close to the Japanese Correctional Association where I work now, there was in the pre-war period a prison with a detention centre attached to it. Gradually, though, the population grew and the neighborhood became increasingly residential. The new residents then galvanized themselves to chase the

[19] This Centre would consist of a correction staff training centre, a centre for dealing with juvenile offenders, a detention centre for prisoners with special medical needs, and the United Nations Asia and Far East Institute for the Prevention of Crime and the Treatment of Offenders (UNAFEI) (which already exists in Fuchu). An image of the planned facility is available at <www.city.akishima.lg.jp/doc/PDF/0700machidukuri/kokusaihoumuimagezu.pdf>.

facilities away, so as to improve the image of their area. As a result, it was closed in 1983.[20]

Why is it, then, that the public could sometimes be so vocal about the building of MOJ detention centres, but were hardly involved in the substitute prison debate or raising concerns about the increase in police facilities? For politician Nobuto Hosaka, this is primarily due to apathy on the latter issue:

Ordinary people have no interest in the substitute prison problem. Mostly they do not know that a problem exists, and even if they do, then they certainly do not want to concern themselves with it.[21]

Such a viewpoint is not contradicted by the events that transpired, in which there was a failure of the general public to engage with the substitute prison issue. This has been a constant source of frustration for those seeking a radical change. Somewhat forlornly, many do not expect the situation to change anytime soon, seeing this not as simple lack of interest, but rather more as a tacit agreement of members of the populace to follow the authorities' lead on the issue. For instance, Kikuta laments that:

In European countries, criminals are treated on the premise that they are human beings, but the philosophy in Japan is different. This means that, even when the international standards for the treatment of detainees are accepted in form, in practice they are not really there. Instead, there is this other culture—the Asian kind of human rights culture. Officials are much more of the mindset that 'you have committed a crime, so you should endure the consequences' and the public do not disagree with this.[22]

It is, of course, too much of a leap to conclude from the events described here that such a cultural outlook can be said to be the fundamental reason behind current police detention practices in Japan. Nevertheless, what is clear is that, for all the opposition of the legal elite, at no point was the NPA fighting against widespread public displeasure. This can only be seen as a contributory factor to the persistence of substitute prison.

Quiet judicial approval

As would be expected from the separation of powers between the three branches of government, the judiciary did not play a direct

[20] Interview with Moritaka Kamoshita, 29 August 2007.

[21] Interview with Nobuto Hosaka, 23 August 2007.

[22] Interview with Kōichi Kikuta, 29 October 2007.

role in the political decision-making process. Nonetheless, judges did have a voice with regard to the substitute prison issue through their courtroom actions. On certain occasions, notably when delivering their judgments on the Big Four exoneration cases during the 1980s, judges criticized the separation of detention and investigation. More routinely, though, it was judges who approved applications from the prosecution requesting prolonged pre-indictment detention, and also it was them who determined whether a suspect should be held in a police cell or one of the MOJ's detention centres. With a detention request approval rate consistently being at around 99 per cent,[23] and virtually all suspects subsequently having been returned to police cells in cases where further detention was permitted, it is clear that they did not see substitute prison as a major problem. Such an interpretation is supported anecdotally by judges, who commonly align with the MOJ in agreeing that they did not see substitute prison itself as equating to a human rights concern.[24] Thus, although being one step removed from the front line in the battle over the future of the system, their rubberstamping of its use indicated tacit agreement with investigative authorities' argument regarding its legitimacy.

That the judiciary generally supported substitute prison was indeed the accepted viewpoint of those partaking in the legislative debates, with participants on both sides acting accordingly on this basis. On the one hand, representatives of the MOJ and NPA used the fact that judges took decisions regarding whether substitute prison was appropriate or not to deflect criticism that prolonged custody in police cells created undue risks for the suspect, compared to the Ministry's detention houses. Crucial to the investigative authorities' position was the autonomy of the judiciary, and the constitutional duty they had to protect citizens. For example, at a hearing of the UNHRC, an NPA spokesman's response to the charge that judges may feel pressured by prosecutors to place suspects in substitute prison for investigative reasons was:

> If true, this is quite [a] serious problem, because it implies that there is no independence of judiciary in Japan, or Japanese judges disregard human rights, because this is what is implied . . . We, however, believe that the judiciary is independent, and that independence is secured, and that Japanese judges make utmost efforts to ensure and establish the human rights

23 MOJ, White Paper on Crime, various years.

24 Interview with Judge A, 7 January 2008.

of people. And if such [a] Japanese judge decides police custodial facility as the place of detention, I hope that you will take this fact into consideration fully.[25]

Of course, the JFBA disagreed with this conclusion, contending that '[j]ust because judges are deciding on substitute prison detention, it cannot be said that this type of detention is free of human rights protection problems'.[26] Nevertheless, it is implicit in such statements that the bar did view judges as being complicit with the investigation through their repeated favouring of the system. So, ultimately, even though judges themselves were not under the political spotlight, this is not to say they did not have an impact on the arguments of the actors that were.

Whilst the preceding discussion might represent the prevailing judicial attitude towards substitute prison, this is not to say that there was never any questioning of the system by judges, or that no one amongst them ever stood against its use. Indeed, the picture could not be complete if it were to exclude what has been perhaps the most significant challenge from the judiciary to the substitute prison system to date. In July 1961 the Yokohama District Court rejected both an initial request and an appeal from the prosecution that a teenage suspect should continue to be held in a police cell, and instead ordered their transfer to the court's juvenile detention centre. The prosecution had made its pleas on the grounds that substitute prison detention was necessary for completing the investigation of the case. In justifying its decision, the Court explained that it could not see a reason why detention in the juvenile detention centre attached to the local court should obstruct this.[27] Although not explicitly following through with the conclusion that the juvenile suspect would be at risk of being placed under duress in police custody, the Court also highlighted that another factor in its judgment was that the juvenile suspect disputed the allegations they faced. This episode remains the most often cited

[25] Record of the UNHRC meetings on the third periodic report of Japan on the implementation of the ICCPR, 1993, Article 645.

[26] '*Kokusai jinken (jiyūken) kiyaku ni motozuki teishutsu sareta dai yon-kai Nihon seifu hōkoku-sho ni tai suru Nichibenren hōkoku-sho*' (JFBA's Report on the Japanese Government's 4th Report on the Implementation of the ICCPR). Document 4, Chapter 3 '*Criminal Procedure*, I: *The "Substitute Prison" Problem*', p. 5, retrieved from <www.npa.go.jp/syokai/ryuchi2/nichibenren/04.pdf>.

[27] The specific content of this ruling is available at <www.shinginza.com/db/01087.html> and <www.shinginza.com/db/01113.html>.

today in discussions within Japan of judicial defiance towards investigation.

Perhaps the reason why there have been very few similar examples of such cases over the succeeding fifty years is that in the rare instances where individual judges have tried to make a stand against substitute prison, they have received little support in doing so. Judge Kazushi Teranishi, well known for speaking out on criminal justice issues, has claimed the experiment of challenging the overuse of substitute prison in Yokohama District Court did not last, and others were reluctant to emulate it, due to the legal officials involved having been either laid off or exiled to remote parts of Japan. Whilst there is something of the conspiracy theory in this explanation, and anyway the case is now over fifty years old, what is not in contention is that when judges have rejected police detention requests, their rulings have been at risk of being overturned on appeal to one of their peers. Reporting on his personal experiences in particular, Teranishi notes that of the fourteen occasions on which he placed a suspect in a detention centre instead of substitute prison, twelve were later overturned upon appeal by the prosecution, pleading that 'sending the suspect to a detention centre constitutes a prejudice against the investigation'.[28] In Teranishi's eyes, this has limited the role of judges in the substitute prison conversation, and undoubtedly contributed to its embedding.

Limited impact of domestic and transnational advocacy

Beyond the JFBA, other domestic advocacy groups also campaigned on behalf of suspects' rights, and against substitute prison in particular. Yet these smaller organizations struggled to even have their voices heard. Indeed, unlike the large, professionally managed, resource-rich, and well-connected lawyers' organization, non-governmental organizations (NGOs) such as the Centre for Prisoners' Rights (CPR), Relief Contact Centre (RCC), and Civil Centre were Lilliputians within the policy-making arena, with scant resources for lobbying politicians, drafting alternative Prison Law amendment legislation, or publicizing their cause. The fact that it is not uncommon for civil society groups within Japan to be on a somewhat small scale does not, it has been observed, necessarily mean that they will be ineffective (Pekkanen 2006).

[28] Judge Kazushi Teranishi, *Asahi Shimbun*, 29 May 1995, p. 4.

However, the lack of public sympathy in this case meant that there was never a point at which they were able to bring to bear significant pressure on politicians in order to effectuate change. This limited access to policy-making on the part of domestic NGOs is illustrated by the following episode that took place at the UN's 2008 examination of Japan's report on the implementation of the ICCPR following Ambassador Akimoto Yoshitaka's rather lighthearted remark that 'the extensive participation of NGOs [in the meeting was] testimony to the dialogue that the authorities [were] engaging in with them', a CPR activist expostulated:

> Actually, the reason why so many of us feel compelled to make the trip to Geneva is precisely the opposite . . . At home, the bureaucrats don't even consider us worthy enough to talk to.[29]

The latter point also exemplifies how the indigenous suspects' rights groups, including the JFBA, sought to increase their leverage by establishing partnerships with international human rights organizations, such as the United Nations Human Rights Committee (UNHRC), the Council of Europe (COE), the International Bar Association (IBA), and Human Rights Watch (HRW). Together they did form something of a transnational substitute prison abolition advocacy network, but, similarly to the domestic efforts, they failed in their attempts to shame the Japanese government into realizing their main objective. Perhaps the main benefit for the groups in question was, rather, communication on the matter—domestic NGOs providing additional information about police detention conditions and case details, and their international partners providing support in the condemnation of the substitute prison system and novel suggestions for how they could influence policy-making.

A Bird's-eye View: Entrenchment through Positive Feedback

It is now pertinent to bring the matter to a conclusion regarding the question of why Japan has the system of remand detention that it currently does. To this end, it is useful to start by taking a step back to note that the American occupiers' oversight regarding doing away with the substitute prison article was pivotal in

[29] Discussion with Emi Akiyama, Geneva, October 2008.

enabling prolonged police detention of suspects to continue during the post-war period. However, as the evidence presented previously has illuminated, this in itself did not predetermine that the system would evolve in the way that it subsequently did. Rather, the NPA actively sought to extend the application of police detention for remand prisoners as a surrogate for its pre-war means for maintaining public peace and order. Indeed, this duty was not merely a burden carried by the police simply because of some historical legal obligation, but one it cultivated through the development of its detention facilities, as well as through corresponding regulation to cater for it. This direction of travel was not only beneficial to the NPA, however, but also, albeit less obviously, to the other governmental actor for whom suspect detention was a concern, namely the MOJ. With these two departments more than content with the substitute prison arrangement, the police cells were constructed for it to become the norm in practice.

In turn, this great divergence between the detention facilities in existence and those that would be needed to do without substitute prison has deeply permeated, and arguably prejudiced, the discourses on the future of substitute prison. Indeed, even by the first time the substitute prison article was seriously debated, during the Prison Law reforms, the logistical challenges of change were a central concern. With the enormous resource shift estimated by the MOJ in order to abolish substitute prison coming alongside the risk of invoking large-scale displeasure amongst an otherwise uninterested electorate, ruling politicians in particular had no incentive to engage in philosophical debate about the merits of retaining the system. Within the ranks of the lawyers, too, although it was at some point argued that there were more cost-effective strategies for substitute prison abolition than those outlined by the MOJ, the ever greater convenience of police cells meant that it would become common for the view to be expressed that it was more realistic and even preferable to use and improve, rather than fight against, substitute prison. Even those wanting to take a hard line in opposition to the system harboured an increasing sense that campaigning for this end was swimming against the tide, with many viewing the system as a pragmatic inevitability—a position that reflected the attitudes amongst judges, who generally saw no problem with sending suspects back to police cells after their first visit to court.

As the proportion of remand prisoners held by the NPA has continued to increase to the present day, it is safe to suppose that this economic issue's importance to the substitute prison debate can only have been exacerbated. Those with a principled objection to the system, including the small collection of civil society groups fighting on this front, now face an even greater hurdle to abolish the substitute prison article than would have been the case in 1908, when it was put into the Prison Law; in 1954, when the American reformers left; or in the late 1970s, when discussions on it began in earnest. For some observers, the very fact that it is now common for the Japanese government to use a monetary barrier to change as part of its defence of substitute prison[30] demonstrates that at least some members of the establishment understand the moral objections to it and ultimately see the abolition of the system as a desirable step, but consider that the scale of the task ties their hands on taking action in this direction.

So it is that one sees there was positive feedback between the NPA's development of facilities for holding suspects and the evolution of the substitute prison debate in policy-making circles. The more the police's detention capacity grew, the more difficult it became for anyone to envisage pushing the NPA and MOJ away from their happy equilibrium. That there was such limited opposition to the substitute prison expansion was crucial to this process taking off, but once it did, the objections only dissipated further. In the end, the practice of placing suspects in police cells rather than MOJ facilities embedded itself within the criminal justice system to the point that it became the norm, and reversing it came to be viewed as completely unfeasible by almost all interested parties.

[30] A recent example can be found in the Comments by the Government of Japan on the Concluding Observations of the HRC (CCPR/C/JPN/CO/5), December 2008, retrieved from <www.mofa.go.jp/policy/human/cove_comment0912.pdf>.

6

Towards the Future

Lay Judges and the End of the Status Quo

Nothing is ever settled until it is settled right.

Various attributions

The wheels of justice grind slowly, but they grind exceedingly fine.

Sextus Empiricus [modern adaptation]

In May 2009, the Japanese government introduced a system of lay participation for criminal trials, which some observers have speculated could trigger further changes across the justice system. In the context of this study in particular, it is natural to consider what implications the reformed court proceedings could have for police detention. Especially amongst the lawyers and judges of Japan, the hypothesis has been put forward that, despite substitute prison having proven impossible to abolish by persuading the investigation directly or through political manoeuvres, such an outcome could still transpire as an unplanned consequence of the lay judge system. This being the case, rather than leaving the police detention story at the Prison Law amendment, this book will conclude by examining whether the evidence that has so far become available lends any credence to the view that substitute prison might have had its day.

Before setting out and scrutinizing the arguments concerning the impact of the introduction of lay judges on substitute prison, let us start this section by briefly outlining the new trial system. The thrust for the overhaul came when a Judicial Reform Council (*Shihō seido kaikaku shingikai*, hereafter JRC) (1999–2001), which had been set up with a wide remit for deliberating both civil and criminal justice process issues, proposed a greater degree of citizen participation in a bid to 'establish a much firmer popular base for the justice system'. In particular, the Council advised that, similarly to European countries, such as France, Germany, and

Italy, a hybrid judge–jury system should be adopted. This recommendation was placed into law with the 2004 Lay Assessor Act, which ordained that in complicated cases, where facts are disputed by the defendant, there are six lay judges handpicked by the courts from a list of 100 names, assisted by three professional judges; and in simpler cases, where there is no substantial controversy, there are only four lay judges and one judge. Currently, the role of the jury is restricted to serious crimes, such as, for example, rape and homicide, with the average annual number of jury trials falling somewhere between 2,000 and 3,000, some of which involve the death penalty. Other key features include the rule that lay judges can independently decide cases with a majority not-guilty verdict. However, if the lay judges reach a majority guilty decision, to proceed to a conviction the support of at least one professional judge is required. Finally, and further reminiscent of continental European-style justice, the system allows for direct questioning of the defendant during the course of the trial by lay judges and citizen participation in sentencing.

Why, then, is it thought that this shift to citizen participation in the deliverance of justice is relevant to substitute prison? Through what mechanism could lay involvement in criminal affairs undermine Japan's police detention arrangements? For some jurists, the heart of the matter is that lay judges will approach contested confessions differently than a professional judge does, being more cautious about accepting their voluntariness at face value. Former criminal judge Takeyoshi Ito is one of those who have spelled out the specific logic behind this thinking. According to him,

> [u]nder the old system, whenever it happened that a defendant withdrew in court their earlier confession on the grounds that the interrogator forced them to sign it, so that an unresolvable dispute emerged between the two sides over whether this was the case or not, judges tended to give their trust to the investigation, upholding the voluntariness of the confession and rendering it legitimate evidence. They sometimes did so rationalizing that even if a little harshness was employed during the interrogation, it was most likely not to the extent that it would compel the defendant to falsely confess. Of course, it should be noted that it was not a rare occurrence that, having been thus affirmed as permissible, such confessions would later, [when the judges come to inspect their cohesion more closely,] be rendered 'untrustworthy', with this taking the trial to an acquittal. This should not distract, however, from the fact that confessions were almost never screened for voluntariness, which is a premise

that must be fulfilled for them to be admitted as evidence for consideration in court.

In contrast to professional judges, the lay judges of the new system will lack the experience of legally trained professionals regarding the investigation process [and its constraints and pressures]. As a result, if the explanation of the investigator is unconvincing, it will be regarded as having a reasonable doubt, and the lay judges will tilt towards a rejection of the voluntariness of the confession [even before examining how consistently it fits the remaining evidence].[1]

Some observers disagree, alternatively contending that lay judges will be dominated by the authoritative professionals who will continue as they did under the old system. However, Ito does not believe the fact that the system is a hybrid one, rather than a pure jury, has any bearing on his argument. Instead, he expects professional judges to be reluctant to push the case of the prosecution that a confession is credible onto lay judges when there is not strong evidence to do so. To quote him again,

[under the new system,] professional judges will probably be more hesitant to support the testimony of the investigator than hitherto when they are not certain of its veracity, because they would not be able to convince the lay judges of this. They would surely be embarrassed to simply assert in front of the lay judges the view that an investigator's testimony, which was conducted secretively and for which there is not even a recording, is trustworthy![2]

Furthermore, such greater focus on the legitimacy of confessions is seen by some as part of a wider expected change, under which prosecutors will come under increased pressure to demonstrate the reliability of their entire cases during trial. As Judge C explains:

In the old days, the prosecutor was of a similar standing to the judge, and would generally be allowed to lead proceedings. There was a great dependence on the confession dossier [prepared by the prosecution], with the role of judges being to check that this established the defendant's guilt, rather than to form judgments based on what was put before them in the courtroom. This is still the case today, but through introducing this new

1 Passage adapted for brevity from '*Jihaku henchō kara no dakkyaku (Saiban'in seido ni kitai suru)*' (Growing out of the Overemphasis on Confessions (Putting hopes on the lay judge system)), Japan's Judges Network, August 2009. Retrieved on 17 December 2009 from <www.j-j-n.com/keijisaiban/saibanin_hossoku/090801/jihakuhencho.html>.

2 Ibid.

system, the prosecutor will not have it so easy, since the lay men and professional judges will much more stringently test the evidence in court to form their own opinion about the case.[3]

To summarize, with the introduction of lay judges, the material brought to court by the prosecution, and particularly any confession, will be placed under closer scrutiny than hitherto before it is admitted as a piece of evidence.

However good the intuition of these judges regarding the workings of the Japanese courts under the lay judge system, a more objective reason that has been put forward for how the new trial format will affect the role of confession in Japanese courts relates to the time constraints that will necessarily come with citizen involvement. Indeed, to put the case more explicitly, it is simply impractical to ask lay judges to devote months, or even years, to court duty so as to determine whether a confession was obtained under duress or not by minutely comparing it with other statements or evidence, as professional judges used to do. This is described in detail by veteran Judge A:

> Probably every judge has, at least once in their career, encountered a barren controversy concerning the reliability of a confession. Dealing with such cases hitherto involved the judge's thorough examination of the mountainous file of deposition statements compiled by the prosecution, until he managed to see the truth through the contradicting claims. In this way the trial would sometimes protract for years, which was harsh on the defendant, especially if they were innocent, as they meanwhile lost their job, and their whole way of life was ruined. Even knowing this, judges did not try to cut corners to resolve the case quicker, as they considered it their duty to take their time and make sure that the truth was reached. However, under the new system it will no longer be possible for years to be spent on trying to spot gaps and contradictions. Lay judges are ordinary citizens with regular jobs, and cannot be asked to take more than a few days off for jury service. So, any evidence [presented at the trial] that leaves doubt as to its legitimacy will be simply discarded from consideration. If it is unclear whether wrongdoing has occurred in eliciting a confession, there will not be time to dig into the documents to find out.[4]

Or, to state it in yet another way, there will not be time for lay judges to pursue the 'precision justice' (*seimitsu shihō*) that Japanese courts have done historically, whereby exhaustive details

[3] Interview with Judge C and Judge D, 5 November 2009.

[4] Interview, 13 December 2007 (an extended version of this judge's discussion appears in Croydon 2008: 101).

of the case are sought over a long period of time so that the 'whole truth', including the motivation for and circumstances surrounding the crime, is revealed and can be taken into account when sentencing.[5] In fact, this aspect of speeding up trials was one of the additional benefits envisioned by the JRC when originally putting forward its jury proposal.

If confessions are to no longer play the same role in Japanese courts, or so the argument goes, then, of course, prosecutors cannot continue with their current strategies. At the very least, it will not be possible for the prosecution to keep putting at the centre of the evidence they present to the court confessions whose reliability is not verifiable, else they risk being repeatedly confronted by lawyers with an argument of the following kind:

> Before the commencement of the investigation, I asked for a thorough recording of the interrogation to be made, which was easily possible. Despite this, [the authorities] did not do so. The policeman just now testified that they have not conducted a coercive interrogation. Members of the jury, who could possibly trust such a claim? If they wanted their conduct to be beyond question, they should have gladly made recordings. Instead they did not, and so I put to you, how could it be said that the policeman's testimony is the truth?[6]

Such challenges, it is argued, could only lead to more acquittals, and a loss of public trust in the investigation. In the words of Judge B,

> [w]ith the lay judge system and transparency being introduced, if the prosecutors continue in the same vein as they have done so far, then the number of innocent verdicts will probably increase. This will lead to the prosecutors looking bad, as if they are not doing a good enough job, by indicting people who have ultimately been established as innocent in court. Would the prosecutors be able to endure the public criticism? This is an important question. There will also be cases whereby the public will think the defendant committed the crime but the investigation's handling of the case was inept—they did not gather enough evidence, and presented a weak case in court, so this is why the culprit got away with it.[7]

[5] Personal communication with Judge A.

[6] A leading criminal attorney from Ōsaka. See '*Jihaku henchō kara no dakkyaku (Saiban-in seido ni kitai suru)*' (Growing out of the Overemphasis on Confessions (Putting hopes on the lay judge system)), Japan's Judges Network, August 2009. Retrieved on 17 December 2009 from <www.j-j-n.com/keijisaiban/saibanin_hossoku/090801/jihakuhencho.html>.

[7] Interview, 7 January 2008.

As a result, it is a widely held view that investigators will be forced to modify their current strategies in order to maintain their high conviction rates in court.

The most common view amongst jurists is that prosecutors will respond to these changing demands by turning to other types of evidence. Of course, investigators could directly counter the attacks of lawyers regarding the truthfulness of confessions by submitting to full electronic recording of interrogations. Jurists point out, however, that such a policy would almost certainly lead to fewer confessions being secured, as not only would investigators be forced to reduce the intensity of their interrogations but also, due to the Japanese 'culture of shame', suspects would be more reluctant to divulge details about the case to officers for fear that these would eventually appear in public (for an extended version of the latter point in particular, see the discussion with a senior judge in Croydon 2008). This might mean in turn that investigators will be forced to cherry-pick to an even greater degree which cases to take to trial, or even indict—and at the moment they already drop 40 per cent of cases at this stage.[8] Because of this potential for a fall in the clearance rate, which is something that the prosecution will certainly seek to avoid if possible, jurists disagree that developments will take this course in practice. Rather, the prevailing opinion is that there could be something of a fundamental shift for Japanese justice towards what has often been described domestically as the inferior 'rough justice' (*ōaji na shihō*) of some Western countries—most notably the USA. In particular, it is considered that, as a result of the new courtroom incentives, investigators will inevitably place a greater reliance on other forms of evidence—particularly of a physical nature, such as finger- and footprints, DNA, and hair samples. This is the only way for them to reduce the number of cases in which their case depends on a confession which a defendant might dispute in court.

To cut to the chase, as the playing field in the courtroom and the demands on the prosecution evolve, so, it has been speculated, will the nature of substitute prison—possibly to the point where it becomes obsolete. That is to say, although some aspects of the substitute prison system—such as the ready-to-access locations of police cells—will continue to hold attractiveness for investigators and lawyers alike, the importance of it as an investigative tool can

[8] This opinion was expressed by Judge B. Interview, 7 January 2008.

only decline if its end-product—the confession—becomes less valuable at later stages of the criminal justice process. Of course, nobody would expect the NPA to simply give up the substitute prison, whatever the restrictions placed on their interrogations or the alternative means for investigating crimes investigators manage to accrue as a result of the introduction of lay judges. Moreover, there are those maintaining that even were full electronic recording to be introduced, the system would retain fundamental flaws, due to the psychological pressures induced on a suspect by their being detained by their investigators (e.g. Nakagawa 2005). Nonetheless, it is thought that the new courtroom dynamics could still bring about a shift from the substitute prison system representing a crucial weapon in the police's arsenal to merely an arrangement of investigative convenience. Especially for those who have been concerned about the potential for human rights abuses in police custody in Japan, this would be an important change. As the JFBA spokesman Yūichi Kaido explains:

> The Prison Law is now amended, but next we will have to revise the Code of Criminal Procedure. If it is made possible [through the Code's revision], for example, that the defense counsel be present at interrogations which are [moreover] recorded, it will become less likely for the human rights violations now seen within the substitute prison system to occur. If this happens, the necessity of substitute prison for the police would disappear. Today's substitute prison is an instrument for obtaining confessions. The JFBA is of the opinion that although it is currently difficult to pursue the abolition of substitute prison system as a whole, it might be possible instead to 'euthanize' it by weakening its function of confession extortion.[9]

Albeit for a different reason, pointing again to the time pressures of running a trial with lay judges, Judge A agrees that the importance of substitute prison to investigators is destined to decline:

> There is no question that substitute prison will eventually lose its meaning in practice. Indeed, with the new system, even if the prosecutor comes to court declaring 'here, all the answers you need are in this dossier of depositions', the court will simply respond 'thank you very much, but we do not care to wade through such a mass of papers'. In the end, prosecutors will come to realize that there is no point in their spending hours upon end with the suspect behind closed doors, painstakingly trying to

[9] Yūichi Kaido, '*Daiyō kangoku no mondai to wa nani ka*' (What is the Substitute Prison Problem?) Livedoor News, 1 May 2006, <news.livedoor.com/article/detail/1904530/>.

build a relationship of trust in order to obtain a confession. So, even though it will take a long time to change the system, change is already on the way.[10]

In May 2014, five years will have passed since lay judges began to participate in sentencing, meaning that it is now possible to start assessing the new arrangement's impact in practice. Indeed, although there was initially some scepticism both from the public and from legal professionals about the specific format of citizen participation, the signs are that it is destined to remain part of the Japanese criminal justice system for the foreseeable future (Croydon 2011), and so it is important to consider its broader implications, including for suspect detention. In particular, can we gauge from the data that has become available whether the future fate of substitute prison is the demise foreseen by these jurists? To what extent are the conjectures in the above chain of logic supported by the evidence to date? Are there signs of confessions becoming less important? Undoubtedly, much more information than that generated within this first five-year period will be necessary to be able to conclude with confidence that the lay judge system has set things on the anticipated course, especially since the ultimate result is expected to manifest itself gradually. However, even at the present stage, it might not be a completely futile exercise to try to catch early precursors of change. The following is an attempt at this.

Firstly, there are signs to suggest that attitudes towards prolonged suspect detention within the judiciary might be starting to shift. In particular, data released by the Ministry of Justice (MOJ) demonstrates that over the past decade there has been a six-fold relative increase in courts rejecting prosecutors' suspect detention requests. Concretely, prior to 2002, the rate of rejection was consistently below 0.2 per cent, but ever since then it has been steadily rising, to the 2011 rate of 1.19 per cent—with the absolute numbers of rejections being 138 and 1,326 for the two years, respectively (see Figure 6.1). Amongst observers, two interrelated contributory factors for this phenomenon have been put forward. One of these concerns is the 2004 introduction of a public defender system that, at the behest of the JRC, increased pre-indictment access to lawyers (for background on this, see Goodman 2008). Specifically, it has been argued that the activities

[10] Interview, 7 January 2008.

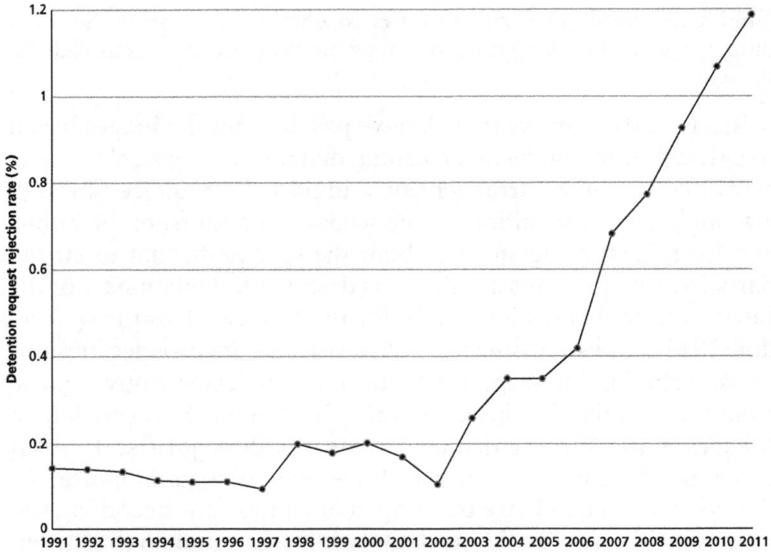

Figure 6.1. Detention request rejection rate

Sources: MOJ, White Paper on Crime, various years.

of these legal professionals on behalf of their clients have secured at least some of the growth in the number of detention request rejections. The other factor identified as important in creating this outcome is a change in the consciousness of judges in anticipation of the new lay judge system. (Given that the increase in rejections started a couple of years earlier than the 2004 introduction of the public defender system, this second factor could be said to fit better with the outcome chronologically.) Reportedly, the opinion was then growing amongst judges that the accompanying new rules of pre-trial disclosure of court evidence demanded greater levels of communication between suspects and lawyers for trials to continue to run smoothly.[11] Judges would, as a result, more often than hitherto deny the prosecution's detention request.

Secondly, with regard to case outcomes, the jury is still out as to whether there has been any significant change. By December 2010, there had been a slight increase in the acquittal rate from 0.1 per cent to 0.3 per cent,[12] which does not stand out as a radical

[11] Personal communication with a senior judge, 18 November 2013. For a more detailed discussion of the revised criminal justice procedure, see Itō 2013.

[12] Akihiro Ishihara and Takayuki Tsukiji, 'Kagoshima Ruling Raises Bar', *Daily Yomiuri*, 12 December 2010, p. 2.

departure from the prosecutorial dominance of the old system. Whether prosecutors are having to work harder to gain these victories is less clear, particularly in terms of having the confessions they present being accepted in court, for there have only been a small number of cases tried by lay judges in which defendants have retracted the statements they made during interrogations in police custody. Indeed, the sixty-one cases in which there was a disputed confession in a lay judge trial represented only 3.7 per cent of the total number of cases, up only marginally from the 3.4 per cent that was the disputed confession rate in similar types of cases prior to the introduction of lay judges.[13] Moreover, even in the rare cases where a disputed confession has resulted in an acquittal, observers have hotly disputed whether the presence of lay judges was crucial to the decision.

Such data-related limitations notwithstanding, there are signs that developments are already progressing in the direction predicted. Perhaps the strongest of these is the evolution in electronic recording practices, which indicates that those working within the criminal justice process recognize that the lay judge system has brought a change to the way prosecutors' evidence is approached in court.

When the Lay Assessor Act was enacted in 2004, the JFBA launched a drive for recording, which was met with strong resistance from investigators. In particular, the lawyers started to distribute notebooks for suspects to self-record the interrogations they were going through, so that possible procedural problems could be exposed.[14] Investigators were adamant that going further in this regard, and especially going as far as full obligatory electronic recording of interrogations, would not only obstruct investigations, but also be detrimental to public safety. They were concerned that, were this to happen, it would become more difficult for those conducting interrogations to establish a rapport with their suspects, members of organized crime gangs would be more reluctant to divulge information for fear of revenge from their

[13] See '*Torishirabe ni kan suru kokunai chōsa hōkokusho*' (An Internal Investigation Report on Suspect Questioning), MOJ, August 2011, pp. 10–12, retrieved from <www.moj.go.jp/content/000077995.pdf>.

[14] In fact, the Ōsaka Bar Association began the distribution of such books even earlier—in October 2003. As for the bar's most recent and refined version of this 'suspect notebook' sample, see <www.nichibenren.or.jp/library/ja/legal_aid/on-duty_lawyer/data/higishanote_000.pdf>.

peers, and privacy issues with regard to third parties could affect the investigation of sexual crimes—see, for example, the work of former high-ranking NPA official Hiroto Yoshimura (2009: 210–13). Such objections have not significantly reduced in the intervening years. For instance, a recent survey conducted amongst prosecutors shows that only 5.6 per cent are in favour of full recording, and 57.9 per cent oppose it entirely.[15]

Nevertheless, four years later, the Public Prosecutor's Office started its own trials of recording, a move that could be interpreted as acknowledgement that it could not continue to resist such measures under the new circumstances. In particular, prosecutors themselves do not dispute that increased transparency of interrogations will make it easier to prove voluntariness and trustworthiness of confessions in court[16]—and this is not without good reason, as in each of the twenty-five cases whereby a lay judge panel has studied a DVD recording of a disputed confession, the prosecution has been the side vindicated.[17] Furthermore, although the recording introduced has been criticized in some quarters for only being partial,[18] it is clear that the Public Prosecutor's Office would not have even taken this step if it did not think that greater transparency was unavoidable for its continued success there.[19] Within police circles too, it seems that recording is increasingly being seen as something that cannot be avoided indefinitely. To see this, one has only to cast a cursory glance at the National Police Academy's journal, *Journal of Police Science* (*Keisatsu-gaku ronshū*), in which efforts are being made to understand, through analysis of the

[15] See '*Torishirabe ni kan suru kokunai chōsa hōkokusho* (An Internal Investigation Report on Suspect Questioning)', MOJ, August 2011, Additional Section 3, p. 20, retrieved from <www.moj.go.jp/content/000077995.pdf>. See also the discussion in 'Report on Interrogation Recording', *Japan Times*, 23 August 2011. <www.japantimes.co.jp/opinion/2011/08/23/editorials/report-on-interrogation-recording/#.UjNUDz_DvD9>.

[16] Ibid.

[17] Ibid.

[18] See 'Comment Regarding the National Police Agency's Announcement of its "Assessment of the Trial Implementation of Audio/Video Recording of Interrogations"', JFBA, 6 December 2012, retrieved from <www.nichibenren.or.jp/activity/document/statement/year/2012/121206.html>.

[19] Former prosecutor Tsuneyasu Ozaki also expressed this view. Interview, 8 August 2007.

experiences in other countries, how recording could potentially be introduced in a way that would be beneficial to its officers.[20]

The debate surrounding electronic recording has also progressed as predicted, with investigators repeatedly linking this issue to a wider reform of their powers and having some success in shifting the argument in this direction. Following an electoral promise to introduce recording, in 2009 the Justice Minister Keiko Chiba, of the Democratic Party of Japan (DPJ), commanded that a panel be created within the MOJ to study how agreement on the matter could be reached between lawyers and prosecutors. The report produced the following year showed something of an impasse, doing little more than simply outlining the two sides' arguments.[21] What was clear from the discussions, however, was that investigators would continue to object to the full recording being demanded by the ruling party unless this was accompanied by their being granted alternative means with which to sustain arrest rates, explicitly naming plea bargaining, sting operations, and increased wire-tapping amongst their desires.[22]

That this is now the battleground has been frequently reconfirmed. For instance, in a 2013 report on reforming the criminal justice system, the MOJ Legislative Council's Special Committee (*Hōsei shingikai tokubetsu bukai*) made an explicit connection

[20] See for example, Shirakawa's analysis of how the British police, after originally opposing the Police and Criminal Evidence Act, which obliged officers to record their interrogations of suspects, eventually came to hold the view that these regulations would be to its own advantage, since more often than not it was helpful in vindicating staff in having done their job properly (Shirakawa 2007a, 2007b, 2007c). Similarly, Kanayama (2007a, 2007b) investigates how electronic recording has been utilized by the police in the USA.

[21] '*Higisha torishirabe no rokuon/rokuga no arikata ni tsuite: Kore made no kentō jōkyō to kongo no torikumi hōshin*' (On the issue of Recording and Videotaping Defendants' Interrogations: The Considerations to Date and the Direction from Now On). Retrieved on 27 September 2013 from <www.moj.go.jp/content/000049080.pdf>.

[22] 'Crime "Tools" Backed', *Japan Times*, 18 September 2009, retrieved from <www.japantimes.co.jp/news/2009/09/18/national/chiba-urges-death-penalty-debate/>. Similarly, a more recent survey indicated that 86.4 per cent of prosecutors felt that they required more investigative tools, such as increased powers of negotiation with suspects and witnesses, to obtain objective evidence and more favourable criminal justice legislation: see '*Torishirabe ni kan suru kokunai chōsa hōkokusho*' (An Internal Investigation Report on Suspect Questioning), MOJ, August 2011, Additional Section 3, pp. 22–3, retrieved from <www.moj.go.jp/content/000077995.pdf>.

between the issue of recording and alternative investigative powers, specifically pointing to its concrete plans to consider whether the so-called 'Wire-tapping Act' should be made less restrictive.[23] Similarly, recent recommendations of a Study Group for Enhancing Investigation Methods and Interrogation set up by the NPA led to the promotion by the police of three main goals, of which the first two concerned the conditions of the interrogation itself, including expanding recording for lay judge trials, and the last further interrogation methods. In particular, the NPA's 2012 White Paper stated on this latter point that there should be attempts made:

> [t]o break away from excessive dependence on interrogations and records of statements, and to respond accurately to crimes that are ever more advanced and complex due to developments in scientific techniques and other factors [for example, use of DNA profiling, security camera analysis, and digital forensics for devices such as laptops, phones, cameras, etc.], and to enable accurate proof through objective evidence, police are striving for the enhancement of investigation methods such as expansion of the DNA profile database and expansion of wire-tapping.[24]

The above strikingly demonstrates the understanding within the investigative authorities that they cannot rely so heavily on confession-based convictions in the future. However, it is also clear from such statements that, although they might be prepared to yield with regard to more widespread recording of interrogations, further travel in this direction will only take place if the reduction in the potency of this investigative technique is compensated for in some way.

These discussions are not likely to be resolved soon. Particularly, as Judge A explains, there is a certain reluctance in Japanese society to give the prosecution what they want to replace it with:

> The Japanese public is very opposed to many of the new investigative techniques being proposed by prosecutors. Plea bargaining in particular is seen in a very bad light of being 'justice by negotiation'. The question is

[23] This law's full title is '*Hanzai sōsa no tame no tsūshin bōju ni kan suru hōritsu*' (Act Concerning Correspondence Interception for the Purpose of Criminal Investigation). Currently, wire-tapping is only allowed in cases of organized crime. For a report on this, see 'Reform Panel Pulls Its Punches', *Japan Times*, 22 February 2013, retrieved from <www.japantimes.co.jp/opinion/2013/02/22/editorials/reform-panel-pulls-its-punches/#.UjW9uT_DvD8>.

[24] Interview with Judge A, 7 January 2008.

whether the investigation will manage to push through this public resistance, and how quickly. My impression is that it will take a very long time for the system to be transformed so that confessions become less important to the case of the prosecution, and this process will be painful.[25]

For some, such objections are deeply rooted in the character of the Japanese, who are seen as being keen for the defendant to express their remorse for their crime and a true apology, rather than doing a business-like deal to ensure their sentence is minimized (Croydon 2010). Whether this is the case or not, it is clear that the prosecution will not be given a free ride on this issue.

In conclusion, the game has definitely changed. The new lay judge system has led judges increasingly to question whether prolonged detention is appropriate, and has pushed Japanese investigators towards greater electronic recording of interrogations. The substitute prison system is thus destined for a fundamental transformation. Indeed, whether or not these developments completely kill substitute prison, one of the central criticisms of Japan's police custody arrangements has been the great control they give the investigation over suspects behind closed doors, but this might not be applicable for much longer.

As a final thought on this matter, it is perhaps pertinent to repeat the note of caution issued by a former MOJ Criminal Affairs Bureau Director even before the incorporation of lay judges into the criminal justice system that, were the substitute prison system to eventually meet its end, the debates about the balance between the human rights of suspects and the powers of the investigative bodies would inevitably remain:

We are happy for substitute prison to be abolished. If that is to be the case, though, a sweeping reform needs to be made to the Japanese criminal justice system, so as to introduce other means of investigation for us. The system needs to be thought of holistically: if certain tools for investigation are taken away from us, then other ones should be given. For, without the appropriate means, we could not possibly fulfill our obligations, and criminals would not face the justice they deserve.

In the end, it is naïve to compare criminal justice systems by focusing on different aspects—yes, we have the substitute prison and other countries do not, but equally they have other investigative tools that we do not. And each of these comes with its own problems . . .[26]

25 Ibid.

26 Interview, 9 November 2007.

7

Conclusion

> A flower falls, even though we love it; and a weed grows, even though we do not love it.
>
> Dōgen Zenji

> The quickest way of ending a war is to lose it.
>
> George Orwell

Recall from the Introduction that the starting point of this study of the prolonged police detention of suspects in Japan was the inextricable link between human rights and politics. Towards the corresponding end of obtaining a political explanation for this divergent policy, it has chronicled how the historical split in the jurisdiction over remand prisoners between the Ministry of Justice (MOJ) and the National Police Agency (NPA) has ultimately preconditioned the suspects' rights decision-making terrain in Japan today. To wit, it has highlighted how the human rights issue in question has been heavily influenced by a domestic institutional constraint. Having already presented a discussion of the future prospects of the substitute prison system, in what remains of the book, attention is devoted to some of the other questions raised at the outset. More specifically, what lessons can be drawn from these findings regarding the impact of culture on human rights discourse in Japan, how can Japan's experiences inform criminal justice policy-makers abroad, and what insight do they provide into how Japan's deadlock with the UN on substitute prison could be broken? Finally, it reflects upon how the events that have been described here, and their repercussions for Japan's prison system, inform the broader debates on human rights implementation, concluding that the latter both shapes and is shaped by the nature of the political discourse that surrounds it.

Whilst the retention of substitute prison can perfectly well be understood via this political interpretation as the logical outcome of the policy formation process, does this mean we should, or even can, disregard the explanatory value of cultural factors? After all, there are certainly 'Asian values' overtones to many of the arguments put forward by the NPA, and investigators are not shy about espousing cultural relativism arguments to support their position. In the words of one police official:

> A perfect system of criminal justice does not exist; every country has to compromise somewhere, and granted, our system is not flawless, but nor is that of any other jurisdiction. In the end, when it comes to a matter such as protecting the individual rights of criminal suspects, each country must simply make a choice as to where to draw the line. In contrast to the West, which places this concern above all else, Japan deems that promoting the right of the community to live in a safe environment is of utmost importance. In a trade-off such as this, there is no right answer, and every country is entitled to choose whichever solution suits it best, depending on their culture and criminal justice situation.[1]

The lack of public interest in the issue, too, might also reasonably be construed *ex post facto* as a general satisfaction with the suspect detention situation in a way that would be predicted by culturalists. Could it thus not be the case that the policy outcome was at least also partly the result of a preconditioning of individuals with some kind of East Asian worldview in which there is a preference for resolving a rights-conflict by prioritizing community rights at the expense of individual suspects' rights? It might be tempting to give a positive answer to this query, but doing so would be somewhat unsatisfactory. For a start, it simply overlooks the fact that there was throughout the decision-making process noticeable domestic opposition to the substitute prison policy. Perhaps more importantly, though, it fails to account for why the particular manifestation of social control that is so prominent within the Japanese criminal justice system is prolonged police detention.

To fill this gap, and provide a supplementary, criminal justice culture explanation for why Japan continues to differ in this particular way from the rest of the developed world, it is perhaps most useful to consider the issue from the standpoint of the investigators. Having been stripped of their pre-war powers, substitute prison proffered itself as a convenient alternative to them. Given the authorities' ability to maintain high crime clearance rates and

[1] Adapted from the comments made during interviews with NPA Official A and NPA Official B, 8 August 2007; Tsuneyasu Ozaki, 8 August 2007; and MOJ Official A, 9 November 2007.

the fact that this measure constituted one of their main investigative tools, it was natural that substitute prison was seen as being pivotal to their effectiveness. This is especially the case in view of the connection between police detention and the elicitation of confessions, which were often central to their victories in court. It is thus hardly surprising that the Japanese authorities did not go on to emulate forces elsewhere, which typically returned inferior criminal justice statistics, by placing greater emphasis on alternative investigative instruments, such as plea bargaining, sting operations, grant of immunity, and broadly applicable wire-tapping—each representing a whole new can of worms. Indeed, might it not be more than simply propaganda of the NPA that it was substitute prison that was crucial to its performance in managing crime? However, the crux of the matter is that it is precisely because the authorities have come to depend so heavily on the system that their fear of losing substitute prison is quite so acute. Had Japanese investigators had more access to different investigative techniques, and corresponding experience of securing convictions based on a wider array of evidence types, then they might well have been more prepared to bargain on substitute prison—a point that is supported by the ongoing developments discussed in Chapter 6. So, if one were to answer the question 'Why is it that prolonged police detention is the investigative tool that has become and remains so prominent?' from the perspective of those whose duty involves holding suspects in it, one might reasonably assert 'Because it is the only option that has been available to us for doing our job'.

Turning now to the lessons for other countries' policy-makers, whilst part of the debate in Japan currently revolves around the issue of what powers might be needed by the investigative authorities if police custody is constrained by electronic recording, on the flip side, a number of other countries are considering extending—or might have already extended—the powers of their police to detain individuals, at least in cases of terrorism. Of course, none of these jurisdictions has adopted, or is likely to adopt, an exact replica of the substitute prison system, but this does not mean there might not be lessons that they might heed from Japan. In the end, as was discussed at the outset, setting a detention limit boils down to drawing a line in the sand in an attempt to balance the competing concerns of public safety and individual freedom. And, on this issue, the substitute prison story offers a valuable message about how a policy can evolve, eventually normalizing a practice that might not have been the intention of its originators. Indeed, in Japan, the way substitute prison was used in the post-Occupation period was certainly not what the architects of the Prison Law envisaged. Moreover, the fact that police detention in Japan has developed slowly over time in the way that it has, has allowed a situation to emerge that no policy-maker would have introduced in one go.

Extrapolating from this, one might thus imagine that even if a measure for terrorists might initially be planned as an exception, investigative authorities are likely to find ways to use it more commonly, or apply it in much broader ways than policy-makers could have foreseen. And, once such a policy is established, then it would become easier for it to be extended, since doing so would no longer be seen as a fundamental philosophical shift. That this is not empty speculation is exemplified by what has happened in the UK over the past fifteen years, for example, where a terrorism policy that permitted seven days' suspect detention when it was introduced in 2000 was gradually stretched over three further iterations by the ruling Labour Party to forty-two days in 2008.[2] Moreover, the UK's Terrorism Act was famously, and controversially, applied to remove an eighty-two-year-old heckler from a Labour Party conference and detain him in custody, which David Cameron, the then leader of the opposition, declared was 'one of those moments which lays bare the full absurdity of the Orwellian [project of the government]'.[3]

So, in a nutshell, legislators cannot afford to think their job is done once their desired statutes are put into force. Attention still needs to be paid as to how their policies are being applied, and whether the motivations for introducing them in their original form are not forgotten. If they perceive developments are headed in a direction they are unhappy with, then it is essential that politicians and the public alike make suitable noises against these early enough for changes to be implemented. Indeed, however noble the original intention of their creation, policy-makers might not be able to fully control them in the future.

[2] From seven days in 2000, to fourteen days in 2003, to twenty-eight days in 2005, to forty-two days in 2008.

[3] 'Hero's Return for Labour Heckler', *BBC News*, 29 September 2005, retrieved from <news.bbc.co.uk/1/hi/uk_politics/4292342.stm>.

That Japanese decision-makers are in exactly this position of being locked into the substitute prison policy by the events of the past is also relevant to the stalemate in Japan–UN exchanges. Indeed, the two sides spend a not insignificant amount of time engaging in debate about the underlying principles of suspect detention that are being compromised under the substitute prison, but they are perhaps fighting the wrong battle, as it does not engage with the very real practical reasons for its persistence. To elucidate, it is clear from this study that many within Japan do understand the inherent problems of substitute prison that have been repeatedly pointed to by the UN. And, as substantiated in Chapter 5, this comment even extends to members of the political and bureaucratic establishment themselves. The focus for domestic actors, though, is the convenience of the extensive police detention network, and the corresponding financial barrier to shifting away from using this for remand prisoner detention. Whilst it might not be the UN's job to direct the way in which Japan should abolish the substitute prison system, the failure to acknowledge this practical consideration as a *bona fide* issue, or initiate a discussion about how it could be resolved, has certainly contributed to the lack of productive exchange on the matter.

As for the promised corollary of this study of substitute prison on the delay in the reform of the convicted prisoners' system, it should already be evident that there was a spillover effect from the issue of police custody onto that of prisons, and that substitute prison was a barrier for wider penal reform. Chapters 3 and 4 in particular made clear that over the decades preceding the eventual legislative change, the NPA exerted a marked influence on convicted prisoners' rights policy-formation. Considering that the police's role in detention was limited to arrestees, not even covered by the Prison Law under deliberation, it could even be said that its impact was somewhat disproportionate. Indeed, despite the treatment of convicted prisoners being irrelevant to the NPA, significant ramifications for the legislative reform concerning such inmates resulted from the stance adopted by the Agency with regard to its substitute jurisdiction over remand prisoners.

From a counterfactual point of view, it would be fair to conclude that, had it not been for the NPA's fight to preserve its turf, the revision of Japan's 1908 Prison Law would have happened as many as three decades before it actually did. If the MOJ had been left on its own to hammer out a solution with the Japan Federation of Bar Associations (JFBA) in the 1980s, its long-coveted desire to see the aging prison legislation updated would most likely have led the Ministry to compromise, even on the substitute prison issue. More specifically, with the MOJ already having made concessions on the content of its legislation and indicating its preparedness to commit in law to an increase in its detention centre capacity, thereby reducing the necessity of substitute prison, it seemed that a deal between the Ministry and the JFBA was possible. However, the NPA's shadowing of the MOJ's every amendment attempt with its own bill, which was an unacceptable move for those campaigning for substitute prison abolition, prompted such opposition from the JFBA and politicians that it was made impossible for the amendment process to reach a conclusion. Thus, it would not be misguided to expect that, if the MOJ's legislation had been seriously considered in the Diet alone at that early stage, its fate would have been different to that of the Two Detention Bills. Moreover, the changes that would eventually be made in the early 2000s, which were widely evaluated by those involved in the decision-making process—including some of the MOJ's harshest critics—as representing improvements in human rights protection, would have been made much earlier.

As it transpired, for the stalemate in the Prison Law reform resulting from the substitute prison issue to be broken, what was required was the near meltdown of the Japanese correctional administration. Only after the Nagoya Prison crisis, when the political leadership intervened so as to ensure legislative progress, was the NPA not involved in the decision-making process. It should be noted, however, that the police only agreed to temporarily withhold its participation once it had already been established that there would be a two-stage reform, with the part of the law relevant to substitute prison being excluded from the first stage. When the Agency returned to the table, its weight was immediately felt again—the exception of its absence simply underlining its importance in the proceedings otherwise.

If there is one message that is to be taken from this book regarding the understanding of variations in respect for human rights across different times and places, it is that models seeking to explain such will fail to be predictive if they do not account for sometimes complex domestic decision-making processes. To understand the importance of the latter, one need look no further than the emergence and embedding of Japan's current system of police custody, as well as the impact of the NPA's defence of this turf upon detention practices more broadly. Indeed, that the substitute prison article, which was originally introduced as a stop-gap measure, could ultimately have such a profound impact on the treatment of not only the suspects to which it applies directly, but also the legal rights protection of all Japanese detainees—convicted as well as unconvicted—starkly illustrates how political constraints within a state can be difficult to disentangle. For those hoping that the international human rights framework will eventually extend across the globe, with universal solutions being found to what are universal problems, it is perhaps disheartening to think that the obstacles to human rights implementation can include factors beyond the recalcitrance of monolithic states. There is of course the hope, though, that as political challenges, overcoming these is simply a matter of political will ...

Interviews and References

Interviews

Below are the details of the main interviews conducted in the course of the fieldwork for this research. At their own request, names of judges and bureaucrats have been withheld to preserve anonymity.

Japan

Interviews conducted in Tōkyō included

Akiyama, Emi. Coordinator, CPR, 24 August 2007.
Death-Row Inmate. Tōkyō Detention House, 16 August 2007.
Eda, Satsuki. President, House of Councillors, National Diet (also Diet Member, DPJ, and formerly a judge), 11 December 2009.
Hiraoka, Hideo. Shadow Justice Minister, DPJ, 31 August 2007.
Hori, Harumi. Board Member, UN Register of Damage (formerly a judge and MOJ lawyer), 23 August 2007.
Hosaka, Nobuto. Diet Member, SDP (also Secretary-General, Parliamentary League for the Abolition of the Death Penalty), 23 August 2007.
Judge A. Senior High Court Judge, 13 December 2007 and 7 January 2008, plus further correspondence.
Judge B. Senior High Court Judge (and later Supreme Court Judge), 13 December 2007.
Judge C. Senior District Court Judge, 5 November 2009.
Judge D. District Court Assistant Judge, 5 November 2009.
Judge E. District Family Court Judge, 16 December 2009.
Kaido, Yūichi. Lawyer, Tōkyō Partnership Legal Office (also Secretary-General, JFBA's Headquarters for the Realization of a Reform of the Criminal Detention System, and Secretary-General, CPR), 18 July 2007.
Kamei, Shizuka. Party leader, People's New Party (also Chair, Parliamentary League for the Abolition of the Death Penalty, and formerly Commissioner, Security Bureau, NPA), 19 October 2007.
Kamoshita, Moritaka. Visiting Lecturer, Chūō and Ryūkoku Universities (also president, Central Research Institute of the Correctional Association, and formerly civil servant, Correction Bureau, MOJ, and Warden, Fuchū Prison), 29 August, 25 October, and 5 November 2007.

Kikuta, Kōichi. Emeritus Professor of Criminal Law, Meiji University (also lawyer, CPR), 29 October 2007.
Koike, Shin'ichirō. Lawyer, Ver Law Office, and JFBA spokesman, 2 October 2007.
Kudō, Mika. JFBA researcher, 19 November 2009.
Kuwayama, Aya. Coordinator, Research Group (also contributor, CPR), 22 July and 3 December 2007.
MacKenzie, Tracy. Second Political Secretary, British Embassy in Japan, 24 October 2007.
Matsuura, Ryōsuke. Staff member, CPR, 11 November 2011.
Makino, Shigeru. Lawyer, Fairness Law Office, 12 December, 2007.
MOJ Official A. General Director, Criminal Affairs Bureau (formerly director, Correction Bureau), MOJ, 9 November 2007.
MOJ Official B. Correction Bureau, MOJ, 31 August 2007.
MOJ Official C. Correction Bureau, MOJ, 31 August 2007.
Moriyama, Mayumi. Diet member (formerly Justice Minister), LDP, 17 December 2007.
Nagai, Jin. Director, United Prisoners' Union, 23 July 2007.
Niitsu, Kumiko. Diet member's secretary, SDP, 7 November 2007.
Nishijima, Katsuhiko. Lawyer, Ochanomizu Joint Legal Office (also acting director, JFBA's Headquarters for the Realization of a Reform of the Criminal Detention System, 31 October 2007.
NPA Official A. Deputy Director, General Affairs Division, NPA, 8 August and 23 October 2007.
NPA Official B. Deputy Director, Criminal Planning Division within the Criminal Affairs Bureau of NPA, 8 August 2007.
Ozaki, Tsuneyasu. Lawyer, Nishimura and Asahi Legal Office (formerly a criminal prosecutor, Tōkyō District Court), 8 August 2007.
Prosecutor A. Supreme Public Prosecutors Office. 16 December 2010.
Sakata, Kōji. Nurse, Fuchū Prison, 18 October 2007.
Sawa, Yasuomi. Deputy Editor, Tōkyō Regional Office, Kyōdo News, 7 November 2007.
Sawada, Kenichi. Warden, Fuchū Prison, 5 November 2007.
Shinomiya, Satoru. Professor of Law, Kokugakuin University Law School, 17 December 2009.
Sugiura, Seiken. Diet member (formerly Justice Minister), LDP, 18 October 2007.
Tagusari, Maiko. Lawyer, Banchō Partnership Legal Office, 18 July and 8 November 2007.
Teranaka, Makoto. Director, Amnesty International, Japan Office, 28 August 2007.
Tōkyō Metropolitan Police Official A. Superintendent, General Affairs Department (also Proxy-Director, Police Detention Administration Division, Tōkyō Metropolitan Police), 23 October 2007.
Ugajin, Hisaichi. Coordinator, RCC, 16 August 2007.

Urushibara, Yoshio. Diet member, New Kōmeitō, 4 November 2009.
Watanabe, Isao. Visiting Professor, Research Institute for Social Safety Policy, Waseda University (also NPA), 11 January 2008.
Yamada, Kenta. Secretary-General, JCLU, 7 November 2007.

Discussions also held with individuals at the following events

Electronic Recording of Interrogations Seminar, JFBA Headquarters, Tōkyō, 19 July 2007.
Feedback session to JFBA of the lawyers attending the examination of the Japanese Government's report on the progress towards the implementation of the Convention Against Torture and Other Cruel, Inhuman or Degrading Treatment or Punishment, 30 July 2007.
Forum 90 Meeting, organized by Yoshihiro Yasuda, Maiko Tagusari, and Kōichi Kikuta (lawyers), 10 October 2007.
Towards the Abolition of the Death Penalty Seminar organized by Forum 90. Included talks given by Sakae Menda (exonerated death-row inmate) and Muneo Suzuki (Diet member, LDP, convicted for a bribery scandal), 13 October 2007.
Reception of Mizuho Fukushima, leader, SDP, 23 October 2007.
Death Penalty Abolition Camp organized by civil activists, led by Yoshihiro Yasuda (lawyer), 3–4 November 2007.
The Criminal Justice and the Criminals within the Society Discussion Session held to mark 70th birthday of Prof. Kōichi Kikuta, held at Meiji University. Discussions with Setsuo Miyazawa (professor, Waseda University), Kōichi Kikuta (lawyer), Kenji Miki (journalist), Yoshihiro Matsubara (professor, Waseda University), Hiroyuki Kusaba (lawyer), 4 November 2007.
Meeting of the Board of Directors of the JCLU. Discussions with directors—Masako Kamiya (lawyer), Jun'ichirō Hironaka (lawyer), Shun Hashiba (lawyer), and Masako Kamiya (professor, Gakushūin University), 7 November 2007.
Third General Meeting of JFBA's Headquarters for the Realization of a Reform of the Criminal Detention System, 13 November 2007.
Meeting of the lawyer representatives of the Boards of Visitors at the Headquarters of JFBA, Tōkyō, 13 November 2007.
Symposium on the Nabari Case featuring talks by journalists and lawyers, JFBA Headquarters, Tōkyō, 15 December 2007.
Meeting of lawyers demanding abolition of the death penalty at JFBA Headquarters in Tōkyō, 23 December 2007.
Convention on the Abolition of Death Penalty in East Asia, Aoyama Gakuin University, Tōkyō, 5–14 December 2009.
Why Innocent People 'Confess': The Reason Why Comprehensive Recording of Interrogations is Necessary Symposium, JFBA Headquarters, Tōkyō, 7 December 2011.

Enzai wa misshitsu de tsukurareru (Miscarriages of Justice are Created behind Closed Doors), Public Gathering, JFBA Headquarters, Tōkyō, 12 March 2012.

Europe

Activity undertaken in Geneva

94th Session of HRC, in which the fifth periodic report of the Japanese Government on the implementation of ICCPR was examined. Attended session and held discussions with Japanese lawyers, NGO members, UN staff.

Interviews conducted in Strasbourg

Dunn, Gerald. Directorate General of Human Rights and Legal Affairs, Human Rights Law and Policy Division, COE, 21 October 2008.

Henrich, Mario. Secretary of the Standing Committee, Committee on Rules of Procedure and Immunities, Secretariat of the Parliamentary Assembly, COE, 20 October 2008.

Layle, Kathleen. Secretary, Research and Documentation Unit, Secretariat of the Parliamentary Assembly, COE, 20 October 2008.

Schirmer, Günter. Secretary, Committee on Legal Affairs and Human Rights, Parliamentary Assembly, COE, 21 October 2008.

References

Akaike, Kazumasa, and Takashi Kusumoto. 1996. '*Kyōsei to iu na no moto ni*' (In the Name of Rehabilitation). In *Nyūmon·kangoku kaikaku (Introduction to Prison Reform)*, edited by *Keiji rippō kenkyū kai* (KRKK), 95–102. Tōkyō: *Nihon hyōronsha.*

Aldous, Christopher. 1997. *The Police in Occupation Japan: Control, Corruption and Resistance to Reform*. London: Routledge.

Aldous, Christopher, and Frank Leishman. 2000. 'Enigma Variations: Reassessing the Kōban'. *Nissan Occasional Paper Series* 31.

Ames, Walter L. 1981. *Police and Community in Japan*. Berkeley, CA: University of California Press.

Amyx, Jennifer. 2004. *Japan's Financial Crisis: Institutional Rigidity and Reluctant Change*. Princeton, NJ: Princeton University Press.

Araki, Nobuyoshi, ed. 2004. '*Chikan enzai jiken to keiji soshōhō no kaishaku/unyō*' (The Cases of Wrongful Groping Conviction and the Interpretation and Application of the Code for Criminal Procedure). In *Chikan enzai no bengo (The Defense of Those Wrongfully Convicted of*

Groping) GENJIN Keiji bengo shirīzu (2) (GENJIN Criminal Defense Series (No.2)), edited by Kenzō Akiyama. Tōkyō: *Gendai jinbunsha.*

Araki, Nobuyoshi. 2006. *'Keiji saiban jitsumu he no gimon'* (A Query about Criminal Justice Practice). In *Hanzai no takakuteki kentō (Multiple-Angle Approaches to Crime)*, edited by Morikazu Taguchi, Inoue Masahito, Ida Makoto, and Shiibashi Takayuki, 109–27. Tōkyō: *Yūhikaku gakujutsu sentā.*

Asahi Shimbun News Desk (*Asahi*). 1992. *Daiyō kangoku (Substitute Prison)*. Tōkyō: *Asahi shimbunsha.*

Avonius, Leena, and Damien Kingsbury, eds. 2008. *Human Rights in Asia: A Reassessment of the Asian Values Debate*. New York, NY: Palgrave Macmillan.

Barrows, Samuel J. 1901. Penal Codes of France, Germany, Belgium and Japan: Reports Prepared for the International Prison Commission. Washington: Government Printing Office: 56th Congress, 2nd Session, House of Representatives.

Bayley, David H. 1976. *Forces of Order: Police Behavior in Japan and the United States*. Berkeley and Los Angeles, CA: University of California Press.

Bell, Daniel. 2006. *Beyond Liberal Democracy: Political Thinking for an East Asian Context*. Princeton, NJ: Princeton University Press.

Botsman, Daniel. 2005. *Punishment and Power in the Making of Modern Japan*. Princeton: Princeton University Press.

Braithwaite, John. 1989. *Crime, Shame and Reintegration*. Cambridge: Cambridge University Press.

Calder, Kent E. 2008. *Embattled Garrisons: Comparative Base Politics and American Globalism*. Princeton, NJ: Princeton University Press.

Cavadino, Michael, and James Dignan. 2006. *Penal Systems: A Comparative Approach*. London: Sage Publications.

Chan-Tiberghien, Jennifer. 2004. *Gender and Human Rights Politics in Japan: Global Norms and Domestic Networks*. Stanford, CA: Stanford University Press.

Croydon, Silvia A. 2008. 'The Impact of Quasi-Jury Introduction on Transparency of Suspect Interrogations in Japan'. *University of Tōkyō Journal of Law and Politics* 8 (Spring): 92–106.

Croydon, Silvia A. 2010. 'Teinei Saiban to Shihō Torihiki' (Justice Implemented Carefully and Plea-bargaining). *Hōgaku Seminā* (April): 146–7.

Croydon, Silvia A. 2011. 'Returning a Verdict on the Jury: How the Japanese Have Reacted to the Introduction of a Lay Judge System'. *Asian Journal of Comparative Law* 7 (1): 1–17.

Croydon, Silvia A. 2014. 'The Death Penalty in a Changing Society: A Survey of Recent Developments in Japan'. *Contemporary Japan* 26 (1): 103–23.

Daikasumi kai, ed. 1970. *Naimushō shi (History of the Home Ministry)*. Vol. 2: *Chihō zaimu kyōkai*.

Daikasumi kai, ed. 1971. *Naimushō shi (History of the Home Ministry)*. Vol. 3: *Chihō zaimu kyōkai*.

Eiji, Takemae. 2002. *The Allied Occupation of Japan*. New York, NY: The Continuum International Publishing Group.

Ellis, Tom, Chris Lewis, Kōichi Hamai, and Tom Williamson. 2008. 'Japanese Community Policing Under the Microscope'. In *The Handbook of Knowledge-based Policing: Current Conceptions and Future Directions*, edited by Tom Williamson, 175–96. Chichester: Wiley-Blackwell.

Farrell, Graham, and Ken Clark. 2004. 'What Does the World Spend on Criminal Justice?' In *HEUNI, paper no. 20*. Helsinki: European United Nations Institute for Crime Prevention and Control.

Finch, Andrew J. 1999. 'The Japanese Police's Claim to Efficiency: A Critical View'. *Modern Asian Studies* 33 (2): 483–511.

First Tōkyō Bar Association (FTBA). 1985. *Ryūchi shisetsu hōan wo kangaeru (Consideration of the Bill for Police Custodial Facilities)*. Tōkyō: JFBA.

Foote, Daniel H. 1991. 'Confessions and the Right to Silence in Japan'. *Georgia Journal of International and Comparative Law* 21: 415–88.

Foote, Daniel H. 1992. 'The Benevolent Paternalism of Japanese Criminal Justice'. *California Law Review* 80 (2): 317–90.

Freeman, Michael. 2002. *Human Rights*. Cambridge: Polity Press.

Freeman, Michael. 2006. 'Putting Law in Its Place: An Interdisciplinary Evaluation of National Amnesty Laws'. In *The Legalisation of Human Rights: Multidisciplinary Approaches on Human Rights and Human Rights Law*, edited by Saladin Meckled-García and Başak Çalı, 49–64. New York, NY: Routledge.

Fukuda, Morio. 2006. *'Ryūchi shisetsu ni okeru hi-ryūchisha shogū ni kan suru hōseido no sara naru kaizen ni tsuite'* (On the Further Improvement of the Legal Framework for the Treatment in Police Facilities). *Keisatsu-gaku ronshū* 59 (9): 59–77.

Garland, David. 2001. *The Culture of Control, Crime and Social Order in Contemporary Society*. Chicago: University of Chicago Press.

Goodman, Carl F. 2008. *The Rule of Law in Japan: A Comparative Analysis (Second Revised Edition)*. The Netherlands: Kluwer Law International.

Goodman, Roger. 2000. *Children of the Japanese State: The Changing Role of Child Protection Institutions in Contemporary Japan*. Oxford: Oxford University Press.

Goold, Benjamin. 2004. 'Idealizing the Other? Western Images of the Japanese Criminal Justice System'. *Criminal Justice Ethics* (Winter/Spring): 14–24.

Gyōkei kaikaku kaigi (GKK). 2004. '*Gyōkei kaikaku suishin iinkai komon kaigi no kaisai ni tsuite*' (Regarding the Meetings of the Advisory Committee for Promotion of Penal Reform). *Keisei* 115 (9): 20–6.

Haley, John O. 1991. *Authority Without Power: Law and the Japanese Paradox*. New York, NY: Oxford University Press.

Haley, John O. 1998. *The Spirit of Japanese Law*. Athens, GA: University of Georgia Press.

Hattori, Takaaki. 1963. 'The Legal Profession in Japan: Its Historical Development and Present State'. In *Law in Japan*, edited by Arthur Taylor von Mehren, 111–52. Cambridge, MA: Harvard University Press.

Hirano, Ryūichi. 1963. *Hanzairon no sho-mondai (Problems in Laws on Treatment of Offenders)*. Tōkyō: *Yūhikaku*.

Hirano, Ryūichi. 1976. '*Kangoku hō kaisei ni tsuite*' (On the Prison Law Reform). *Hōritsu jihō* 48 (7): 8–11.

Hirano, Ryūichi. 1985. '*Gendai keiji soshō no shindan*' (Diagnosis of the Current Criminal Procedure). In *Collection of Articles Celebrating Professor Dandō Shigemitsu's 70th Anniversary*, edited by Shigemitsu Dandō, 407–23. Tōkyō: *Yūhikaku*.

Hirano, Ryūichi, Kantarō Nagano, and Isomi Suzuki. 1989. '*Kokusai jinken renmei hōkokusho* (Parker-Jaudel Hōkokusho)' (The Report by the International Federation of Human Rights–The Parker-Jaudel Report). *Hōritsu jihō* 92 (7): 92–102.

Hirano, Ryūichi, Toshiki Odanaga, and Testsuya Fujimoto. 1988. '*Keiji·ryūchi shisetsu no kentō – Shakai fukki gyōkei no jitsugen to daiyō kangoku no zengen wo mezashite*' (Analysis of Penal Institution and Police Station Detention Facilities—Aiming at the Realisation of a Social Rehabilitative Correctional Administration and the Attrition of Substitute Prison). *Hōritsu jihō* 60 (3): 6–22.

Hōritsu jihō, ed. 1978. *Tokushū: Kangoku hō kaisei mondai (Special Edition: The Issue of the Prison Law Revision)*. Vol. 50. Tōkyō.

Hōritsu jihō, ed. 1983. *Tokushū: Keiji/ryūchi shisetsu hōan no kentō (Special edition: A Consideration of the Penal and Police Facilities Bills)*. Vol. 55. Tōkyō.

Hōritsu jihō, ed. 1988. *Tokushū: Keiji/ryūchi shisetsu hōan no kenkyū (Special edition: A Study of the Penal and Police Facilities Bills)*. Vol. 3, 60. Tōkyō.

Hunter, Janet. 1984. 'Police'. In *Concise Dictionary of Modern Japanese History*. Berkeley, CA: University of California Press.

Igarashi, Futaba. 1989. '*Daiyō kangoku haishi to kōchisho fusoku mondai*' (The Abolition of the Substitute Prison and the Issue of the Shortage of Detention Houses). *Hōritsu jihō* 61 (7): 103–5.

Igarashi, Futaba. 1991. *Daiyō kangoku (Substitute Prison)*. Vol. 183, *Iwanami Booklet*. Tōkyō: *Iwanami Shoten*.

Inata, Toshihide. 1971. '*Daiyō kangoku seido ni tsuite*' (Regarding the Substitute Prison System). *Keisei* 82 (10): 9–12

Ishii, Ryōsuke. 1958. *Japanese Legislation in the Meiji Era*. Translated by William J. Chambliss. Tōkyō: *Kasai* Publishing and Printing Co.

Ishii, Ryōsuke. 1980. *A History of Political Institutions in Japan*. Tōkyō: University of Tōkyō Press.

Itō, Kazuko. 2013. 'Wrongful Convictions and Recent Criminal Justice Reform in Japan'. *University of Cincinnati Law Review* 80 (4): 1245–75.

Itoh, Hiroshi, and Lawrence W. Beer. 1978. *The Constitutional Case Law of Japan: Selected Supreme Court Decisions, 1961–70*. Seattle, WA: University of Washington Press.

Iwase, Jūmei. 2006. *'Keiji shisetsu oyobi jukeisha no shōgū nado ni an suru hōritsu no ichibu wo kaisei suru hōritsu no seiritsu igi'* (The Significance of the Establishment of the Act Partially Amending the Act on Penal Institutions and the Treatment of Sentenced Inmates). *Keisatsugaku ronshū* 59 (9): 46–59.

Jansen, Marius B. 2009. *The Making of Modern Japan*. Cambridge, MA: Harvard University Press.

Jansen, Marius, and John W. Hall. 1989. *The Cambridge History of Japan: The Nineteenth Century*. Cambridge: Cambridge University Press.

Japan Federation of Bar Associations (JFBA), ed. 1995. *Daiyō kangoku no haishi to keiji shihō kaikaku he no teigen—Kokusai hōsō kyōkai (IBA) no chōsa repōto to seminā kara (A Proposal for the Abolition of Substitute Prison and Reform of the Criminal Justice—From the IBA's Investigation Report and Its International Seminar)*. Tōkyō: *Akashi shoten*.

Japan Federation of Bar Associations (JFBA), ed. 2008. *Enzai shibushi jiken: Tsukurareru jihaku (The Miscarriage of Justice in the Shibushi Case: The Creation of Confessions)*. Edited by Aya Kuwayama. Vol. 55, *Genjin Booklets*. Tōkyō: *Gendai jinbunsha*.

Jaudel, Etienne, and Karen Parker. 1989. *Police Cell Detention in Japan: The Daiyō Kangoku System*. San Francisco, CA: Association of Humanitarian Lawyers.

Johnson, Chalmers. 1972. *Conspiracy at Matsukawa*. Berkeley and Los Angeles, CA: University of California Press.

Johnson, Chalmers. 1982. *MITI and the Japanese Miracle: The Growth of Industrial Policy 1925–1975*. Stanford, CA: Stanford University Press.

Johnson, David T. 2002. *The Japanese Way of Justice: Prosecuting Crime in Japan*. Oxford: Oxford University Press.

Johnson, David T. 2007. 'Crime and Punishment in Contemporary Japan'. *Crime and Justice* 36 (1): 371–423.

Kamoshita, Moritaka. 1971. *'Daiyō kangoku wo kangaeru'* (Considering Substitute Prison). *Keisei* 82 (5): 96–9.

Kamoshita, Moritaka. 2005. '*Gyōkei hō kaisei no keii to mondaiten – Sono hitotsu*' (The Course of the Correctional Administration Law and One of the Points at Issue). *Kyōsei kōza* 26: 19–38.

Kanayama, Taisuke. 2007a. '*Beikoku ni okeru torishirabe no rokuga·rokuon ni tsuite (Ge)*' (Regarding the Examination of Suspects with Video and Audio Recording in the USA (Part II of II)). *Keisatsu-gaku ronshū* 60 (1): 128–43.

Kanayama, Taisuke. 2007b. '*Beikoku ni okeru torishirabe no rokuga·rokuon ni tsuite (Jō)*' (Regarding the Examination of Suspects with Video and Audio Recording in the USA (Part I of II)). *Keisatsu-gaku ronshū* 60 (1): 202–16.

Kangoku hō kaiaku to tatakau gokuchūsha no kai, ed. 1985. *Zenkoku kangoku jittai (The Situation of Prisons Nationwide)*. Tōkyō: *Ryokufu shuppan*.

Kangoku zasshi, ed. 1897. *Keisatsu ryūchijo wo motte kōchikan ni daiyō no ken ni tsuite (About the Issue of Substituting Police Cells for Prisons)*. Vol. 8. Tōkyō.

Katagiri, Yutaka. 2006. '*Miketsu kōkin seido kaisei no keii to gaiyō: Ryūchijo shisetsu ni okeru shogū wo chūshin ni*' (The Course and the Significance of the Revision of the Remand Detention System). *Keisatsu-gaku ronshū* 59 (9): 6–45.

Keck, Margaret E., and Kathryn A. Sikkink. 1998. *Activists Beyond Borders*. Ithaca, NY: Cornell University Press.

Keiji rippō kenkyū kai (KRKK). 1988. '*Keiji/ryūchi hōan no kenkyū tokushū*' (The Detention of Remand Prisoners and the Problem of Criminal Accommodation (Special Issue for Research on the Two Detention Bills)). *Hōritsu jihō* 60 (3): 6–62.

Keiji rippō kenkyū kai (KRKK). 1991. '*Keiji kōkin hōan yōkō Kenkyūkai shian no shushi*' (Content of a Tentative Bill Proposal for Criminal Detention). *Hōritsu jihō* 63 (6): 50–85.

Keimu kyōkai, ed. 1943. *Nihon kinsei gyōkei shi kō (Ge) (A History of Modern Japanese Penal Administration (Part II))*. Tōkyō.

Keisatsu kangoku gakkai Tōkyō shikai. 1894. *Kangoku gaku (A Study of Prisons)*. Tōkyō: *Gozandō*.

Kitajima, Keisuke, Susumu Yamashita, and Toshihiro Kawaide. 2006. '*Shinhō no shikkō ni mukete: Kysōei ni tai suru kitai*' (Towards the Implementation of the New Law: Expectations for Correction). *Keisei* 117 (1): 48–87.

Kitamura, Atsushi. 2005. '*Kangoku hō kaisei*' (The Revision of the Prison Law). *Hanzai to hikō* 146 (Special Edition): 42–50.

Krauss, Ellis S., and Robert Pekkanen. 2011. *The Rise and Fall of Japan's LDP: Political Party Organizations as Historical Institutions*. Ithaca, NY: Cornell University Press.

Leishman, Frank. 1999. 'Policing in Japan: East Asian Archetype?' In *Policing Across the World: Issues for the Twenty-first Century*, edited by Rob I. Mawby, 109–26. London: UCL Press.

Maeda, Ai. 2004. *Text and the City: Essays on Japanese Modernity*. Durham: Duke University Press.

Masajirō, Takigawa. 1961. *Nihon gyōkei shi (History of Penal Criminal Administration)*. Tōkyō: *Seiabō*.

Matsuo, Kōya. 2004. *Keiji soshōhō kōenshū: Kōen keishiki de tokiakasu Matsuo keiso no shinzui (Collection of Lectures on the Code of Criminal Procedure: Unravelling the Essence of Matsuo's Code of Criminal Procedure through His Lectures)*. Tōkyō: *Yūhikaku*.

Mitchell, Richard H. 1973. 'Japan's Peace Preservation Law of 1925: Its Origins and Significance'. *Monumenta Nipponika* 28 (3): 317–45.

Mitchell, Richard H. 1976. *Thought Control in Pre-war Japan*. Ithaca, NY: Cornell University Press.

Mitchell, Richard H. 1992. *Janus-Faced Justice: Political Criminals in Imperial Japan*. Honolulu, HI: University of Hawaii Press.

Miyazawa, Setsuo. 1992. *Policing in Japan: A Study on Making Crime*. Albany, NY: State University of New York Press.

Miyazawa, Setsuo. 2012. 'The Enigma of Japan as a Testing Ground for Cross-Cultural Criminological Studies'. *International Annals of Criminology* 50 (1/2): 154–75. (Originally published in the same journal in 1994.)

Morishita, Tadashi. 1989. '*Beifutsu bengoshi no daiyō kangoku chōsa*' (An Investigation of Substitute Prisons by American and French Attorneys). *Hanrei jihō* 1302: 19–20.

Moriyama, Mayumi. 2004. *Hōmu Daijin to shite no 880 nichi (880 Days as Justice Minister)*. Tōkyō: *Kawade shōbō shinsha* Publishers.

Moston, Stephen, and Terry Engelberg. 2011. 'The Effects of Evidence on the Outcome of Interviews with Criminal Suspects'. *Police Practice and Research: An International Journal* 12 (6): 518–26.

Murai, Toshikuni. 2003. '*Kokusaiteki na kanten ni tatte*' (From an International Perspective). In *21-seiki no keiji shisetsu: Gurōbaru standādo to shimin sanka (Criminal Facilities of the 21st Century: The Global Standard and Civil Participation)*, edited by Kenji Rippō Kenkyūkai, 2–7. Tōkyō: *Nihon hyōronsha*.

Murayama, Masayuki. 1990. *Keira keisatsu no kenkyū (A Study on Patrol Policing)*. Tōkyō: *Seibundō*.

Nakagawa, Takahiro. 2005. '*Miketsu kōkin seido ni tsuite no ronriteki kadai*' (The Theoretical Problems of the Remand Detention System). *Liberty and Justice* 56 (September): 47–54.

Nakahara, Hidenori. 1956. 'The Japanese Police'. *Journal of Criminal Law and Criminology* 46 (4): 583–94.

Nakao, Bunsaku. 1948. '*Kangoku hō kaisei yōkō ni tsuite*' (Concerning the Proposal for the Revision of the Prison Law). *Keisei* 59 (3): 9–18.

National Police Academy. 2006. *'Tokushū: Keiji shūyō shisetsu oyobi hi-shūyōsha nado no shogū ni kan suru hōritsu'* (Special Edition: The Act on Penal Detention Facilities and Treatment of Inmates and Detainees). *Keisatsu-gaku ronshū* 59 (9).

Neary, Ian. 1989. *Political Protest and Social Control in Pre-war Japan: The Origins of Buraku Liberation*. Manchester: Manchester University Press.

Neary, Ian. 2002. *Human Rights in Japan, South Korea and Taiwan, Routledge Advances in Asia-Pacific Studies*. Abingdon: Routledge.

Nishimura, Hideki. 2006. 'The Retrial of the "Yokohama Incident": A Six-decade Battle for Human Dignity'. *The Asia-Pacific Journal. Japan Focus*: www.japanfocus.org/-Nishimura-Hideki/2025/article.html.

Niwayama, Hideo, and Igarashi Futaba, eds. 1981. *'Daiyō kangoku to shimin-teki jiyū' (The Police Custody System and Civil Liberties)*. Tōkyō: *Seibundō*.

Odanaka, Toshiki. 1977. *Gendai keiji soshō hō ron (A Theory of a Contemporary Criminal Procedure): Keisōshōbō*.

Ogawa, Shigejirō. 1976. *Nihon kangoku hō kōgi—Meiji 22 nen kaisei kangokusoku no fukkoku kaisetsu (A Lecture on Japanese Prison Law—Re-issued Explanation of the 1889 Reform of the Prison Regulations)*. Tōkyō: *Nihon gyōkei shi kenkyūkai*.

Oguri, Takao. 1996. *Daiyō kangoku no haishi wo motomete: Watashi no hōkoku·rombun kara (Demanding the Abolition of the Substitute Prison System—From My Report)*. Tōkyō: *Arakawa* Printing.

Ōno, Seiichirō. 1930. *'Futō kōkin no mondai'* (The Problem of Unjustifiable Detention). *Hōritsu jihō* 2 (11): 3–6.

Ōno, Seiichirō, and Kyōichi Asakura. 1966. *Kangoku hō—kaitei, fukkan (Prison Law—Revision, Reprint)*. Tōkyō: *Yūhikaku*.

Pedlar, Neil. 1990. *The Imported Pioneers: Westerners Who Helped Build Modern Japan*. Folkestone: Japan Library.

Peerenboom, Randall. 2003. 'Beyond Universalism and Relativism: The Evolving Debates about "Values in Asia"'. *Indiana International & Comparative Law Review* 14 (1): 1–86.

Pekkanen, Robert J. 2006. *Japan's Dual Civil Society: Members Without Advocates*. Stanford, CA: Stanford University Press.

Putnam, Robert D. 1992. *Making Democracy Work: Civic Traditions in Modern Italy*. Princeton, NJ: Princeton University Press.

Risse-Kappen, Thomas, Stephen C. Ropp, and Kathryn Sikkink, eds. 1999. *The Power of Human Rights: International Norms and Domestic Change, Cambridge Studies in International Relations*. Cambridge: Cambridge University Press.

Röhl, Wilhelm, ed. 2005. *History of Law in Japan since 1868*. Leiden-Boston: Brill.

Samuels, Richard. 1987. *The Business of the Japanese State*. Ithaca, NY: Cornell University Press.

Sasaki-Uemura, Wesley M. 2001. *Organizing the Spontaneous: Citizens Protest in Postwar Japan*. Hawaii, HI: University of Hawaii Press.

Satō, Motoharu. 2005. '*Daiyō kangoku no rippō jijitsu/shushi to genzai*' (The Legislative Facts and Intents regarding Substitute Prison and Modern Day)'. In *Daiyō kangoku·kōchisho kaikaku no yukue—Kangokuhō kaisei wo megutte (The Direction of the Reform of the Substitute Prison System and Detention Houses—Regarding the Revision of the Prison Law)*, edited by *Keiji rippō kenkyū kai* (KRKK), 30–60. Tōkyō: *Gendai jimbunsha*.

Shihōshō, ed. 1939. *Shihō enkaku shi (History of Legal Development)*. Tōkyō: *Hōsōkai*.

Shimato, Jun. 2007. '*Keiji shisetsu ni okeru miketsu kōkinsha to bengonin to no gaibu kōtsū no kakudai*' (Expansion of the Remand Prisoners' Communication with Counsel in Criminal Facilities). *Keiji hō jānaru* 8: 97–103.

Shirakawa, Yasuhiro. 2007a. '*Igirisu ni okeru higisha torishirabe ni tsuite (Jō)*' (Regarding the Examination of Suspects in England (Part I of III)). *Keisatsu-gaku ronshū* 60 (4): 75–103.

Shirakawa, Yasuhiro. 2007b. '*Igirisu ni okeru higisha torishirabe ni tsuite (Chū)*' (Regarding the Examination of Suspects in England (Part II of III)). *Keisatsu-gaku ronshū* 60 (5): 117–56.

Shirakawa, Yasuhiro. 2007c. '*Igirisu ni okeru higisha torishirabe ni tsuite (Ge)*' (Regarding the Examination of Suspects in England (Part III of III)). *Keisatsu-gaku ronshū* 60 (6): 65–95.

Sissons, David C. S. 1959. 'The Dispute Over Japan's Police Law'. *Pacific Affairs* 32 (1): 34–45.

Smethurst, Richard J. 1974. *A Social Basis for Prewar Japanese Militarism: The Army and the Rural Community*. London: University of California Press.

Soeda, Yoshiya. 2007. *Naimushō no shakai shi (Social History of the Home Ministry)*. Tōkyō: *Tōkyō daigaku shuppan kai*.

Stockwin, J. Arthur A. 2003. *Dictionary of the Modern Politics of Japan*. London: Routledge.

Suehiro, Izutarō. 1930. '*Kore demo sashitukae nai no deshō ka?—Keisatsu ryūchijo ni tsuite Watanabe Shihō Daijin he no kōkaijō*' (Do You Not Have Objections Even to This?—An Open Letter to Justice Minister Watanabe regarding the Police's Houses of Custody). *Suehiro* 2 (11).

Takesako, Yoshiya. 2006. '*Miketsu kōkinsha ni kan suru yūshikisha kaigi no teigen to giron ni tsuite*' (On the Proposal of the Council Concerning the Treatment of Remand Prisoners and their Reasoning). *Keisatsugaku ronshū* 59 (9): 78–108.

Tan, Hsien-Li. 2011. *The ASEAN Intergovernmental Commission on Human Rights: Institutionalising Human Rights in Southeast Asia*. Cambridge: Cambridge University Press.

Tipton, Elise K. 1990. *The Japanese Police State: The Tokkō in Interwar Japan*. Honolulu, HI: University of Hawaii Press.

Tipton, Elise K. 1997. 'Tokkō and Political Police in Japan'. In *The Policing of Politics in the Twentieth Century: Historical Perspectives*, edited by Mark Mazower, 213–40. Providence, RI: Berghahn Books.

Van Dijk, Jan, John Van Kesteren, and Paul Smit. 2008. 'Criminal Victimisation in International Perspective: Key Findings from the 2004–2005 ICVS and EU ICS'. In *Wetenschappelijk Onderzoek-en Documentatiecentrum, publication number 257*.

Wakayama, Shigeo. 1899. '*Keisatsu-chō ni kan suru ryūchijo*' (The Houses of Custody in Police Stations). *Kangoku zasshi* 10 (4): 27–8.

Westney, D. Eleanor. 1982. 'The Emulation of Western Organisations in Meiji Japan: The Case of the Paris Prefecture of Police and the Keishi-chō'. *Journal of Japanese Studies* 8 (2): 307–42.

Yokoyama, Minoru. 2004. 'Changes in Functions of Japanese Corrections with Criminalisation'. In *Adult Corrections: International Systems and Perspectives*, edited by John Winterdyk, 231–67. Monsey, NY: Criminal Justice Press.

Yoshida, Shigeru. 2007. *Yoshida Shigeru: Last Meiji Man*. Lanham, MD: Rowman & Littlefield Publishers.

Yoshimura, Hiroto. 2009. *Keisatsu kaikaku: Chian saisei ni mukete (Police Reform: Towards a Restoration of the Order)*. Tōkyō: *Tachibana shobō*.

Index